FEMINISM WITHOUT WOMEN

FEMINISM WITHOUT WOMEN
Culture and Criticism in a "Postfeminist" Age

TANIA MODLESKI

Routledge ▪ New York & London

Published in 1991 by

Routledge
An imprint of Routledge, Chapman and Hall, Inc.
29 West 35 Street
New York, NY 10001

Published in Great Britain by

Routledge
11 New Fetter Lane
London EC4P 4EE

PN
1995.9
· W6
M55
1991

Library of Congress Cataloging in Publication Data

Modleski, Tania, 1949–
    Feminism without women / Tania Modleski.
      p.   cm.
    Includes bibliographical references and index.
    ISBN 0-415-90416-1; ISBN 0-415-90417-X (pbk.)
    1. Women in motion pictures. 2. Sex role in motion pictures.
    3. Feminism and motion pictures. 4. Women in popular culture.
    5. Motion pictures—Social aspects—United States. I. Title.
    302.23′082—dc20   91-13126
                                         CIP

British Library Cataloguing in Publication Data

Modleski, Tania *1949*–
    Feminism without women : culture and criticism in a
    "postfeminist" age.
    1. Feminism
    I. Title
    305.4201

    ISBN 0-415-90416-1
    ISBN 0-415-90417-X pbk

To the women

TABLE OF CONTENTS

Preface   ix

PART I: THEORY AND METHODOLOGY

CHAPTER ONE: POSTMORTEM ON POSTFEMINISM   3

CHAPTER TWO: FEMININITY AS MAS(S)QUERADE   23

CHAPTER THREE: SOME FUNCTIONS OF FEMINIST CRITICISM; OR, THE SCANDAL OF THE MUTE BODY   35

PART II: MASCULINITY AND MALE FEMINISM

CHAPTER FOUR: A FATHER IS BEING BEATEN: MALE FEMINISM AND THE WAR FILM   61

CHAPTER FIVE: THREE MEN AND BABY M   76

CHAPTER SIX: THE INCREDIBLE SHRINKING HE(R)MAN: MALE REGRESSION, THE MALE BODY, AND FILM   90

PART III: RACE, GENDER, AND SEXUALITY

CHAPTER SEVEN: CINEMA AND THE DARK CONTINENT: RACE AND GENDER IN POPULAR FILM   115

CHAPTER EIGHT: LETHAL BODIES: THOUGHTS ON SEX, GENDER, AND REPRESENTATION FROM THE MAINSTREAM TO THE MARGINS   135

Notes   165

Index of Films   183

Index

PREFACE

In a recent book on popular culture entitled *The Female Gaze*, a collection of essays by a new generation of avowedly feminist critics, many of the contributors hold a preceding generation of feminist critics responsible for depriving them of the enjoyment of much popular culture. Insisting on the right to the pleasures promised women by the culture industry, one contributor proposes that "Joan Collins [in her role in *Dynasty*] represents a far-reaching challenge to feminism." Participating as it does in a growing reaction against the politicized culture criticism of the 1970s and early 1980s, such a "challenge" cannot be dismissed, even if it cannot be taken up on its own terms. It would seem to offer one more sign that the time is right for a feminist rethinking of the articulations of popular culture and political criticism. The essays in this book were each designed to shed light on different facets of the "postfeminist" moment by looking at mass culture (mostly movies) in the context of various developments in cultural criticism. I attempt to show the latter's complicity with the former in assuming the goals of feminism to have been attained—an assumption that seems premature, to say the least.

By juxtaposing two very different kinds of discourse—the theoretical and the popular—I do not intend to make the former trivial, or to deny important differences. It has, however, always been my firm conviction (one which I spell out in Chapter 3) that the critic is never wholly outside the culture she analyzes, or completely resistant to its forces, retrograde as these may often be. If Jean-Paul Sartre was right that the "surest way to be bowled over by one's age is to turn one's back on it," then a radical cultural politics might begin to face its age by examining its connection to even the lowest forms of culture, rather than disavowing any implication in it (or— what amounts to the same thing—celebrating this culture *as* politically progressive so as to legitimate and protect one's private pleasures).

In the first chapter, I outline some of the trends in contemporary critical studies that provide the context for the discussions in subsequent chapters. The next two chapters are concerned primarily with questions of methodology and theory in popular culture studies; and the remaining chapters present readings of popular movies and analyze the relation of these texts to current theoretical debates. The main problem I have had to confront in choosing to focus on contemporary mass culture is the transitory nature of the objects of study: thus, for example, the chapter on the war film was written before the war with Iraq—a development that has somewhat altered the media's representation of the "warrior," who is now, occasionally, a woman (although in other ways we see how films like *Top Gun* and *Heartbreak Ridge* have provided psychological preparation for military aggression). Despite the ephemerality of the texts, however, I believe the attitudes they express toward women, men, and feminism are important to examine because they mark a major conservative shift in the cultural climate; what distinguishes this moment from other moments of backlash is the extent to which it has been carried out not *against* feminism but in its very name.

One of the great advantages of working on contemporary popular culture is that so many people can be drawn in to do some of your work for you. Nancy Vickers and Hilary Schor contributed significantly to this project, and I thank them for filmgoing beyond the call of friendship and for much inspiration. They also read the manuscript in various versions and gave valuable advice, as did Susan Rosenfeld and Lynn Layton. I would like, as always, to gratefully acknowledge Nadia Medina and Jane Nardin for their emotional and intellectual support, as well as for specific help on the manuscript. I am particularly indebted to Patrice Petro, who time and again dropped everything to read and critique individual chapters, and all the revised chapters, as soon as they arrived via express mail at her door. It has been my great pleasure to work with Bill Germano at Routledge on two projects now, and I want to extend my thanks for his support, tact, sense of humor, and professionalism.

Some portions of this book have appeared elsewhere in a different form. The following sources are gratefully acknowledged. "Femininity as Mas(s)-querade," in Colin MacCabe, ed. *High Theory/Low Culture* (Manchester: Manchester University Press, 1986); "Some Functions of Feminist Criticism, Or the Scandal of the Mute Body," in *October* 49 (Summer 1989); "A Father is Being Beaten: Male Feminism and the War Film," in *Discourse* 10 Spring/Summer 1988; "Three Men and Baby M," in *Camera Obscura* 17 (May 1988), and "The Incredible Shrinking He(r)man, Male Regression, the Male Body and Film," in *Differences* 2, no. 2 (Summer 1990).

PART I

Theory and Methodology

Chapter One

Postmortem on Postfeminism

In 1987, the *New York Times Magazine* published an article entitled "Literary Feminism Comes of Age." The article begins with a vignette of the feminist critic Elaine Showalter teaching a course at Princeton University on the literature of the *fin de siècle*. The female author of the article quotes Showalter's remarks about the "lunatic fringe of radical feminism" at the turn of the century. Some of these women, Showalter points out to the class, "labelled sperm a 'virulent poison' and advocated sexual abstinence as a political goal."[1] After offering this example of feminist lunacy from another era, the author immediately turns to a male critic, Peter Brooks, for an assessment of the present state of feminist criticism. (Although feminism is no longer in its minority it still seems to need a male authority figure to speak on its behalf and certify its legitimacy as well as its sanity.) Brooks, whose previous book on narrative theory contains only a single sentence about feminist criticism,[2] remarks, "Anyone worth his [!] salt in literary criticism today has to become something of a feminist" (p. 110). And he goes on to assert, "The profession is becoming feminized" (p. 112). Yet the male critic's confusion here, of feminism with feminization, may belie the author's major claim—that feminist criticism in becoming absorbed into the academy has lost its ability to threaten the male literary establishment.

The article is in fact a perfect example of the kind of texts I will be discussing in much of this book—texts that, in proclaiming or assuming the advent of postfeminism, are actually engaged in negating the critiques and undermining the goals of feminism—in effect, delivering us back into a prefeminist world. Thus the *Times* author, in tacit defiance of feminism's critique of the institution of the family, consistently adopts familial meta-

3

phors, domesticating women and putting them back in their "proper" sphere: "For feminist literary criticism," she writes, "once a sort of illicit half sister in the academic world, has assumed a respectable place in the family order" (p. 110). Later she remarks, "Despite its growing respectability, feminist criticism retains a hint of scandal, like an old aunt who breaks into bawdy stories over tea" (p. 116). By the end of the article, then, literary feminism has not only come of age, but passed its prime and entered its dotage. And in the process the lunacy invoked at the beginning of the article reemerges as harmless senility.

The very format of the *Times* article belies the claim made in its title, especially when one remembers that not long before this piece appeared, the *Times Magazine* had run an elaborate spread on members of the Yale School of Criticism. Five or six full-page color photos of very important looking, prosperous, and, of course, male critics, most nearing retirement age (old uncles?), accompanied the article, which treated the subject of deconstruction with much fanfare. In contrast, the "Literary Feminism" article is illustrated by a single half-page black and white photo of "Princeton's Elaine Showalter in her study." Literary feminists may indeed have been accepted into the "family order," but for all that they would seem to be rather poor relations.

GYNOCIDAL FEMINISMS

The decision to feature Elaine Showalter in the *Times* article is intriguing in light of this critic's career trajectory, which is paradigmatic of the developments in feminist criticism that have motivated the writing of this book. Showalter, it may be remembered, was one of the most emphatic and articulate advocates of a female-oriented criticism she labeled "gynocritics." By "gynocritics," Showalter meant a kind of criticism that would move away from an "angry or loving fixation on male literature" and on "male models and theories" and would develop "new models based on the study of female experience."[3] For Showalter, feminist criticism found "its most challenging, inspiriting, and appropriate tasks" in concentrating on "female culture"—female literature, female "theory," etc. (p. 135). To be sure, many found Showalter's program to be too prescriptive, and ultimately untenable, since patriarchal texts clearly *comprise* a large part of "female experience"—which is not to say that the experience is identical to that of men. (Thus, for example, my own work on the films of Alfred Hitchcock was motivated by the desire to understand this very misogynist director's popularity with female viewers.) Nevertheless, Showalter's strong defense of women and women's experience, combined with her forceful critiques of male critics who seemed to be coopting feminism and rendering women silent and invisible, were inspiring to those feminist critics struggling to theorize a viable and theoretically sophisticated notion of the female as social subject at a period when the very idea of the subject was undergoing a series of philosophical challenges.

Then, soon after the "Literary Feminism" article appeared, Showalter shifted her focus to "gender studies," and in 1989 published an edited volume entitled *Speaking of Gender*. In her introduction, Showalter announces feminism's departure from the "gynocritics" of the 1970s and early 1980s, argues for the necessity of considering questions of masculinity, and heralds a "renewed feminist interest in reading male texts, not as documents of sexism and misogyny, but as inscriptions of gender and 'renditions of sexual difference.' "[4] While Showalter is aware of the danger of cooptation on the part of male critics and understands the feminist concern that male critics might "appropriate, penetrate or exploit feminist discourse for professional advantage" (p. 7), she clearly approves of the direction taken by a generation of younger male critics focusing on masculinity as a construct rather than "a universal norm" (p. 8). Most disturbing about this introduction, however, is its marginalization of feminism in the sense that Showalter is no longer focused on the question (which is *the* question of the present volume): what's in these new developments *for feminism* and for women? Showalter writes, "While men's studies, gay studies, and feminist criticism have different politics and priorities, together they are moving beyond 'male feminism' to raise challenging questions about masculinity in literary texts, questions that enable gender criticism to develop" (p. 8). Feminism, in this formulation, is a conduit to the more comprehensive field of gender studies; no longer is the latter judged, as in my opinion it ought to be, according to the contributions it can make to the feminist project and the aid it can give us in illuminating the causes, effects, scope, and limits of male dominance.

Showalter certainly seems to be accurate in assessing gender studies to be a new phase (although it might prove yet to be the phase-out) of feminist studies. Her book takes a place alongside, for example, journals with names like *Genders* and *Differences*, titles that stand in marked contrast to those of journals created in the 1970s like *Signs: Journal of Women in Culture and Society* and *Feminist Studies*. An even more telling sign of the times, however, has been the advent in the 1980s of a new form of anthology organized around debates between men and women who read one another's texts and take each other to task for their positions on a whole array of issues relating to male feminism and sexual difference. (The first and most notorious of these is *Men in Feminism* which I discuss in Chapter 4).[5] While these books, in staging the perennially fascinating "battle of the sexes," make for very compelling reading, they can be considered "postfeminist" in several respects. First, insofar as they focus on the question of male feminism as a "topic" for men and women to engage (as the first one did), these books are bringing men back to center stage and diverting feminists from tasks more pressing than deciding about the appropriateness of the label "feminist" for men. Second, the books in their very format betray a kind of heterosexual presumption—a presumption pointed out by the gay male critic Lee Edelman, who in one of these books speaks on behalf of the absent lesbian (and we should note in passing that the practice of including an inoculating critique of its own blind spots, so as to allow business to proceed as usual, has become a common tactic in contemporary political criticism).[6] Third, the anthologies tacitly assume and promote a liberal notion of the formal equality of men and women, whose viewpoints are structurally accorded equal weight. Thus while terms like "dialogism" (drawn from the work of Mikhail Bakhtin) are commonly invoked in the rationale for these volumes, it is hard to see how such a term functions as anything other than a euphemism for "dialogue"—a concept that in eliding the question of power asymmetry has rather conservative implications.[7]

Collections like these have drawn a great deal of notice and publicity, but the kind of work most useful to feminism has, in my opinion, been the work men are doing without clamoring for women's attention and approval. As Paul Smith, who is given the last word in the *Times* article, is quoted as saying: "My feeling is that men should be kind of quietly doing the things that support feminism, without at this point being able to get any credit for that" (p. 117).

But a little credit where credit is due. A body of male criticism supportive of the feminist project *is* beginning to develop, and the criticism I have personally found most useful in thinking through my own subject is the kind that analyzes male power, male hegemony, with a concern for the effects of this power *on the female subject* and with an awareness of how frequently male subjectivity works to appropriate "femininity" while oppressing women. This male feminist criticism reveals such appropriations, which I will be investigating in this book, to be deeply embedded in the American cultural tradition. Thus, in an extremely interesting essay entitled "The Politics of Male Suffering: Masochism and Hegemony in the American Renaissance," Christopher Newfield examines Nathaniel Hawthorne's *The Scarlet Letter* to show how the character of Arthur Dimmesdale undergoes an exemplary process of "male feminization" that is empowering to men and disempowering to women. "Hegemonic patriarchy can survive," Newfield argues,

> without male assertion, but not without feminization: only feminization enables men to evade the one-directional dominations of stereotypical masculinity, to master the non-conflictual, and to occupy both sides of a question. Whereas tyranny depends on male supremacy, liberal hegemony or "consensus" depends on male femininity.[8]

These insights confirm my own conviction that however much male subjectivity may currently be "in crisis," as certain optimistic feminists are now declaring, we need to consider the extent to which male power is actually consolidated through cycles of crisis and resolution, whereby men ultimately deal with the threat of female power by incorporating it. Such a process will become clearer in later chapters, where I discuss *Three Men and a Baby*, the phenomenon of Pee-wee Herman, and current theorizations of male masochism, but I wish to give some indication here of how the process works in recent writing by established male theorists and critics.

To begin, we might, for purposes of comparison, consider the following quotation from the work of another critic of American culture, David Leverenz, whose work, like Newfield's, shows a real concern for and knowledge about how male power frequently works to efface female subjectivity by occupying the site of femininity. In an analysis of Ralph Waldo Emerson, Leverenz challenges the tendency within criticism to label Emer-

7

son's power "female," and he notes the way in which a certain conceptualization of femininity as an attribute of the mind operated in Emersonian thought at the expense of women:

> Though Emerson challenges the social definitions of manhood and power, he does not question the more fundamental code that binds manhood and power together at the expense of intimacy. Emerson's ideal of manly self-empowering reduces womanhood to spiritual nurturance while erasing female subjectivity. "Self-Reliance" takes for granted the presence of faceless mothering in the mind, an ideal state of mental health that he sums up in a memorable image: "The nonchalance of boys who are sure of a dinner."[9]

To understand how a male feminist approach like Leverenz's differs from "postfeminist" male appropriations of feminism, I would like to contrast this passage to one from Stanley Cavell, taken from his analysis of the 1937 film *Stella Dallas*, which forms part of a larger work on "melodramas of unknown women." In this new project, Cavell analyzes a genre, melodrama (a.k.a. the woman's film), which has been important in feminist film theory because, as "texts of muteness," melodramas seem to strive to articulate a voice repressed within patriarchal culture. Women are attracted to the genre, it has been suggested, because melodrama is about the drive for total *expression* and for recognition of that which in women's lives and feelings has been misrecognized, misunderstood, and repressed.[10] But Cavell, in focusing on melodramas of the 1930s and 1940s, appears, like many other conservative thinkers at the present time, to be attempting to contain the threat posed by feminist thought and to reposition the struggle between feminism and the patriarchal tradition as a struggle inhering *in* that tradition. This, in turn, involves a remystification of precisely the mode of thought analyzed by Leverenz, and it reveals a confusion between feminism and feminization similar to the one we saw in the quotation from Brooks at the outset. In the following passage Cavell, who has indicated that his analysis of *Stella Dallas* is meant to "preserve" philosophy as he knows it, tries to rescue the "feminine" Emersonian tradition from "male philosophy" and in the process to make common cause with feminist critics:

> I have written as though the woman's demand for a voice, for a language, for attention to, and the power to enforce attention to, her own subjectivity, say to her difference of existence, is expressible as a response to an Emersonian

demand for thinking. I suppose that what for me authorizes this supposition is my interpretation of Emerson's authorship as itself responding to his sense of the *right* to such a demand as already voiced on the feminine side, requiring a sense of thinking as a reception . . . , and as a bearing of pain, which masculine philosophy would avoid.[11]

We will put aside the dubious reliance on stereotypes of femininity as passive and masochistic to look at the way Cavell's text enacts what Leverenz's deconstructs. In Cavell, female subjectivity and feminism itself are assimilated to the "feminine" mind of a male philosopher—and we might note that the "faceless mothering" of the mind referred to by Leverenz is an especially apt term given Cavell's use of the text *Stella Dallas*, the archetypal story of a mother's self-*effacing* sacrifice of her child for the child's own social advancement. Cavell is canny enough to suspect himself of negating the voice he is claiming to help bring forth, for he asks, "Does this idea of the feminine philosophical demand serve to prefigure, or does it serve once more to eradicate, the feminine difference?—to articulate or to blur the difference between the denial to the woman of political expression and a man's melancholy sense of his own inexpressiveness?" The question is posed only to be immediately dropped but its very language suggests the answer: Cavell is indeed appropriating—we might say garrulously appropriating—the muteness of the "unknown woman." In poetically invoking the male philosopher's "melancholy inexpressiveness," Cavell solicits our recognition of the male as the superior candidate for our feeling of pathos, the melodramatic sentiment par excellence. In a brilliant analysis of the gendering of melancholia, Juliana Schiesari demonstrates "melancholia" to be precisely the category by which the male thinker is culturally empowered to represent his "losses" at the expense of the female subject. She writes, "[The] ideology of melancholia appropriates from women's subjectivities their 'real' sense of loss [say, Stella Dallas's unbearably painful loss of her child; or the feminist sense of a voice appropriated or denied] and, in Lacanian terms, recuperates that loss . . . as a privileged form of male expression"—an expression that, in the case of a Cavell, employing a cunning ruse of male power, masquerades as *in*expressivity.[12] He is, as the saying goes, at a "loss" for words. The paradox works in the opposite way for women: their demand for a language they claim to lack *is*, we remember, "expressible" *by Cavell himself* as a demand emanating

9

from a (feminized) male philosophical tradition. That this demand is, in Cavell's phrase, "already voiced" would seem further to nullify the feminist sense of dispossession in relation to language and discourse (and at this point the circularity of the entire argument becomes clear).

The case of Stanley Cavell is of interest to me here for a number of reasons. First, there is his use of (a feminized) popular culture to illuminate a philosophical tradition. My own work is engaged in a more thoroughgoing "leveling" of high and low cultures, but I want to show how the very act of appropriation revealed in Cavell's readings of women's films is characteristic of both these cultures today. Second, we see that the kind of thought that privileges the "feminine" (understood in rather clichéd terms) within philosophy is by no means unique to French deconstructive thought, but is very much part of one strain of American thought (indeed, it is intriguing to compare the passage I quoted from Cavell with the one from Lyotard I quote at the end of Chapter 7; the very same stereotypes of passive and masochistic femininity are invoked to make precisely the same point about thinking as "reception," as a "suffering of time"). Third, in identifying so strongly with the heroines of popular melodramas, Cavell reveals more explicitly than most how much American thought still falls squarely within the genre of what Nina Baym calls "melodramas of beset manhood." What is of course besetting manhood today is feminism, which the melancholy male "hero" responds to by appropriating so that he can make its losses (for which he is thus partly responsible) his losses.

I want to stress that I see Cavell's work as representative of a certain male critical response to feminism and that I could have chosen to discuss in some detail several other essays—from Marxists or deconstructionists— that have enacted similar dramas and have sometimes elicited angry responses from feminists. One lamentable postfeminist spectacle was conducted on the pages of *Critical Inquiry* and involved Frank Lentricchia making a kind of low joke out of feminism, particularly the work of Sandra Gilbert and Susan Gubar. The source of the controversy was an essay by Lentricchia on Wallace Stevens, "Patriarchy Against Itself—The Young Manhood of Wallace Stevens," which suggests by its very title the move we saw in Cavell to relocate the struggle of feminism against patriarchy to a place entirely *within* patriarchy and within the psyche of the patriarch himself.[13] Another controversy erupted over an essay that appeared in

Representations entitled "Medieval Misogyny" by R. Howard Bloch. In this essay, which adopts the by now clichéd view of a certain strain of deconstructionism that writing can be seen as feminine, Bloch attempts to reveal the paradoxes inherent in medieval misogynist writings: "If woman is defined as verbal transgression, indiscretion, and contradiction, then . . . any writer can only be defined as a woman."[14] Like Cavell and Lentricchia, then, Bloch sees a certain patriarchal tradition as divided within itself, or turning against itself, so that, finally, the problem of misogyny becomes, as Elaine Hansen phrases it, a problem of *self*-loathing.[15] Elsewhere in the essay Bloch effectively wipes out the entire history of feminist film theory when he remarks, beginning again with one of his slippery conditional clauses and exhibiting the same defiance of the basic rules of logic, "If woman is conceived to be synonymous with the senses of perception, then any look upon a woman's beauty must be the look of a woman upon a woman, for there can be no such thing as a male gaze or desire" (p. 15). In all my researches into postfeminism I have encountered only a single instance of more tortuous patriarchal gender-bending: in Donald Pease's admiring summary of Lentricchia's argument about Stevens. According to Pease, insofar as men *submit* (since submissiveness is a feminine trait) to the cultural imperative to be men, they are really undergoing "cultural feminization."[16] Or, insofar as men are men, they are women.

Because I am focusing so much on the dangers facing feminism, I especially wanted to make it clear that I do not consider them to comprise the whole picture. For this reason it seemed important to cite Leverenz's work as well as Cavell's, so as to indicate the range of response found in men's criticism today: thus, one man, Leverenz, in focusing on masculinity, on the construction of patriarchal power, *and on the place of the female subject* within this construction, makes a significant contribution to gender studies and feminism; the other man, while purporting to engage in a "dialogue" with feminism (although how voiceless women and inexpressive men are to manage such a thing is not clear), is mostly engaged in conversations with himself. That the difference is not, as Showalter would have it, entirely a generational matter may be seen in the most recent entry in the male publishing game, Joseph A. Boone and Michael Cadden's *Engendering Men*, a collection of essays about male feminism written entirely by men (the book could thus have taken my title in all seriousness, whereas I

11

meant it as an exaggeration of certain trends in contemporary feminist studies).[17] In an unusually strong postfeminist irony, the final essay of this volume which banishes women from its list of contributors is a complaint about the way heterosexual men have become invisible within feminism![18]

Before concluding this section, we need to note one aspect of contemporary gender studies that is especially promising from a feminist point of view: the work on gay sexuality undertaken largely by gay men, and influenced by Eve Kosofsky Sedgwick's groundbreaking study, *Between Men: English Literature and Male Homosocial Desire*. In this book Sedgwick analyzes how homophobia and misogyny are intertwined consequences, as well as causes, of the bonding among heterosexual men. While Sedgwick has been criticized in at least one quarter precisely *for* driving a wedge between gay men and straight men, for the most part *Between Men* has had the more salutary effect of making feminists sensitive to issues of homophobia and making gay men aware of how constructions of homosexuality intersect with misogynist constructions of femininity.[19] An example of the kind of essay that shows how a feminist analysis combined with a gay analysis can help deconstruct a postfeminist text is a recent essay by Lee Edelman, who in a critique of the Lentricchia controversy reveals a kind of "fiscal Emersonianism" at the heart of Stevens's writing and Lentricchia's "Marxist" interpretation. Edelman detects "a deeply rooted concern on the part of bourgeois heterosexual males about the possible meanings of dependence [emotional or economic] on other males"—a dependence whose danger lies not only in the threat of a " 'feminization' that would destabilize or question *gender*, but in the threat of a 'feminization' that would challenge one's (hetero)sexual identity."[20] I will be exploring the intersections of gay and feminist criticism at greater length, particularly in the final chapter.

But the new direction within gender studies also carries with it postfeminist dangers—in this case, especially, the silencing of the lesbian perspective. Thus Sedgwick's dismissal in *Between Men* of lesbianism as a nonissue—she suggests that since all women supposedly exist on a lesbian continuum, lesbianism as a topic blurs into feminism itself—betrays a disturbing lack of concern for the special difficulties homosexual women face in a sexist homophobic culture. A similar sign of the postfeminist times is the recent publication of a special issue of *South Atlantic Quarterly* entitled "Displacing Homophobia," which has only gay men as contributors except for Eve Sedgwick, who although she has made her reputation largely in studying gay male relations, *here* discusses a lesbian writer, Willa Cather. But the focus on Cather, the only lesbian considered in the book, results in a critique of this very male-identified writer's political and sexual conservatism and of her intense "effeminophobia," which is manifested particularly in her disdain for Oscar Wilde.[21]

I would hope, however, that in correcting its habit of neglecting the lesbian perspective (which, revisionist histories notwithstanding, held sway in the women's movement for only a brief moment in time with only a segment of its members) feminism will not fall into an error of equally serious postfeminist consequence, and see lesbianism as existing at the same political and theoretical level as other so-called marginalized groups. While in the last few years, engaged political criticism has become increasingly insistent on the necessity for each oppressed group to become aware of its privileges in relation to other oppressed groups, there seems to me to be a crucial difference between telling, say, a white woman she should be aware of her racial privilege and telling her she should be aware of her privilege as a heterosexual female. For feminism has emphasized from the beginning the *oppressiveness* of the ideology of compulsory heterosexuality and the institution it supports—that of the nuclear family. The family is the structural unit keeping women economically and physically dependent on men; separating women from other women; and, in extreme (but by no means uncommon) cases, providing the space in which men may abuse women with impunity. The special difficulties faced by lesbians under such a system are analogous to those of a prisoner who has escaped incarceration and, being "at large," faces more extreme punitive measures than many of the more docile inmates. The hazards faced by lesbians cannot be overestimated, but we might remember the time when feminism deemed it no great "privilege" to be a wife in patriarchy.

UNBECOMING WOMEN

In its May 31, 1990, issue, the *New York Review of Books* published a review of some books of feminist literary criticism, an event so unusual that some people might have taken this as another token of literary feminism's having "come of age." The review, however, was assigned to Helen

13

Vendler, a literary humanist who could be expected to vent great hostility towards *any* political project operating within literary studies. As a woman, of course, Vendler could serve as a kind of "front man" for the male literary establishment which could then feel confirmed in its antagonism towards feminism, since, after all, this *was* a woman saying such nasty things. To anyone familiar with Vendler's work, then, her anti-feminist attack on feminist criticism in the name of a humanist view of literature and aesthetics could certainly have been predicted; what *may* have been more surprising was this humanist woman's approving remarks on the collection *Feminism/ Postmodernism*, edited by Linda J. Nicholson.[22] Nicholson's book is largely composed of essays devoted to promoting an anti-essentialist version of feminism and thus, according to Vendler, "can be seen as taking part in one of the perpetual outbreaks of nominalist skepticism against Aristotelian universalism." Comparing these "anti-essentialists" to feminist essentialists she observes, "The 'sect of one' is the logical reduction of the nominalist position, while the party line is the logical end of the universalist position." And she ends by exulting over the book as a symptom of the breakdown of the women's movement, "The most cheering thing, finally, about all political movements is their unsuppressible tendency to splinter, as their broad original manifestoes are more and more rigorously scrutinized."[23] Vendler's assessments are of course open to debate. But inasmuch as radical feminism is frequently called upon to account for its being on the same side of certain issues as the New Right, postmodern feminists might well wish to ponder how they wound up in this new "alliance" with anti-feminist humanism.

Beyond this, however, we need to deal precisely with the problem posed by a Helen Vendler to a feminism that might want to hold onto a belief in "woman" rather than discredit and discard the category for its "essentialist" implications. Does the existence of a scholarly woman so hostile to feminism's agenda, a woman whom the male establishment would no doubt like to see as exemplary, confirm the anti-essentialist view that "woman" is at best a meaningless term?

The debates over female essentialism, along with the rise of gender studies, are the major contextualizing events of this book: thus, "Feminism Without Women" can mean the triumph either of a male feminist perspec-

14

tive that excludes women or of a feminist anti-essentialism so radical that every use of the term "woman," however "provisionally" it is adopted, is disallowed. Indeed, the two meanings of my title are interrelated: the rise of gender studies is linked to, and often depends for its justification on, the tendency within poststructuralist thought to dispute notions of identity and the subject. From Jacques Lacan, for whom the individual subject is produced by language, to Louis Althusser, for whom the subject is produced by ideology, to Jacques Derrida, for whom the subject is an effect of writing (itself seen as "feminine," a concept that may be unrelated to actual women), to (especially) Michel Foucault for whom the subject is a regulatory fiction produced in and through discourse, poststructuralist writings have been read by many as sounding the death knell of the humanist notion of identity, a term that invariably carries with it an assumption of gender and a hetero-sexual imperative: one is always either male or female. Once "the subject" is called into question in such a radical way, and once gender and sexual difference are seen in some sense as "arbitrary" (as linguistic difference was for Ferdinand de Saussure, the intellectual "father" of all these male theorists), it is easy to see how a "man" can be a "woman" or, as in the case of Jonathan Culler, can perform an activity *as* a woman ("reading as a woman").[24]

It is also easy to see why poststructuralist theories have appealed to feminists. Since feminism has a great stake in the belief, first articulated by Simone de Beauvoir, that one is not *born* a woman, one *becomes* a woman (for if this were *not* the case it would be difficult to imagine social change), thinkers like Lacan and Foucault have provided the analytical tools by which we may begin the arduous task of unbecoming women. However, as feminists are increasingly pointing out, the once exhilarating proposition that there is no "essential" female nature has been elaborated to the point where it is now often used to scare "women" away from making *any* generalizations about or political claims on behalf of a group called "women." (Indeed, we shall see in Chapter 3 a sometimes feminist critic proposing Don Juan as a model practitioner of literary speech acts precisely because he is considered to be an enemy of generalization.)

It is not altogether clear to me why women, much more so than any other oppressed groups of people, have been so willing to yield the ground on which to make a stand against their oppression. But it is certainly clear that for many "women" the very term arouses a visceral, even phobic reaction. Thus, in her book *"Am I That Name?"* Denise Riley speaks of "the exhaustion with reiterations about 'women' which must afflict the most dedicated feminist." She continues, "Surely it's not uncommon to be tired, to long to be free of the merciless guillotines of those gendered invocations thumping down upon all speech and writing, to long, like Winifred Holtby for 'an end of the whole business . . . the very name of feminist . . . to be about the work in which my real interests lie.' "[25] It is clear to me whose "real interests" would be served by our ending "the whole business" of feminism. But be that as it may, we may remember the famous title of an article by Hélène Cixous ("Castration or Decapitation?") who suggests that for women in patriarchal society "decapitation" rather than castration is at stake, and we might see a strong irony in Riley's assigning to *feminism* possession of the guillotine and the means to commit political terror. The phobic aspect underlying some of the attacks on the category of "woman" is further confirmed when we consider Riley's choice for a title, *"Am I That Name?"*—that name being, of course, "woman." In the original source, Shakespeare's *Othello*, "that name" refers to another "w" word altogether, which Riley, like Desdemona, cannot bring herself to say. Thus in her epigraph to the book she omits the final, telling line:

Desdemona:	Am I that name, Iago?
Iago:	What name, fair lady?
Desdemona:	Such as she says my lord did say I was.
Emilia:	He called her whore.

(Act IV, Scene II, 1622)

At one point in the book, Riley expresses a wish for women to get to a point in their politics where they are able to say to themselves, "[To] interpret every facet of existence as really gendered produces a claustrophobia in me; I am not drawn by the charm of an always sexually distinct universe" (p. 111). In my view, however, although women have had to take up the term "women" emphatically to rescue it from opprobrium, they

16

have done so in *opposition* to patriarchy's tendency to "saturate" us with our sex; and in fact all the great feminist texts in history have decried this tendency, from Wollstonecraft's *A Vindication of the Rights of Women* to Woolf's *A Room of One's Own* to Beauvoir's *The Second Sex* and beyond. Riley even goes so far as to imply that female essentialists are less aware of their dominated condition than those who resist claims to a commonality of "women's experience." The very use of the phrase "women's experience," she says, "masks the likelihood that these [experiences] have accrued to women not by virtue of their womanhood alone, but as traces of domination, whether natural or political" (p. 99). But surely for many women the phrase "women's experience" is shorthand for "women's experience of political oppression," and it is around this experience that they have organized and out of this experience that they have developed a sense of solidarity, commonality, and community. It may be true, as Riley argues— and here she seems to be erroneously taking the extreme positions of some cultural feminists to be representative of intellectual feminism today—that there are no "moments when some, as it were, non-ideological kind of woman-ness erupts, such that you are for that moment a woman unironically and without compromise" (p. 97) but since, as Althusser has so convincingly shown, there is *no* "outside" to ideology, I do not see how this observation works specifically to discredit the term "woman." Moreover, if anti-essentialists are correct—as I believe they are—to point out the historical variability of definitions of women, this variability is no less than, say, for blacks (since it means one things to be a black person in Haiti today, another in the American South during slavery times, etc.). This fact, however, hardly prevents black people from organizing around the category of race.

In fact, though, far from recognizing the analogy, anti-essentialists often bolster their arguments by pointing to the supposed inability of "essentialists" to deal in a sufficiently nuanced way with issues like race or class. Thus feminists accused of essentialism incur charges of ethnocentrism or colonialism when they use words like "commonality" or even "women's experience" since they (white middle-class women) are said to be denying the specificity of the experiences of their female "others." Judith Butler sums up the anti-essentialist case:

> If one "is" a woman [a concession she does not ultimately grant], that is surely not all one is; the term fails to be exhaustive, not because a pregendered "person" transcends the specific paraphernalia of its gender, but because gender is not always constituted coherently or consistently in different historical contexts, and because gender intersects with racial, class, ethnic, sexual, and regional modalities of discursively constituted identities.[26]

While this would seem to be an unimpeachable observation, Butler herself never follows it up by discussing most of these "modalities" in her book *Gender Trouble* once they have served their theoretical purpose of dissuading feminists from claiming commonalities across class and racial lines. Her book instead becomes a highly abstract Foucauldian meditation on theories of sexuality and sexual difference (in Lacan, Freud, Kristeva, Wittig, and Foucault himself). Ironically, then, anti-essentialists may be no more prepared to deal with such issues as race or ethnicity than the "essentialists" whom they criticize for neglecting these issues. (We may note, for example, that the anthology *Feminism/Postmodernism*, which frequently claims for postmodern feminism a superior ability to deal with issues of race, contains no substantial discussion of these issues.)

Other feminists have been more caustic than Butler. Donna Haraway peremptorily writes, "We do not need a totality in order to work well. The feminist dream of a common language, like all dreams for a perfectly faithful naming of experience, is a totalizing and imperialist one."[27] I think more subtle distinctions need to be made here, however. Obviously there are other ways of achieving a common language beyond the imperialist imposition of one's own language and cultural references on others. One could always learn the *other*'s language, for example (which does not mean that it would have to be able to achieve "a perfectly faithful naming of experience"—and I think Haraway actually knows this; however, so strong is her postmodern mistrust of communicational transparency that, as this quotation shows, she tends to sound at times as if any effort to work toward linguistic commonality is very nearly a fascistic enterprise). Ideally, a common language would not be a monologic entity but the product of various cultural encounters of the sort discussed by Gloria Anzaldúa in her book *Borderlands/La Frontera*, which talks about meeting others "halfway." Explaining her decision in the book to "code switch" between languages, "from English to Castillian Spanish to the North Mexican dialect

18

to Tex-Mex to a sprinkling of Nahuatl to a mixture of all these," Anzaldúa writes:

> There at the juncture of cultures, languages cross-pollinate and are revitalized; they die and are born. Presently this infant language, this bastard language, Chicano Spanish is not approved by any society. But we Chicanos no longer feel that we need to beg entrance, that we need always to make the first overture—to translate to Anglos, Mexicans and Latinos, apology blurting out of our mouths with every step. Today we ask to be met halfway. This book is our invitation to you—from the new mestizas.[28]

Women of color have, as this passage suggests, played a vanguard role in reconceptualizing the notion of identity, so that it becomes a more flexible term, capable of including the experience of people who (as in the collection *This Bridge Called My Back*) possess multiple cultural allegiances and, often, suffer multiple kinds of oppression. It is up to white middle-class women to make sure that their own uses of terms like "identity" and "experience" do not work to shut out the experiences of people of various colors, classes, and sexualities. It is also of utmost importance to work to understand how these experiences may in more or less complex ways conflict with one another.[29] One part of this book is devoted to delineating the ways various groups are played off against one another to the ultimate benefit of white hetero-patriarchy.

In a much read and widely admired essay, *Feminist Politics: What's Home Got to Do with It?*, Biddy Martin and Chandra Mohanty discuss how one white Southern feminist woman, Minnie Bruce Pratt, tries to respond to demands on the part of women of color, Jewish feminists, and lesbians that white middle-class women avoid colonizing and appropriating others' experiences and, instead, learn the others' "languages" and cultural references and acknowledge the duality or multiplicity of identities and oppressions in a Christian-dominated, straight, white culture. While they show how Pratt scrupulously avoids colonizing the "other," Martin and Mohanty also warn against a "monolithic (and overly theoretical) critique of identity," which they argue is based "on a refusal to accept responsibility for one's implication in actual historical or social relations, on a denial that positionalities exist or that they matter, the denial of one's own personal history and the claim to a total separation from it."[30]

19

Martin and Mohanty's essay, along with the work of women of color like Anzaldúa, has influenced the work being undertaken by some white feminists who are becoming sensitive to the way the notion of "experience" has operated in exclusionary ways. Thus in *Beyond Feminist Aesthetics*, Rita Felski quotes bell hooks's observation that "white women who dominate feminist discourse today rarely question whether or not their perspective on women's reality is true to the lived experiences of women as a collective group." As a result of critiques like hooks's, says Felski, "it has become apparent that female community cannot simply transcend existing power structures but is deeply implicated within them." But she also observes that hooks's criticisms do not imply a rejection of the notion of "female experience," but, on the contrary, are based upon a presupposition of "a preexisting ideal of a public sphere which claims to represent all women and can thus be criticized and made answerable for its failure to do so." Felski concludes, "An appeal to a shared experience of oppression provides the starting point from which women as a group can open up the problematic of gender, at the same time as this notion of gendered community contains a strongly utopian dimension."[31]

I would like to stress the importance of this final observation about the utopian dimension of the feminist "community," as well as of the term "woman" itself. Teresa de Lauretis echoes Felski's insight when she says, in an important discussion of essentialism, that the " 'essence' of woman is, and has always been, more of a project than a description of existent reality"; this insight provides us with a way to hold onto the category of woman while recognizing ourselves to be in the *process* (an unending one) of *defining and constructing the category* (which, as noted earlier, includes very disparate types of people).[32] In the final analysis it seems more important to struggle over what it *means* to be a woman than over whether or not to be one. This is a struggle, I have indicated, all too briefly, being enacted within feminism today by women of various sexualities, classes, ethnicities, and races—most of whom, it is important to recognize, have *not* taken up the banner of anti-essentialism, although they have strenuously resisted efforts of white middle-class women to colonize them.[33]

In this connection it is interesting to note that despite the accusations of ethnocentrism and colonialism sometimes leveled at "essentialists" by anti-essentialists, Denise Riley begins her book by noting the similarity of her

20

title, *"Am I That Name?"* to the words of Sojourner Truth's speech, "Ain't I a Woman?" Reaching out across racial lines, historical eras, and national boundaries to claim commonality of belief with a black female abolitionist on the nature (or anti-nature) of "woman," Riley writes, "It's my hope to persuade readers that a new Sojourner Truth might well—except for the catastrophic loss of grace in the wording—issue another plea: 'Ain't I a fluctuating identity?' " (p. 1). How a writer who is concerned to emphasize the historically variable meaning of "women" can envisage a *new* Sojourner Truth, abolitionist, feminist, ex-slave, is difficult for me to grasp. This caveat aside, I would want to insist on the crucial *difference* between the question posed by Riley and the one posed by the "real," historically specific Sojourner Truth (whose very name suggests a kind of doubleness—a being at once "essentialized" and *in process*). Sojourner Truth, employing a negative and a question invites no simple answer—invites in fact both a yes *and* a no: "yes," in terms of her "experience," which in some major respects reduces her to her biology—to being the white man's breeder with little freedom to "fluctuate" in any way (although in other respects it requires her to possess the physical strength of a man); and "no" in terms of an ideology based on a notion of frail white Southern womanhood. Given the doubleness of response required by the question as it is posed by a black woman and an ex-slave, it seems to me politically irresponsible for (white) feminism to refuse to grant to Sojourner Truth the status of a woman for it would then be in complicity with the racist patriarchal system that Sojourner Truth was protesting and that has denied, and in important ways continues to deny, this status to the black female (in this respect, excluding women from a contested category on the grounds that there *is no category* may well be the latest ruse of white middle-class feminism). On the other hand, to answer the question in the affirmative has, whatever the ontologically correct position, morally and politically devastating consequences to patriarchal values, for it points up the monstrous hypocrisy of a system which could so exploit a woman's body while infantilizing, idealizing, and sentimentalizing women with its belief in female fragility and spirituality.

In continually repeating the refrain "And ain't I a woman?" as she recounts her personal history as a slave, Sojourner Truth contests ideology by an appeal to experience, and experience by appeal to ideology, and in the very space of this negation affirms herself *as a woman*. In this respect,

21

the "loss of grace" resulting from Riley's substitution of the phrase "fluctuating identity" for the word "woman" is *in truth* "catastrophic," since it is, I will argue, precisely the performative, rhetorical effects of woman's speech that express the utopian aspirations of feminism and the utopian dimension of the term "woman" within feminism.

It is possible, of course, to argue that a nineteenth-century black woman needed to believe in herself as a woman, while in the twentieth century intellectual (white?) women who "know better" should go a step farther, moving beyond the naivete of a Sojourner Truth to a point where they are fully conscious of the allegedly fictional status of the term "woman"— acting when necessary, in Riley's phrase, "as if" they are women while knowing they are not. But I am very wary of this development within feminism. I worry that the position of female anti-essentialism as it is being theorized by some feminists today is a luxury open only to the most privileged women. I worry about the consonance of this position with the ones being advanced by certain white male poststructuralist intellectuals who have proclaimed the death of the subject: if Nancy K. Miller is correct to counter proclamations about the death of the subject by insisting that "only those who have it can play with not having it," could we not also say of anti-essentialist feminists that only those possessing vastly wider options than the majority of women living in the world today can play at "being it" while theorizing themselves into the belief that they are not it?[34] And, finally, I worry that the complicated belief structure Riley and others counsel us to adopt as a *female* form of disavowal (which in its Freudian version would be "I know very well I'm not a woman, but all the same . . . ") might be said not so much to counter masculine disavowal as to participate in the same phobic logic. Given that fetishistic disavowal in the male is the means by which the psyche avoids facing the fact of the woman's difference, the fact of her *being* a woman, the feminist anti-essentialist, with her fears of being decapitated by her "essentialist" sisters, might be confirming the very horror that is at the root of male castration anxiety and the dread of woman.

22

Chapter Two

Femininity as Mas(s)querade

In discussions of mass culture, gender has typically been theorized as simply one positioning among many, one possible point of resistance to mass culture's attempts to homogenize social reality. Thus Fredric Jameson writes:

> The only authentic cultural production today has seemed to be that which can draw on the collective experience of marginal pockets of the social life of the world system: black literature and blues, British working-class rock, women's literature, gay literature, the *roman québecois*, the literature of the Third World; and this production is possible only to the degree to which these forms of collective life or collective solidarity have not yet been fully penetrated by the market and by the commodity system.[1]

Marxism today has abandoned its exclusive reliance on the working class as agents of revolutionary change, and grants women and a few other groups some importance as well. However, Jameson's invocation of the women's movement occurs toward the end of an essay with no feminist perspective, and women are brought in at the last to be offered as one of the few rays of hope in what has been portrayed as a bleak situation. Perhaps the very measure of its bleakness is that women, gays, and rock groups—these "marginal pockets" of social life—*are* our best hope.

But the issue of gender in relation to mass culture goes much deeper and ramifies in a number of quite surprising directions. By looking at several different kinds of discourse, I want to show how our ways of thinking and feeling about mass culture are so intricately bound up with notions of the feminine that the need for a feminist critique becomes obvious at every level of the debate.[2] To begin with, women find themselves at the center of many historical accounts of mass culture, damned as "mobs of scribbling women," in Hawthorne's famous phrase, and held responsible for the debasement of taste and the sentimentalization of culture. As the example of Hawthorne suggests, historians of culture are not the only ones who blame women for creating the conditions of what Ann Douglas calls "the cultural sprawl that has increasingly characterized post-Victorian life."[3] Artists themselves adopt this view, which holds such sway not necessarily because of its truth value but because it rests on powerful stereotypes, habits of language, and unexamined—because unconscious—psychic associations.

In this chapter I want first to examine the orthodox position of the literary historian for the way in which mass culture is condemned as a "feminized" culture. Then I will discuss the work of two other contemporaries—an artist, Manuel Puig, and a theorist, Jean Baudrillard, who, far from condemning mass culture because it is "effeminate," try to reevaluate and to some extent affirm it precisely on the grounds of its association with or resemblance to the feminine. This is certainly an interesting twist to the old debate, although it must be remembered that the feminine has always been a term alternately denigrated and exalted. Whether the latest development represents a gain for women or for feminism remains to be seen.

The orthodox view has been argued by feminist critic and literary historian Ann Douglas in *The Feminization of American Culture*. The book, which *The New York Times* called "indispensable reading for modern feminists," is an impassioned defense of certain nineteenth-century male artists who in the book's account waged a heroic but losing battle against the effete sentimentalizers of culture—women writers and their clerical allies. The condemnation of women writers for their piety and sentimentality is not new, of course, but Douglas goes beyond the customary accusations and not only judges the writings of the majority of nineteenth-century women to be of inferior quality when measured against the artistic achievements of a Herman Melville; she also holds them accountable for the advent of modern mass culture. Discussing Little Eva in Harriet Beecher Stowe's *Uncle Tom's Cabin* as the archetypal heroine of women's fiction and Little Eva's death as the archetypal event, Douglas writes:

Stowe's infantile heroine anticipates that exaltation of the average which is the trademark of mass culture. Vastly superior as she is to most of her figurative offspring, she is nonetheless the childish predecessor of Miss America, of "Teen Angel," of the ubiquitous, everyday, wonderful girl about whom thousands of popular songs and movies have been made. . . . In a sense, my introduction to Little Eva and to the Victorian scenes, objects and sensibility of which she is suggestive was my introduction to consumerism. The pleasure Little Eva gave me provided historical and practical preparation for the equally indispensable and disquieting comforts of mass culture. (pp. 2–3)

Instigating the Civil War was obviously not the last charge for which Stowe would be answerable. Despite Douglas's homage in the book to a kind of intellectual "toughness" that she herself considers masculine, this passage is remarkable for its reliance on impressionistic associations and its lack of concern for the questions of who profits from Miss America and of the extent to which the image of the "teen angel" antedates Stowe and the vast majority of women writers.

Little Eva's death from "consumption" would appear to take on a retroactively symbolic significance. But rather than examine the forces that conspire to condemn women to be the preeminent consumers in consumer society, women's habit of consumption is often seen to be nearly as unavoidable as death. In an illuminating passage, Douglas remarks that "content was *not* the most important aspect of their work. Ministerial and feminine authors were as involved with the method of consumption as with the article consumed." Thus, even women's *production* of texts is transformed into an act of consumption, or in Roland Barthes's terminology, their writing of books into a readerly practice.

Douglas goes on to contrast the nineteenth-century minister, who preferred "light reading" (i.e., fiction and poetry) to the well-educated eighteenth-century minister of Calvinism (a religion that she elsewhere terms "repressive, authoritarian, dogmatic, patriarchal to an extreme" [p. 12]. The latter read "dense argumentative tracts" that "forced him to think, not to 'read' in our modern sense; metaphorically speaking, he was producing, not consuming." Finally, Douglas speaks of the "countless Victorian women" who "spent much of their middle-class girlhoods prostrate on chaise-longues with their heads buried in 'worthless novels.' " Douglas supports her arguments by referring to the writings of contemporary "observers" contrasting these girls unfavorably with their supposedly more industrious grandmothers who "spent their time studying the Bible and performing useful household chores" (p. 9). Now, evidence of this kind would seem to be of questionable value, drawing for its force more on imagery than on empirical fact; indeed, it would seem to be precisely the vivid *image* of girls prostrate on chaise-longues, immersed in their worthless novels, that has provided historical preparation for the practice of countless critics who persist in equating femininity, consumption, and reading, on the one hand, and masculinity, production, and writing on the other.

Although Douglas singles out Stowe's *Uncle Tom's Cabin* (the book that was said to have produced a war) to indict for introducing the pleasures of consumerism, recent criticism has shown that far from being a work that simply participates in a kind of "complicated mass dream life," which for Douglas means that such books are readerly even in their writing, the novel is actually carefully and artfully crafted. Moreover, feminist analysis has revealed that its utopian vision is based upon an idea of *feminine* production in the home which gets extended into an ideal for national and international government. As Jane Tompkins notes, the home "is conceived as a dynamic center of activity, physical and spiritual, economic and moral, whose influence spreads out in ever widening circles."[4] Feminist criticism of this sort leads us to reevaluate and clarify our terms and to rid ourselves of some of the unconscious associations they carry. Too often, politically oriented criticism invokes "production" as an ideal pure and simple, without concerning itself with what is being produced. Thus, the Calvinist minister is praised for "producing the texts he read," even though they may have been "repressive, authoritarian, dogmatic, patriarchal in the extreme." On the other hand, Stowe is condemned for allowing readers to become "absorbed" in her thrilling novel (i.e., to "consume" it) despite the fact that she was presenting them with an ideology based upon a feminine mode of production and intended "to effect a radical transformation of . . . society." Such a view exposes the masculinist bias of much politically oriented criticism which adopts metaphors of production and consumption in order to differentiate between progressive and regressive activities of reading (or viewing, as the case may be).

Tompkins's strategy is to correct this bias by expanding the definition of "production" to include the kind of work that women do. An alternative strategy might consist of deconstructing the hierarchical relation that exists in the oppositions production/consumption and writerly/readerly in order to search out the radical potential of the subordinate terms, each of which, as we have seen, is typically associated with the feminine. Indeed, as one might expect in our postmodern age, such a project has already been initiated by artists and theorists alike.

Manuel Puig's acclaimed novel *Kiss of the Spider Woman* provides an excellent example of such a deconstructive text. The novel takes place in an Argentinian prison, where the homosexual "queen" Molina helps pass the time by relating film plots to his cellmate, the Marxist revolutionary Valentin. The setting of the novel obviously gives new meaning to the usually pejorative designation of mass-produced art as "escapist." The novel draws on the conventions of the prison film, only here the films themselves function as the "great escape."

Kiss of the Spider Woman is the story of the growing love of Valentin for Molina, although this is rendered obliquely, since the book presents us primarily with the dialogue between the two. At the beginning of the book the men tend to disagree and quarrel a great deal, but they gradually come to know and like each other better, largely as a result of their discussions about films, which frequently provoke personal associations and revelations. Molina has been bribed by the prison warden to elicit information about Valentin's political activities in return for his parole. He appears to go along with the plan, yet it becomes clear that he is doing so for his own purposes; thus he manages to procure food from the warden (so Valentin will not be suspicious of his absence from the cell when he is brought out by the warden but will simply assume that his mother has come to see him), and he uses this food to "soften up" Valentin for the seduction that finally occurs. At the end, the warden changes his tactics and releases Molina in the hopes that he will lead them to Valentin's comrades. And this is precisely what happens, since Valentin has extracted a promise from Molina to deliver a message to his cohorts, who, possibly because they spot the police when they arrive at the designated meeting place, gun him down in the street. Subsequently, Valentin is tortured, a merciful doctor gives him some drugs, and he has a dream constructed out of the images and plots of the films Molina has described throughout the book.

At the beginning of the novel, although Valentin very much enjoys

27

indulging in the "escapist" pleasures offered him by Molina, he deeply distrusts this enjoyment and insists on restricting the storytelling to bedtime, for he adopts the standard leftist view of popular culture. Not unlike Douglas's Calvinist minister, Valentin forces himself to struggle with his difficult political science tracts, repudiating the attractions of the film stories. "It can become a vice, always trying to escape from reality like that, it's like taking drugs or something. . . . If you read something, if you study something, you transcend any cell you're inside of, do you understand what I'm saying?"[5] At one point, Valentin condemns himself for his "weakness" in becoming attached to the characters in one of the stories and feeling sad that the "film" has ended (p. 41). It becomes clear that Valentin associates this "weakness" with femininity and fears the passivity involved in the processes of identification and empathy—those *bêtes noires* of Marxist literary and film criticism. Surrendering oneself *to* the texts is to assume an uncomfortable resemblance to the women *in* the texts—for example, the zombie woman, who is powerless to resist the will of others, even though it means burning herself alive at her husband's command.

It is to assume, as well, an uncomfortable resemblance to Molina, who, as the consumer *par excellence*, yields himself to the films with utter abandon, resents Valentin's attempts to analyze the stories, and weeps when Valentin criticizes his favorite film, which is, significantly, a Nazi propaganda film that he admires for its aesthetic beauty and for the love story. Furthermore, Molina's attitude toward men, like his attitude towards films, is one of complete surrender of self. For example, he tells Valentin of a fantasy he has of living with a waiter with whom he is infatuated. He dreams of helping him study and arranging things so that the man will never have to work again. "And I'd pass along whatever small amount of money was needed to give the wife for child support, and make him not worry about anything at all, nothing except himself, until he got what he wanted and lost all that sadness of his for good, wouldn't that be marvelous?" (p. 69).

Having set up the traditional polarities that we saw were operative in Douglas's work (masculinity = production and work; femininity = consumption and passivity), Puig proceeds to effect a transvaluation of the terms. The project of the novel is to get Valentin to accept the otherness that Molina represents—femininity, homosexuality, and mass culture—

28

and, ultimately to allow himself to be sexually and textually seduced by Molina, whom he calls "the spider woman." The spider woman is featured in the drug-induced dream Valentin has at the end of the book: at first she appears to Valentin to be trapped in a spider's web, but then it becomes clear that the spider's web is growing out of her own body, "the threads are coming out of her waist and hips, they're part of her body, so many threads that look like hairy ropes and disgust me, even though if I were to touch them they might feel as smooth as who knows what, but it makes me queasy to touch them" (p. 280). The description of the spider woman, an image of femininity and of homosexuality taken from mass culture, suggests what is at stake in Valentin's attitude toward his others: the fear of entrapment and absorption, which is simultaneously desired and dreaded.

Throughout the novel Puig is satirizing traditional Marxism in the figure of Valentin, and in both the narrative and the accompanying footnotes the book indicates that a revolution must occur in the personal realm as well as the political and must be concerned with sex and gender as well as class. For Marxism, which is classically preoccupied with production, this sexual revolution would involve a new and more positive attitude toward consumption. Hence the book's obsessive concern with food. Valentin at first resists being nurtured by Molina, as he resists the film stories. Finally, however, he comes to accept the various consumer pleasures offered and embodied by Molina and changes his mind about the importance of "sensory gratification" which he earlier repudiated. At the beginning, for example, he protests that Molina's food offerings and his storytelling are getting him into "bad habits":

> There's no way I can live for the moment because my life is dedicated to political struggle. . . . Social revolution, that's what's important, and gratifying the senses is only secondary. The great pleasure's something else, it's knowing I've put myself in the service of a noble . . . ideology . . . Marxism. . . . And I can get that pleasure anywhere, right here in this cell and even in torture. (pp. 27–28)

One of the ironies of Valentin's manifesto is his lack of awareness that his machismo contains strong elements of passivity and even masochism (pleasure in torture). Thus the traits that Valentin rejects as feminine are revealed early in the novel to be important parts of his character. By the

29

end, Valentin has been reduced to helplessness at the hands of Molina, who feeds him, wipes and bathes him after he has been incontinent, and continues to tell him "films" at bedtime "like lullabies" (p. 279). He learns to view his "weaknesses" as less shameful and, at least to a certain extent, comes to enjoy being submissive.

As for Molina, his identification with the passive and often masochistic heroines of his films, his swooning rapture over the films he describes, would appear to make him the ideal manipulated consumer. On the contrary, however, it becomes increasingly apparent as the novel progresses that Molina uses the films in order to do his own manipulating. On occasion he admits to resorting to strategy, as when he confesses that he likes to leave Valentin "hanging" so he will enjoy the film more. "You have to do it that way with the public, otherwise they're not satisfied. On the radio they always used to do that to you. And now on the T.V. soaps" (pp. 25–26). In other words, Molina uses the techniques of manipulation he has learned from his adored mass culture in order to seduce Valentin into his web. Mass culture becomes not the enemy, as it is for the Marxist, but the very agency through which Molina accomplishes his coup and conquers Valentin. The triumph that Molina achieves precisely through his utter devotion both to men and to movies, as well as by his apparent submission to the law represented by the warden, is perhaps attributable to what Jean Baudrillard, quoting Hegel, calls "the eternal irony of femininity" that supposedly characterizes the masses—"the irony of a false fidelity to the law, an ultimately impenetrable simulation of passivity and obedience . . . which in return annuls the law governing them."[6] Molina's exaggeration of the feminine—his simulation of womanhood, derived from emulating film heroines, realizes an ideal of femininity as mas(s)querade: the homosexual "queen" as exemplar of the hyperreal.

In the above passage, taken from *In the Shadow of the Silent Majorities, or, the Death of the Social*, Baudrillard himself is praising the masses, rather than condemning them on account of their putative femininity. This is the only reference to the feminization of culture in the entire work, and yet it is crucial, for the essay builds upon this Hegelian notion of feminine seduction, which is really a synonym for the term Baudrillard has imported into mass culture studies: "simulation." Thus, the word "simulation" itself dissimulates, masking the extent to which Baudrillard's theorization of the masses and mass culture duplicates the theorization of the feminine in much contemporary thought.

Just as Molina refuses to accept Valentin's analyses of the films ("Why break the illusion for me, and for yourself too?" [p. 17]), Baudrillard's masses resist the intellectual's attempts to impose on them "the imperative of rational communication" (p. 10). Instead, they demand spectacle; they prefer to be fascinated rather than provoked to thought. Thus far, of course, Baudrillard is in complete agreement with most critics of mass culture. He differs from them crucially, however, in placing, often, a positive value on the masses' refusal of meaning. Again like Molina, whose ingenuousness continually exposes Valentin's Marxist principles as narrow and inflexible, the masses, according to Baudrillard, "scent the simplifying terror which is behind the ideal hegemony of meaning" (p. 10). Baudrillard here aligns himself with various contemporary thinkers, like Roland Barthes, who implicitly denounces the terrorism of the "hegemony of meaning" when he speaks of the "regime of meaning."[7] Barthes, however, considers this regime to be in the service of mass culture and repeatedly calls on high art to challenge and overthrow it. For Baudrillard, on the contrary, the *masses* are in the best position to answer Barthes's call; they "realize here and now everything which the most radical critics have been able to envisage," as they "wander through meaning, the political, representation, history, ideology, with a somnambulant strength of denial" (p. 49). They annihilate everything that seeks to control them, not by their strength of will but by their very will-lessness and passivity.

The masses function as a "gigantic black hole," a simile ostensibly taken from physics, but perhaps owing something to (female) anatomy as well: "an implosive sphere," a "sphere of potential engulfment" (p. 9). According to Baudrillard, the rabid consumerism suggested by the term "engulfment" is truly radical in its potential. For a "system is abolished only by pushing it into hyperlogic. . . . You want us to consume—O.K. let's consume always more, and anything whatsoever; for any useless and absurd purpose" (p. 46). Here the values espoused by Ann Douglas and other traditional leftist thinkers are reversed. Meaning, regardless of who "produces" it or how, is explosive and terroristic; consumption is implosive and revolution-ary. (At least it *may* be revolutionary. Baudrillard is aware of the fact that this implosive tendency of the "somnambulant" masses means that they are likely enough to destroy themselves in destroying the system, like the zombie woman in one of Molina's films who has to burn herself alive in order to eradicate the evil that possesses the village.[8])

And, as we have seen, Baudrillard, unlike Douglas, is far from denigrating the putative femininity of mass culture. The masses who push the system into a hyperlogic are engaging in the same "excessive fidelity to the law" that characterizes Hegel's eternal feminine, the same "simulation of passivity and obedience" that "annuls the law governing them." It is the mute acquiescence of the masses to the system—the silence of the majority—that renders them most feminine. The masses, outside of meaning, are outside of language and of representation: hence the end of politics as we know it. "Withdrawn into their silence . . . they can no longer be spoken for, articulated, represented, nor pass through the political 'mirror' stage, and the cycle of imaginary identifications" (p. 22). Baudrillard here is extending contemporary psychoanalytic definitions of woman to a political analysis of the masses. For in current theory it is *woman* who has been consigned to silence because of her inability to pass through the mirror stage, to enter language, the symbolic and the social. Thus she has been called "the ruin of representation." In her "formlessness" she can only, paradoxically, represent lack—that is, the horrible possibility of *un*representability, the "abyss" or "void" of meaning, to use Baudrillard's term.[9]

Declaring the masses to be the ruin of (political) representation, Baudrillard rather gleefully and apocalyptically proclaims the death of the social. In former times, "the devices of classic sociality" ensured that "social meaning still flows between one pole and another." But with the devices of "simulation" there is "no longer any pole nor any differential term, hence no electricity of the social either: it is short-circuited by the confusing of poles, in a total circularity of signalling" (p. 21). In another essay Baudrillard makes clear that the "circularity of signalling" characteristic of our electronic age means the end of both domestic space and the public sphere. On the one hand, television (for example) exposes the privacy of domestic space to the scrutiny of the entire world (as in the case of the Loud family), while, on the other hand, all the events of the universe unfold nightly on our private television screens. The individual experiences "this forced extroversion of all interiority, this forced injection of all exteriority" as a kind of rape: "the unclean promiscuity of everything which touches, invests

32

and penetrates without resistance, with no halo of private protection, not even his own body to protect him any more."[10] Once again, then, the masses are shown to be utterly feminized in their mediatization: in the past, of course, it was woman who was forced to live the loss of both public and private space—denied participation in the public sphere, and, although confined to domesticity, forbidden real privacy (a room of her own) and even legal possession of her body.

Baudrillard's work has recently had an enormous impact not only on mass culture theory but on art criticism as well. Baudrillard has been received by many as a kind of ultimate authority, a guru, his disciples exhibiting an "excessive fidelity" to his theory that, not surprisingly, does nothing to "annul" its power. It is important for feminists to draw out and scrutinize the implications of Baudrillard's conceptualization of the masses and mass culture, and in particular to question its significance for feminism. Feminists disturbed by contemporary theory's (especially Lacanian theory's) relegation of women to the realm of the presocial might be tempted to rejoice prematurely in the end of the social and the consignment of almost *everyone* to the place hitherto reserved for women (we will return to this question in the discussion of *Three Men and a Baby* in Chapter 5). But that would be to gloss over crucial distinctions.

In an important essay that is useful for my purposes, Nancy K. Miller questions the relevance to feminism of Foucault's work on the death of the author. She argues that contrary to what some feminists have claimed, it is Foucault's "sovereign indifference" to the matter of "who's speaking," and not the concept of authorship itself, that is the mask "behind which phallocentrism hides its fictions":

> the authorizing function of its own discourse authorizes the "end of woman" without consulting her. What matter who's speaking? I would answer that it matters, for example, to women who have lost and still routinely lose their proper name in marriage and whose signature . . . has not been worth the paper it was written on; women for whom signature—by virtue of its power in the world of circulation—is *not* immaterial. Only those who have it can play with not having it.[11]

The death of the social is another of phallocentrism's masks, likewise authorizing the "end of woman" without consulting her: "the social itself no longer has any name. Anonymous. THE MASS. THE MASSES."[12] Only those who have had privileged access to the social can gleefully announce its demise. For women, who throughout most of history have not been given political representation or a political voice—a state of affairs that has made them the *true* silent majority—there is little reason to be sanguine about the possibilities of a revolution based on the mute tactics of the eternal "feminine."

Not the least of the problems involved in equating the masses and mass culture with the feminine is that it becomes much more difficult for women to interrogate their role within that culture. As Freud put it in his essay on "Femininity" (employing patriarchal strategies of deviousness), if women *are* the question, they cannot *ask* the questions. And yet it is crucial for us to ask them, because, as feminist critics have shown, women are victimized in many and complex ways in mass culture. Valentin was undoubtedly right the first time: the spider woman *was* in fact entrapped in that web, as almost all the women in the movies Molina discusses are ensnared in various patriarchal traps, and as Molina himself is destroyed at the end, letting "himself be killed because that way he could die like some heroine in a movie" (p. 279).

Despite the suggestion in *Kiss of the Spider Woman* of a role reversal and a shift in power dynamics—with Molina temporarily in the ascendancy as a result of his feminine strategies, which are also the strategies of the consumer—nothing much ever really changes. Throughout, Molina remains in the feminine role of nurturer and caretaker, while Valentin reaps all the benefits of consumerism. And despite Baudrillard's implicit denial of the contemporary relevance of sexual difference, as all difference and all politics—including feminist politics—are supposedly absorbed into a feminized mass, women daily experience a sense of oppression in a social order that is at least alive enough to ensure the continuance of that oppression. A feminist approach to mass culture might begin, then, by recognizing and challenging the dubious sexual analogies that pervade a wide variety of discourses, however seductive they may at first appear. And this is especially important when, as in the case of Baudrillard, such discourses masquerade as theories of liberation.

CHAPTER THREE

Some Functions of Feminist Criticism;
Or, the Scandal of the Mute Body

REDUCING THE VARIABLES: FEMINISM, "ETHNOGRAPHIC" CRITICISM AND ROMANCE READERS

She got off the bus and entered a large restaurant with a noble foyer thronged with people, none of them seeming to know which direction they were going in. They wandered, bewildered, rudderless, in need not only of someone to tell them which of the many separate cafes would supply their immediate material wants, but of a guide to the deeper or higher things of life. While a glance at the menus displayed or a word with an attendant would supply the former, who was to fulfill the latter? The anthropologist, laying bare the structure of society, or the writer of romantic fiction, covering it up? Perhaps neither, Catherine thought. And why should she assume that these people, temporarily confused and wandering, were in greater need of guidance than she was herself?

Barbara Pym, Less Than Angels

At the University of Copenhagen in Denmark which I visited some time ago, the feminists tell an anecdote about a male colleague engaged in big battles with other literary scholars over the value of reception theory in mass-culture studies, a theory which in his view is, almost self-evidently, more scientific, rigorous, and democratic than the supposedly impressionistic and elitist pursuits of ivory-tower "textual" critics. At a conference in which he delivered a paper on the reception of a certain television program, the scholar began by explaining that he had surveyed sixteen young men about their reactions to the program. Putting aside objections to the paltry number of respondents in a study claiming to possess scientific rigor, one

35

of the feminists protested against the exclusion of women from the survey and demanded to know the man's reasons for limiting it to males. His answer was: "I wanted to reduce the variables as much as possible."

One can't, of course, hold reception theory particularly responsible for neglecting the female viewpoint; the whole history of criticism—as well as of mass culture itself—consists of reducing women either to total absence, or to an unthreatening, anorexic, presence. Yet because reception theory or, to use the current terminology, "ethnographic" criticism, seems to hold a particular attraction for feminists, who are concerned to account for the specificity of women's response to a largely oppressive popular culture, it seems worthwhile to ask whether this particular tool of the "master" can aid us in "dismantling" his house. Some preliminary investigation of the basic presuppositions of the ethnographic approach is in order before feminists pick up their tape recorders and head fearlessly out to, say, the midwest to begin their fieldwork among the female fans of *Falcon Crest*. Furthermore, a consideration of this approach, which appears to many to possess obvious political authority, since it puts the analyst in direct contact with "the people," is a good place to begin a general discussion of the functions of feminist criticism: just what is it we feminists hope to accomplish by examining popular texts—or, for that matter, any text at all?

In its most recent, Marxist, version, ethnographic criticism may be said to have arisen partly in response to the perceived excesses of so-called "textual criticism" and to the pessimism of many culture critics whose negative attitude about mass culture has seemed to contribute to the political paralysis these critics have purported to explain. The approach has been developed in its most sophisticated and highly theorized form in Great Britain, where a strong cultural studies tradition has served as the background against which a growing number of critics are voicing their dissatisfaction with the formalistic analyses associated with the work of the film journal *Screen* in the 1970s. In the dissenters' view, *Screen*'s psychoanalytically informed theory, concerned largely with describing the way subjects are "inscribed" in and "constructed" by popular film texts, tended to ignore actual social subjects who by virtue of their complex histories and multiple cultural affiliations (educational, religious, vocational, political, etc.) always, it is argued, exceed the subject implied by the text.[1] In this respect the critique mounted by *Screen* has been linked to the earlier critique of the Frankfurt School, which seldom made a distinction between the "ideally" manipulated consumer of mass culture and the actual consumer, who in real life is always caught up in a network of discourses inharmoniously clamoring for the subject's allegiance, an allegiance that the individual, exercising a certain degree of autonomy, may choose either to grant or to withhold. An ethnographic criticism would, its proponents urge, be able to overcome the politically disabling critiques associated with traditional Marxist textual analysis and to ascertain not only how social subjects take up the meanings proffered by a given mass cultural text but also, and more important, how and in the name of what *other* system of meanings and values people might come to refuse the dominant or "preferred" readings of that text. Ethnographic criticism takes as its slogan the phrase coined by Stuart Hall that people are not "cultural dupes," and insists that popular texts must therefore somehow "allow . . . audiences to make meanings that connect with *their* social experience."[2] The aim of ethnographic criticism is, then, to locate these areas of resistance to the dominant ideology that, once identified, could theoretically be pressed into the service of radical political struggle.

Such an ambition is clearly unimpeachable, although the task of accounting for the way large, multiply-determined groups of people interact with a given text—to say nothing of compiling all the information into a coherent account—might seem a little daunting. Moreover, there is a danger that by focusing on the audience member's response to texts, the critic might wind up re-subscribing to an apolitical view of the individual as sole producer of meanings and unwittingly endorsing a pluralist, anything-goes kind of criticism. The notion of "subculture" has thus come to be seen as crucial since it furnishes analysts with a means of categorizing and interpreting data that avoids positing the individual either as totally autonomous in relation to the text or (the view often ascribed to the Frankfurt School and *Screen*) as totally determined *by* the text. In the words of one critic:

> In order to provide anything like a satisfactory account of the relationship between people's mass media involvements and their overall social situation and meaning system, it is necessary to start from the social setting rather than the individual; to replace the idea of personal needs with the notion of structural contradiction; and to introduce the notion of subculture.[3]

37

By focusing on subcultures and studying the values and beliefs associated with them, the analyst is able to make sense of the ways in which "messages" are "decoded" according to the shared cultural orientation of particular groups—the contradictions between the decoded messages and the dominant ideology being the points of rupture into which revolutionary ideologies might insert themselves.

One of the most fascinating studies taking an ethnographic approach to a mass cultural text is David Morley's ground-breaking book on the audience for the British "news-magazine" program, *Nationwide*. In *The Nationwide Audience*, Morley examines the responses of over twenty separate groups of people, chosen with regard to education, class background, political affiliation, vocation, and race. The study reveals an astonishing variety of responses among the groups of viewers, ranging from largely uncritical acceptance of the show's messages and ideological presuppositions to criticism of its political bias, its condescending tone, and its superficial treatment of its subjects (often from conservative, well-educated groups), to outright repudiation of its messages and ideological slant (mainly by left-wing trade unionists). Morley's conclusions about the various kinds of social systems that subcultural groups are able to draw upon in resisting the onslaught of mass culture go a long way toward refuting those critics like Jean Baudrillard who, as we have seen, has vociferously proclaimed the "death of the social"—killed, it would seem, by the ever encroaching and suffocating web of media simulation. Even so, however, certain basic methodological questions that might temper the optimism with which Morley's work is imbued are never adequately addressed. First, to what extent is the respondents' critical attitude merely a function of the fact that the ethnographer places them in a situation where they are *required* to be critical? When people are watching television in ordinary situations, as one of Morley's respondents observes, the critical attitude is relaxed. The media's messages might easily slip past the vigilant censor into the viewer's unconscious, an area unfortunately neglected by most ethnographers—*Screen*'s psychoanalytic emphasis having been the first victim to ethnographic criticism.

Second, to what extent are the responses elicited by the ethnographic critic testimony to the predisposition of the masses to be surveyed and tested, to submit themselves voluntarily and even eagerly to the relentless efforts of the media (and now of the media critics) to know and hence control them? Indeed, it seems possible that ethnographers may even be reproducing in their investigative procedures the methods of control they are seeking to undermine. This possibility is strikingly evidenced in a study by John Fiske, who has conducted an ethnographic study of teenaged female fans of the rock singer Madonna. Fiske explains that in order to ascertain how young girls find in Madonna's work meanings which allow them to "escape ideological control," the ethnographer should engage in "listening to [the girls], reading the letters they write to fan magazines, or observing their behavior at home or in public."[4] Without irony, Fiske proceeds to employ these techniques of patriarchal panopticism, which date back at least as far as Samuel Richardson's *Pamela*, to show that Madonna and her female fans are engaged in a "*subversion*" of male visual power, that they somehow *escape* the control of the male gaze—the ethnographer's gaze being apparently benignly neutral.

Quite obviously, the need for a self-reflexive attitude on the part of the ethnographer acquires a particular urgency when the ethnographer is male and his subjects women, since he inevitably participates in a power structure he appears to contest. In Morley's case, however, such an admonition might seem irrelevant, since his is less a strategy of male appropriation of women's culture than a simple matter of the usual neglect—of reducing the variables so as to exclude considerations of gender. However, Morley does in fact interview several groups of females, some of whom, interestingly, refuse to engage with the program at all. For example, a group of black, mainly West Indian/African women complain that "*Nationwide* or anything like that's too boring":

"We're not interested in things like that."

"I just didn't think while I was watching it."

"I'd have liked a nice film to watch—*Love Story* . . ."

Morley comments: "This cultural distance means that the premise of *Nationwide*—the reflection of the ordinary lives of the members of the dominant white culture, which is what gives the programme 'appeal' for large sections

39

of that audience—is what damns it for this group." The group, says Morley "simply do not possess the appropriate cultural capital to make sense of the programme" and therefore, he concludes, are engaged in a "critique of silence" (pp. 71–72). But Morley never asks how it is that the group possesses the "cultural capital" to understand the romanticized life of a white male from Harvard and his love affair with a doomed Radcliffe student. To Morley, the only variable here is race, despite the fact that the groups which supposedly criticize the program by their very silence happen to consist overwhelmingly of women (who also strongly endorse the British soap opera *Crossroads*). It does not occur to him that this "critique of silence," which repudiates the culture's dominant representations of political and social events, is readable as a "feminine" critique—and a very old one at that: we might recall, for example, the heroine of Jane Austen's *Northanger Abbey* who rejects "male" history books as unacceptable alternatives to Gothic and romantic novels.

But it seems possible to go even further, albeit in a slightly fanciful direction, and see in the women's preference for romances and for soap operas an implicit judgment not just on the television program in question, but on the ethnographic approach itself. That romance and ethnography *are* opposed in some fundamental way is the point of the quotation from Barbara Pym's novel *Less Than Angels* that began this essay—the ethnographer being one who demystifies the social relations glamorized and obfuscated by the romance writer. Pym suggests that these two approaches are strongly gender-linked and although "neither" may provide adequate guidance for the "confused" and "wandering" multitudes, Pym's sympathies clearly lie with her heroine, the romance writer, rather than with the male anthropologist whom she treats rather sardonically:

> "Your people wait for you," said Catherine. "How soothing it will be to get away from all this complexity of personal relationships to the simplicity of a primitive tribe, whose only complications are in their kinship structure and rules of land tenure, which you can observe with the anthropologist's calm detachment."[5]

Now, if we recall that romances are usually precisely about the way the aloof male loses his "calm detachment," is forced to stop *assessing* the heroine and to admit his emotional involvement with her; and if we take

40

seriously feminist claims that women's popular culture expresses some of the legitimate grievances of women in patriarchy (although at the same time neutralizing these grievances), then a feminist critic might be tempted to see in the formula-story of romances an allegorical lesson for the male ethnographer: a lesson about the necessity of acknowledging his personal investment in his subject(s) and developing more interactive, mutually implicating methods of cultural inquiry. In any case, to a feminist reader of *The Nationwide Audience*, the female viewers' desire for different forms of popular culture and for a "politics" a little "closer to home," as one respondent puts it, may express precisely the kind of resistant, or at least contradictory relation to the dominant culture (in this case to patriarchy) that Morley seeks, but that his traditionally masculinist-Marxist approach prevents him from discerning. In not heeding the women, Morley effectively guarantees their silence, which he then explains as resulting from a lack of cultural competence.[6]

If it is true, as Pym suggests, that ethnography is a particularly "male" activity, a question arises as to whether it is possible for the methodology to be recuperated by the feminist critic interested in "laying bare" the mystified social relations of popular romances. Is the female feminist critic able to give an authentic voice to the women traditionally silenced by patriarchal culture and sometimes even by that culture's sternest dissidents? A widely admired book on women's romances, *Reading the Romance* by Janice Radway, gives an emphatically affirmative answer to both questions. In her study, Radway reports and elaborates on her "ethnographic" researches into a midwestern community of romance readers (called by the fictitious name of Smithton), headed by "Dot," a woman who writes a newsletter evaluating romances each month. Radway's book is both rich in detail and ambitious (interviewing romance readers, giving a history of the paperback industry, considering the texts in the light of Nancy Chodorow's psychoanalytic study *The Reproduction of Mothering*, etc.), and it is not my intention here to conduct a detailed critique of it. Rather, I want to analyze a few of the presuppositions of Radway's ethnographic methodology and in particular to examine the viability for feminist critique of the intimately linked theories of subcultural formations and what has variously

41

been called the acquisition of "literary competence," the accumulation of "cultural capital," or the development of particular "reading formations."[7]

Throughout her study Radway is concerned to justify the superiority of her approach over that taken by the elitist "professors of English," as she calls them, since the latter in her view fail to take into consideration the real women who read romances and who are in the best position to inform scholars about what the women call their reading "habit." According to Radway, there is "no evidence" that we (critics, professors) "know how to read as romance readers do." To support such a position, Radway refers to the work of Stanley Fish, who, she says, first taught her the importance of studying what "real readers do with texts," for meaning, according to Fish, "is constructed from textual materials by a reader who operates not alone and subjectively but according to assumptions and strategies that he or she has adopted by virtue of prior participation in a specific interpretive community," a term that has certain affinities with the more Marxist notion of "subculture."[8] The work of Fish and other theorists of literary competency has in fact appealed strongly to other feminists besides Radway, in part because it provides a way of deconstructing the canon and explaining women's exclusion from this canon and in part because it can help explain how women learn to read the writings of other women. Thus, in a feminist critique of the male literary canon, Annette Kolodny approvingly quotes Murray Krieger's narrative of how people come to understand interpretive conventions and hence to acquire literary competency: "Once one has read his [sic] first poem, he turns to his second and to the others that will follow thereafter with an increasing series of preconceptions about the sort of activity in which he is indulging. In matters of literary experience, as in other experiences, one is a virgin but once."[9] But surely, this is a naive account in a post-Althusserian, post-Derridean literary world; for, as the continental thinkers have taught us, often using the same unfortunate meta-phorical language, in reading as in writing one is always already a whore.

Given that Radway's "community of romance readers" is, it must be pointed out, an extreme rarity in the world, since reading romances is a perfect example of the serialized activity Jean-Paul Sartre saw as character-istic of mass culture, we need to note that the interpretive conventions enabling us to read romances are not formed in a community or subculture like the one studied by Radway but are, for *most* of us, set in place from birth, that in patriarchal society a female child is born into and simultaneously interpellated by a world where many of the conventions of romance hold powerful sway—in, say, her mother's fantasy life (which in turn shapes her own life at the level of the unconscious), in popular songs and fairy tales, and, later, in novels and movies. These conventions are, then, part of our cultural heritage as women. In short, there is *every* reason to suppose, if we are honest with ourselves, that we know how to read as romance readers do: any woman who has ever responded emotionally to Rhett Butler sweeping Scarlet O'Hara up the stairs knows how to "read" romances (and in fact the Smithton women list *Gone with the Wind* among their all-time favorite novels).

The point here is not only that it is questionable from a moral and political point of view to treat romance readers as if they were natives of Bora-Bora rather than middle-class housewives from somewhere around Kansas (although, of course, ethnographic studies of the natives of Bora-Bora are *also* often morally and politically problematic).[10] The point is also that romances are the property of us all—and not of just white Anglo-Saxon and American women either: Morley's female West Indian and African subjects, we recall, seemed just as avid for mass-produced female fantasies as Kansas housewives, and, of course, Harlequins and other serial romances are translated into dozens of languages. In this regard, the limits of a "subcultural" approach to women's romances ought to be clear, since the popularity of romances is a *cross*-cultural phenomenon, and romances provide women with a common fantasy structure to ensure their continued psychic investment in their oppression.

Moreover, assuming its effectiveness, this fantasy, which promises women complete fulfillment through heterosexual love, ensures the impossibility of women ever *getting together* (as women) to form a "subculture" (if it makes any sense to speak of the majority of the world as a "subculture") and hence to develop a system of values that will effectively challenge and undermine an increasingly hegemonic patriarchal ideology. Because women's experience has been privatized, and because, as Terry Eagleton has argued, criticism belonged to the bourgeois (male) public sphere before it became almost wholly academicized, a woman-oriented criticism could emerge only when feminists began to public-ize and collectively explore their private experience and, through consciousness-raising, to come to terms with the myriad ramifications of feminism's most basic insight, "the personal is political."[11] Located, until recently, on the margins of the academy, the feminist critic has contributed to the forging of a woman's culture based on this insight and has felt herself to be part of a broader movement of women on whose behalf she could sometimes speak because, through consciousness-raising, she in fact *did* speak *to* them—as one of them. Her work is, then, ideally plurivocal, not denying the differences of other women but learning about them through dialogic exchange, rather than through ethnographies that posit an unbridgeable gap between the critic's subjectivity and the subjectivity of "the others."[12]

But because Radway never admits the similarity between herself and the women she studies and, like Fiske and Morley, adopts the pose of the disinterested "scientific researcher," she winds up condescending to the very people she wants to rescue from critical scorn—this despite her claims never to have contradicted the women: "I have always worked first from their conscious statements and beliefs about their behavior, accepted them as given, and then posited additional desires, fears, or concerns that complement rather than contradict those beliefs and assertions" (p. 10). For someone who proceeds to utilize a psychoanalytic methodology in analyzing the texts' appeal to their readers, this is quite an extraordinary claim. It flies in the face of the most basic insights of psychoanalysis—that the unconscious is made up of feelings and desires that the conscious mind finds difficult to tolerate (i.e., the unconscious *contradicts* the conscious mind), and that it is itself, as Freud continually asserted, *characterized* by contradiction. In general, the crucial element missing here is a sense of the various ways a notion of contradiction *must* be brought to bear in any attempt to understand the full complexity of women's relation to culture: contradictions at an intrapsychic level; contradictions between conscious or unconscious fantasies and the discourses that conflict with or discredit these fantasies; and contradictions between competing ideologies and discourses as they are reflected both in popular texts and in the audience's relations to these texts. A recognition that romance readers may be self-contradictory in their attitudes and behavior does not necessarily open up the analyst to the charge of elitism, as Radway seems to fear, *especially* if we are willing to acknowledge how much we ourselves are implicated within those very structures we set out to analyze, how much our own feelings, desires, anxieties, etc., are caught up in contradiction—in short, how much our fantasy lives, for all our cherished feminist ideals, may resemble those of the women we study.

Far from being narcissistic, as it might at first appear, the self-analysis involved in the kind of feminist criticism I would advocate may well provide an antidote to the narcissism I suspect to be at the heart of much reader-oriented popular culture criticism—a criticism which, although claiming a certain objective validity by appealing to the pleasures and tastes of others, often seems to be based on an unspoken syllogism that goes something like this: "I like *Dallas*; I am a feminist; *Dallas* must have progressive potential."[13] It seemed important at one historical moment to emphasize the way "the people" resist mass culture's manipulations. Today, we are in danger of forgetting the crucial fact that like the rest of the world even the cultural analyst may sometimes be a "cultural dupe"—which is, after all, only an ugly way of saying that we exist inside ideology, that we are all victims, down to the very depths of our psyches, of political and cultural domination (even though we are never *only* victims).

All of this is simply to propose a place for the feminist textual critic who recognizes her commonality with other women. Because she is so deeply invested in her methodology, Radway finds it necessary utterly to discredit textual critics—an attack that is curious in light of her decision to accord "Dot," the Smithton community's romance reviewer, great authority. For Dot, it turns out, may be as idiosyncratic in her tastes as any other reader and may in fact have imposed these tastes upon the group as a whole: "Therefore," writes Radway, "while the members of the Smithton group share attitudes about good and bad romances that are similar to Dot's it is impossible to say whether these opinions were formed by Dot or whether she is simply their most articulate advocate" (p. 55). But what, finally, is the *feminist* critic but an articulate advocate of opinions about texts?—opinions which she sometimes shares with other women, and sometimes helps to form.

AT THE CROSSROADS: ON THE PERFORMATIVE ASPECT OF FEMINIST CRITICISM

In *Less Than Angels*, Pym refers to a newlywed couple who "set out for the field to gather material about the married life of a primitive people,

45

giving in exchange generous information about their own, which filled the natives with delight and astonishment" (p. 166). In Pym's comic vision, anthropology is seen as a *form* of gift giving rather than, as has traditionally been the case, the study of such forms. Now, since, as I have argued, feminism can evolve only through a process of dialogue, and since traditional forms of ethnography militate against this process, I would like, in the spirit of Barbara Pym, to replace the unidirectional, ethnographic notion of feminist criticism with one situated in the realm of symbolic exchange— the realm, that is, of the gift. A view of feminist criticism as symbolic exchange—between the critic and the women to whom she talks and writes—is, I would argue, more egalitarian than much reader-response criticism which frequently condemns as elitist the very idea that the critic might have anything to give to anyone. Thus Robert C. Allen speaks disparagingly of the textual critics' view of their task as "finding the 'figure in the carpet'—the meaning of the work that lay hidden in its structure— and relating that meaning to other readers who had not discovered it for themselves (or who did not possess the interpretative gifts of the critic)."[14]

As we have seen, reader-response critics have countered textual critics by insisting that meaning resides not in any given text but in the reader as s/he interacts with the text, although this meaning may be determined within a larger context—that of the interpretive community to which the reader belongs. I have already discussed some of the limitations of this view for feminist criticism; but now I would like to go further and argue that another problem with such formulations lies in their assumption that an *already-existent* meaning resides *somewhere*, and that the critic's job is to locate it (in the text, in the reader, in the interpretive community, or in the relations among the three). On the contrary, a fully politicized feminist criticism has seldom been content to ascertain old meanings and (in the manner of the ethnographers) take the measure of already-constituted subjectivities; it has aimed, rather, at bringing into being *new* meanings and *new* subjectivities, seeking to articulate not only what *is* but "what has never been."[15] In this respect it may be said to have a performative dimension—i.e., to be *doing* something beyond restating already existent ideas and views, wherever these might happen to reside.

The term "performative" has received its fullest elaboration in the philosophy of J. L. Austin, whose work has recently been revived by Jacques

46

Derrida. While Derrida's appreciation/ critique of Austin has aroused some controversy and been addressed at length in Shoshana Felman's book, *The Literary Speech Act*, the implications of this work have gone largely unnoticed by feminist criticism.[16] According to Austin, many utterances, or speech acts, are not merely descriptive statements of fact ("constatives") but expressions whose function is to carry out a performance. As his first example, and one to which he continually returns, Austin cites the act of saying "I do" in a wedding ceremony—words by which the speaker commits him/herself to another person in a ceremony that makes the promises uttered legal and binding. When judging the success of such an act, Austin says, the criteria we invoke are not the truth or falsity of the claim, but the "felicity" or "infelicity" of the performance: thus, if a man utters the words "I do" when he is already married, the act is an infelicitous one. Generally, for an act to be felicitous, "there must exist an accepted conventional procedure having a certain conventional effect, the procedure to include the uttering of certain words by certain persons in certain circumstances."[17] But, going on to question the term "exist" in this formulation, Austin concedes that there are cases "of procedures which someone is initiat-ing"[18]—a concession of great importance to the feminist critic, who, partici-pating in a community whose values she both shares and "helps to form," is in the process of challenging "accepted conventional procedures" and forging new ones.[19]

In the broadest sense, feminist critical writing is performative insofar as it embodies a promise. In this respect, Austin's privileging of the promise, involving as it does a commitment to the future, is of special interest to feminism, although the fact that Austin chooses to concentrate on marriage vows is not without a certain irony. For feminist criticism has, of course, rejected the ideology—purveyed in romances and many other forms of popular and high art—that holds marital commitments to be women's chief goal and greatest desire. It has sought to show how such performatives may be "infelicitous" from the *woman*'s point of view and has attempted to redefine our "commitments." Nevertheless, despite the redefinition, it re-mains importantly the case that feminist critical writing is committed writ-ing, a writing committed to the future of women.

In seeking to answer the question, "Why write?" Jean-Paul Sartre (who was referring to the creative writer, but in terms that suit our purposes as well) proposed a definition of "committed" or "engaged" writing as writing that presupposes the freedom of the other (the reader)—recognizes this freedom, has "confidence in it" and requires of it "an act in its own name, that is, in the name of the confidence that one brings to it." In the final analysis "the end to which [writing] offers itself is the reader's freedom."[20] By assuming, to use our old slogan, that people are not (only) cultural dupes, by assuming a degree of freedom in the reader (an assumption ethnography continually works to prove and hence seldom gets around to building upon) *at the same time that the writer takes this freedom*—woman's liberation—*as a goal*, feminist critical writing is simultaneously performative and utopian, pointing toward the freer world it is in the process of inaugurating. Thus it may be said to contain, as the Frankfurt School would put it (speaking, however, strictly of high art), a *promesse de bonheur*.

According to Sartre, "committed writing" involves the transmission of a dream or a vision to others and hence participates in a

> ceremony of the *gift* and the gift alone brings about the metamorphosis. It is something like the transmission of titles and powers in the matriarchate where the mother does not possess the names, but is the indispensable intermediary between uncles and nephew. Since I have captured this illusion in flight, since I lay it out for other men and have disengaged it and rethought it for them, they can consider it with confidence. It has become intentional. (pp. 33–34)

Obviously feminists cannot accept Sartre's account without revising it significantly, for feminist criticism is involved in a twofold process: first, it reveals the ideological workings of a system in which women, far from being in a position to *give* the gifts, *are* the gifts, "indispensable intermediaries" between men; and, second, by engaging in relationships of reciprocity with other women, it works toward a time when the traditionally mute body, "the mother," will be given the same access to "the names"—language and speech—that men have enjoyed.

Recent work influenced by continental theory has, however, challenged the very premises on which this project could proceed. The most pertinent of these challenges is contained in Shoshana Felman's book, *The Literary Speech Act*, entitled in the original French, *Le scandale du corps parlant*, or *The Scandal of the Speaking Body*, which represents an attempt to save

Austin's work from Derrida's criticism, in part by analyzing it in light of the theories of Jacques Lacan. In this book Felman, who has done important work in the past as a feminist critic, implicitly disavows the Sartrean notion of committed writing and instead frankly celebrates a speech of broken commitments and broken promises, proposing Austin as theorist of a "radically negative" view of language and Molière's Don Juan as exemplar of the literary speech act. For Felman, Don Juan's heroism (i.e., Lacanianism) lies in his refusal to make his speech conform to or refer to anything outside itself, thus engaging solely in performative speech and thus, too, exposing language as purely self-referential: "The trap of seduction . . . consists in producing a *referential illusion* through an utterance that is by its very nature *self-referential*: the illusion of a real or extralinguistic act of commitment [the promise of marriage] created by an utterance that refers only to itself [the act of seduction, which takes place within language]."[21] In a way, Felman seems to be arguing, Don Juan's refusal to keep his commitments to women is analogous to the refusal of writing (whether literary or critical) to honor what Christopher Butler has called "mimetic commitments."[22] With the advent of Derrida and Lacan, and the privileging of self-referential writing, the very notion of committed writing seems to become passé.

For both Derrida and Felman, the interest of Austin's work lies in the way it has problematized the notion of the referent. Derrida writes, "As opposed to the classical assertion, to the constative utterance, the performative does not have its referent . . . outside of itself, or, in any event, before and in front of itself."[23] Derrida, however, criticizes Austin for subverting the radical nature of this insight when the latter turns to contextual information—information "outside" of the utterance—in judging the felicity of a speech act: for example, when Austin notes, "[I]t is hardly a gift if I *say* I give it you but never hand it over." According to Derrida, by holding fast to the felicity/infelicity opposition and by appealing to a realm beyond the speech act, i.e., "the total context," in order to judge the success of the act, Austin demonstrates a belief in "absolutely meaningful speech master of itself" and falls victim to the usual philosophical error which refuses to see the "irreducible polysemy" of language, the " 'dissemination' escaping the horizon of the unity of meaning."[24]

One surely cannot quarrel with Derrida's view that writing does not simply reflect a prior reality, nor with his implication that—to use Austin's example—in literary and critical writing the giving of the gift is in a sense identical with the claim to be giving it: to write *is* "to hand it over." Neither can it be disputed that claims to take into account "the total context" in analyzing speech acts involve an illusory ideal of mastery. But various critics have argued that although there will always be elements of language and its contexts that escape our control and although our contact with the real will always be mediated by language, we are not thereby obliged to abandon all hope of understanding, in limited ways, events "before and in front of" literary and critical speech acts—in other words, all hope of, on the one hand, acknowledging the impact of history (a text's contexts), and, on the other, writing in reference to a (better) future.

Because they are ultimately concerned with altering material reality, most political critics seem to be reluctant to abolish the category of the referent altogether, although like Christopher Butler in his book *Interpretation, Deconstruction, and Ideology*, most *do* seek to go beyond "simple mimetic theory." Noting the tendency of some contemporary theorists to invoke naive notions of reference and the real, which are then undermined by the theorist as sophisticated deconstructor, Butler proposes that the relation between world and text is not one of exact correspondence "to the facts," but one that always, necessarily, involves the "interpreter's mediating statements" (p. 53). Like Fish and others, Butler says these statements will be produced in relation to the codes, conventions, and ideological presuppositions of the interpreter, who invokes interpretive norms developed from within a given community or institutional framework. "There are," Butler writes, "all sorts of relationships between the text and the world, from the relatively trivial (Betsey Trotwood is just like my Aunt Mabel) to the historically and ideologically significant (as when Goldmann argues that Racinian tragedy reveals the essential structure of the relationship of the *noblesse de la robe* to the Kings of France)" (p. 54).

Now a feminist critic, who believes history and ideology to be important stakes in feminist criticism, may well find parts of Butler's argument compelling, but will certainly be inclined to raise an eyebrow at his examples. From a feminist point of view, nothing could be *more* "historically and ideologically significant" than the existence of the single woman in patriarchal society, her (frequently caricatured) representation in patriarchal art, and the relationship between the reality and the representation. This example helps to suggest the limitations of literary theories that restrict themselves to a search for meaning instead of inquiring into the illocutionary force of a text, and it suggests as well the necessity of understanding how performative and referential aspects of texts are interrelated. For feminism, it is not simply a question of affirming or denying the accuracy of patriarchal representations, but of understanding what texts like *David Copperfield do*, how they *produce* the very resemblances they are then seen to reflect (how they influence our perception of Aunt Mabel and Aunt Mabel's perception of herself). I am not arguing for a crude understanding of cause and effect here. Just as Butler argues against "simple mimetic theory," one can claim that texts have all sorts of complicated effects on readers without subscribing to the simplified theories of sociological and ethnographic critics or to the kinds of arguments advanced by, say, some anti-pornography groups (e.g., that pornography leads directly to rape). In a critique of those who ridicule the anti-pornography groups for their oversimplifications, Monique Wittig suggests one way of theorizing pornographic discourse—and by implication, any discourse—as "performative act":

> The pornographic discourse is part of the strategies of violence which are exercised upon us: it humiliates, it degrades, it is a crime against our "humanity." As a harassing tactic it has another function, that of a warning. . . . [The] experts in semiotics . . . reproach us for confusing, when we demonstrate against pornography, the discourses with the reality. They do not see that this discourse *is* reality for us, one of the facets of the reality of our oppression. They believe that we are mistaken in our level of analysis.[25]

As with pornographic discourse, so too with other, more "respectable" discourses, like Dickens's novels: they not only reflect women's subordinate status but may actively denigrate and demean women—a process to which Butler contributes in his own small way when, casting about for an example of the trivial, he strikes irresistibly upon the image of the spinster.

In seeking to reevaluate the very criteria by which we judge historical and ideological significance, and to counter the violence of patriarchal rhetoric (and break the vicious cycle whereby the performative and mimetic aspects of texts mutually reinforce each other, representation producing reality and reality affirming representation), feminism must martial its own illocutionary force to "detrivialize" women. In doing so it should avoid falling into "the trap of seduction" and reject as an ideological ruse the attempts to render language and literature trivial that often take place in the very name of the feminine. For example, at one point Felman praises Don Juan/Austin for revealing "History" to be "made up of trivialities," since "unlike saying, doing is always trivial: it is that which, by definition, cannot be generalized," and she quotes Roland Barthes:

> A writer—by which I mean . . . the subject of a praxis—must have the persistence of the watcher who stands at the crossroads of all other discourses, in a position that is *trivial* in respect to purity of doctrine (*trivialis* is the etymological attribute of the prostitute who waits at the intersection of three roads).[26]

Notwithstanding the sleight of hand here, by which the *writer* as the speaking body is identified with the "trivial" prostitute, let us not forget that the practice praised by Felman throughout the book is the devaluation of women *by* Don Juan, who in seducing them relegates them to the status of "mere" bodies.[27] It is difficult to see what Felman means in claiming performance to be anti-generalization, since she earlier praises Don Juan for acting according to "the principle of substitutability" (p. 37). But isn't this to say that Don Juan, the "master of rupture" (p. 43), treats all women as conquests and deprives them of their uniqueness, fulfilling, in fact, the performative definitions of "generalize" given in the *American Heritage Dictionary*: "to render indefinite or unspecific," "to reduce to a general form, class or law"—the class being in this case the female gender? In any event, of course, the real, historical scandal to which feminism addresses itself is surely not to be equated with the writer at the center of discourse, but with the woman who remains outside of it, not with the "speaking body," but with the "mute body."

Not, then, Don Juan, Austin, Kierkegaard, Lacan, Nietzsche, or Marx— all of whom are mentioned by Felman as scandalous speaking bodies—but maybe Judith Shakespeare, the woman imagined by Virginia Woolf. We might recall that the crossroads, in addition to being the place where the prostitute waits and the place where, says Felman, the murder of the father occurs, is also the place where Shakespeare's sister lies buried after having been ruined by the male stage manager who laughed at *her* "performative" ambitions, her attempts to become a speaking body, and who seduced and abandoned her and drove her to suicide. To him she was just another of the infinitely substitutable female bodies he would encounter in the course of his life.

Woolf's distinctive accomplishment in *A Room of One's Own* (an accomplishment ignored by some recent Woolf criticism which focuses on "the limits of Woolf's feminism," meaning, very often, the limits of her socialism) was to have given a name, a desire, and a history to one of the mute females who lived and died in obscurity.[28] In so doing, Woolf deliberately engaged in "a dynamic movement of the modification" of historical reality[29] and thus realized one of the chief performative and utopian ambitions of feminist criticism. So too, in a sense, it could be said that *every* time a feminist critic speaks and writes as a woman in a world that has always conspired to silence and negate women she brings into being a new order and enacts the scandal of the speaking body in a far more profound way than those people already authorized to speak by virtue of their gender.

The question of authorization is indeed very much at stake in the theory and practice of the performative, as Felman herself points out, quoting Austin, whose "scandalous" words she allows to dominate the second half of her book: "A performative utterance . . . has existence only as an act of authority" (p. 50). To be sure, Felman is concerned primarily with the way the speech of great men undermines its *own* authority, an authority that is, we might add, thereby confirmed since, as Terry Eagleton has pointed out, it can "immolate itself only because it is always already in place . . . secure . . and perhaps likely to reinforce that security the more flamboyantly it parades its blindness."[30] A feminist criticism, by contrast, aims at seizing authority from men at the same time that it seeks to redefine traditional models (like the ethnographic one) of authority, power, and hierarchy. Again, Woolf's distinction is that she accomplished both tasks so brilliantly, laughing at male posturing, deflating (hence, making "trivial") masculine pretensions, while affirming women in prose so striking and so dazzling that it has empowered countless numbers of feminists. Nor will it do to characterize this prose as mere aestheticization, as Donna Landry does when she claims:

What Woolf's texts offer feminist critics is a discursive elision of conflict, a magical transformation of intractable historical realities into elegant and exhilarating prose. But this aestheticization is at heart a suppression, and theories based on suppressions are what feminist criticism cannot afford.[31]

Now, the first point, about Woolf's "discursive elision of conflict," is highly debatable, but what concerns me here is the utter dismissal of "elegant and exhilarating prose." Instead of condemning such prose as "aestheticization," we might follow Jacques Derrida in his resuscitation of the concept under the name of "rhetoric." And instead of viewing this dimension of speech acts as a suppressive force, we might view it as a *productive* force, and, most definitely and performatively, as *force*:[32]

> I thought of that old gentleman, who is dead now, but was a bishop, I think, who declared that it was impossible for any woman, past, present or to come, to have the genius of Shakespeare. He wrote to the papers about it. He also told a lady who applied to him for information that cats do not as a matter of fact go to heaven, though they have, he added, souls of a sort. How much thinking those old gentlemen used to save one! How the borders of ignorance shrank back at their approach! Cats do not go to heaven. Women cannot write the plays of Shakespeare.[33]

In asserting her writerly authority with wit and subtlety Woolf enacts a seizure of power that, as many women will understand, is perhaps the most difficult act of all for women to perform, mistresses of the "masquerade" as they may be. It is important, in fact, to distinguish between the concepts of the "performative" and the masquerade, the latter having received much attention from feminist critics in recent years. In Joan Rivière's influential analysis, the masquerade is, precisely, a "feminine" *compensation* on the part of the woman for having usurped what she perceives to be a "masculine" authority and thereby "unsexed" herself.[34] The term "performative" as I use it contains no such disavowal.

Nor, I think, is Woolf engaged in disavowal, although her writing creates a kind of splitting of the subject that has sometimes been linked to the process of fetishization and disavowal. Woolf's emphasis on writing as a process serves to foreground the act of enunciation and challenges dominant modes of authority, which tends to represent itself unilaterally as uncontestable law, drawing on what Homi Bhabha calls "the artifice of the archaic." In an article on what it means to be a committed writer in a post-Derridean, post-Lacanian world, Bhabha discusses this concept of enunciation:

54

It is the very authority of culture as a knowledge of referential truth which is at issue in the concept and moment of *enunciation*. The enunciative process introduces a split in the performative present, of cultural identification; a split between the traditional culturalist demand for a model, a tradition, a community, a stable system of reference—and the necessary negation of the certitude in the articulation of new cultural demands, meanings, strategies in the political present, as a practice of domination, or resistance. . . . [T]he enunciation of cultural difference problematizes the division of past and present . . . at the level of cultural representation and its authoritative address.[35]

In making her poet the sister of Shakespeare, Woolf acknowledges the importance to her of male literary traditions, models, and canons at the same time that, by inventing a poet who would articulate women's experience, she inevitably contests these traditions and negates the cultural certitude they inspire. For women's writing, in critiquing the representation of women in many male texts, possesses the potential to undermine the "stable system of reference" Butler so confidently invokes, even while he argues for the cultural relativism of such invocations. Interestingly, although Shakespeare's sister is created in response to the felt need of feminism to possess its *own* models and traditions, she is a deliberate "artifice of the archaic," which functions to dislodge male cultural authority from the site of "truth."[36] At one point, for example, Woolf remarks on the way Dr. Johnson—that archetype of the male authority figure whose words are always performatively becoming law—uses the same phrase the imaginary stage manager had uttered to Judith Shakespeare:

A woman acting put him in mind of a dog dancing. Johnson repeated the phrase two hundred years later of women preaching. And here, I said, opening a book about music we have the same words used again in this year of grace, 1928, of women who try to write music. . . . So accurately does history repeat itself. (p. 56)

In the very act of appearing to cede the omnipotence of patriarchal authority, Woolf undermines it by claiming prior authority and placing herself at the originary moment. In giving priority to fiction (her own) Woolf suggests the fictiveness, and hence arbitrariness, of the patriarchal cultural tradition, i.e., suggests that its authority does indeed rely on an "*artifice* of the archaic," on "representational *strategies*," on the "*guise* of a pastness that is not necessarily a faithful sign of historical memory" but a fictive force that gains power through iteration—history repeating itself *in*accurately (Bhabha, p. 19, emphasis added). Far from eliding the question of history and avoiding historical conflict, then, Woolf actually stages a conflict *with* the past, complicating the notion of history, and simultaneously demonstrating a commitment to its very absences.

Because these *are* absences, however, Woolf must ultimately look to the future for a female poet who will "put on the body which she has so often laid down" and give voice to the women who have led such "infinitely obscure lives" that "no biography or history has a word to say" about them. As she describes the poet's task, Woolf performatively becomes the woman she seeks:

> I . . . went on in thought through the streets of London feeling in imagination the pressure of dumbness, the accumulation of unrecorded life, whether from the women at the street corners with their arms akimbo, and the rings embedded in their fat swollen fingers, talking with a gesticulation like the swing of Shakespeare's words; or from the violet-sellers and match-sellers and old crones stationed under doorways; or from drifting girls whose faces, like waves in sun and cloud, signal the coming of men and women and the flickering lights of shop windows. . . . [I]n imagination, I had gone into a shop. . . . And there is the girl behind the counter too—I would as soon have her true history as the hundred and fiftieth life of Napoleon or seventieth study of Keats and his use of Miltonic inversion which old Professor Z and his like are now inditing. (pp. 93–94)

Not unlike Austen's Catherine in *Northanger Abbey*, who found standard history boring because it excluded women, Woolf directs her attention to the lives of the Aunt Mabels rather than to the French kings and emperors, and in rejecting accepted views of the insignificance of women's lives, begins to put new values and new ideologies into "play"—"getting away with things," so to speak. "Getting away with things is essential, despite the suspicious terminology," observes J. L. Austin, using a typical masculine analogy to illustrate the point, "like, in football, the man who first picked up the ball and ran" (p. 30). Mindful of Woolf's re-valuations of male and female activities ("football and sport are important, the worship of fashion, the buying of clothes *trivial*" [p. 77]), we might prefer to replace Austin's example with a sartorial one and think of feminist performative writing as a sort of "fashion statement," a styling of unconventional femininities. In

56

any event, a speech act, like any act, may sometimes inaugurate whole new forms of play and creativity—and this is the performative point of Woolf's rhetoric, as well as its pleasure.

Colin Mercer writes:

> No longer can the contradictory *play* of ideology be reduced to questions of meaning and truth. You can ask whether people "believe" what they hear on the News or on *Nationwide*, but it's by no means clear what people would "believe" in light entertainment or comedy. Once enjoyment and pleasure are reintroduced—those jokers in the game—we have to change the rules and go beyond the message.[37]

As these words suggest, ideology is as effective as it is because it bestows pleasure on its subjects rather than simply conveying messages, and so it cannot be combated only at the level of meaning. For this reason, the theory and practice of the performative are crucial to a politically engaged criticism. Felman points out that the "radical negativity" of the performative philosophers—who are, we remember, concerned with "felicity" and "infelicity" rather than truth and falsity—is intimately related to questions of pleasure and power. Discussing Austin's humor, she writes, "humor constitutes not only an assault on knowledge but also an assault on power, on repression in every sense of the word—political or analytical" (p. 118). But as feminists have repeatedly pointed out, humor is in fact very often an "assault" on the powerless, and hence is part of the reality of women's oppression. Feminism has sought to overthrow this oppression by offering alternative pleasures, and through its myriad subtle and deft rhetorical strategies, its scathing and often exhilarating humor, has indeed begun to "transform" the "intractable historical realities" of women's lives. "Our mothers and grandmothers . . . mov[ed] to music not yet written," says Alice Walker in one of her critical essays, again reminding us of the way "the division of past and present" is problematized in the enunciation of cultural difference.[38]

Toward the end of *A Room of One's Own*, Woolf considers the kinds of tasks the female writer faces:

> She will not need to limit herself any longer to the respectable houses of the upper middle classes. She will go without kindness or condescension, but in

57

the spirit of fellowship into those small, scented rooms where sit the courtesan, the harlot and the lady with the pug dog. (p. 92)

Although we surely want to go further than Woolf and imagine a time when there will *be* no classes to which the woman writer may restrict herself, we have not come close to realizing the vision that would make the radical struggle possible. Years after Woolf wrote of her hopes, the mute women remain mostly mute, despite the kindly ethnographers and the Lacanian/ Barthesian/Austinian critics who embrace the role of prostitute: the real courtesan still sits in her small, scented room and the prostitute stands at the crossroads, where the fathers continue either to be solicited or murdered. And Woolf's prophecy of a female "fellowship" in which women speak freely to and of one another remains to some extent a promise—and nothing less.

PART II

Masculinity and Male Feminism

CHAPTER FOUR

A Father Is Being Beaten

Male Feminism and the War Film

In 1959 J. Glenn Gray published his classic study, *The Warriors: Reflections on Men in Battle*, dedicated to his wife, Ursula, whom he designates as "formerly one of 'the enemy.' " Reading the words of this dedication today, from the vantage of people who have gone through the latest wave of feminism, we might take them to refer not only to Ursula Gray's nationality but to her gender as well: she was an enemy, according to the contemporary view, as much because she was a woman as because she was German. Gray's book, however, scarcely even touches on the relationship between male sexuality and male violence in war, although, to be sure, the little it does say is astonishingly candid, given the time in which it was written. In a chapter entitled "Love: War's Ally and Foe," Gray writes, "[There] is enough of the rapist in every man to give him insight into the grossest manifestations of sexual passion. Hence it is presumptuous for any of us to scorn the practitioners of the lowest kind of passion as beings with whom we have no kinship."[1] In contrast to Gray, who has virtually nothing more to say on the subject, contemporary texts devoted to analyzing "the enduring appeals of battle" tend to focus obsessively on the issue of sexuality—to the point indeed of excluding almost every other factor. The titles of two of the most recent books on war, Klaus Theweleit's *Male Fantasies* and Anthony Wilden's *Man and Woman, War and Peace*, underscore the shift in focus. But perhaps the shift is made most evident and dramatic in Stanley Kubrick's film, *Full Metal Jacket,* when in the final sequence the marines, believing themselves to be facing an enemy force, discover that they are up against one lone sniper who turns out to be a young Vietnamese woman.

For these men, whose transformation in boot camp came when they graduated from being a bunch of "ladies," as the gunnery sergeant calls them, to a platoon of hardened marines, the moral of the encounter might be summarized, "We have met the enemy and she is us." In this way, Kubrick's film shows that an important objective of war is to subjugate femininity and keep it at a distance. However, at the same time that the film is critical of male sexual attitudes in war, it is, like most patriarchal representations, in complicity with the attitudes it attacks. As the young woman writhes on the floor begging the men to shoot her, the camera lingers on the scene at agonizing length until she is finally put out of her misery. The ending of the film thus corroborates Theweleit's finding that the war fantasies he studied invariably build to a climax in which the woman/enemy is rendered a bloody mass.[2]

When Rafter Man, the Mama's boy turned gung-ho killer, critically wounds the young female sniper, he boasts, "Am I a heart-breaker, am I a life-taker?" The words recall the title of another film about marines, *Heartbreak Ridge*, which refers to a battle site in Korea where the hero, played by Clint Eastwood, has distinguished himself for bravery. The words of the title are picked up by the country and western love song, "Sea of Heartbreak," that plays during the credit sequence over documentary footage of war. Like *Full Metal Jacket*, but in a less critical vein, *Heartbreak Ridge* and other current war films show the activities of breaking hearts and taking lives—that is, sexual domination and wartime aggression—to be so intertwined as to make it nearly impossible to speak, in an older way of conceptualizing the problem, of a "displaced sexuality." In fantasies of war, sexuality is manifested in violence, and violence carries an explosive sexual charge. To take a particularly vivid example from a sequence in *Top Gun*: as each of the two male characters goes off to have sex with the woman he is involved with, the song "Great Balls of Fire" plays on the soundtrack; then the music merges into that of the theme song, while the men go back to practicing their war games and are forced to parachute out of the plane, which explodes as the hero's partner dies.

Speaking of the writings of the men in Germany's Freikorps, Klaus Theweleit notes a similar merging of the "idea of 'woman' with representations of violence," a violence that stems, in his view, from "a fear of dissolution through union with a woman" and that propels man—or, to use

Julia Kristeva's term, abjects him—into a homosocial relation with other men.[3] The film *Top Gun*, which Jim Hoberman in his review for *The Village Voice* aptly retitled *Phallus in Wonderland*, provides the best contemporary example of the dynamics analyzed by Theweleit. In this film the presence of the love interest protects man from suspicions of homosexuality, while male homoeroticism protects him from too great an intimacy with woman. For example, after the film's hero "Maverick" meets "Charlie," the female instructor in the pilot training school known as Top Gun, the film takes great pains to establish his command of the relationship. On the first date he has with her, he is late because he is playing volleyball with some other men. In this rather lengthy sequence, the camera lovingly dwells on the glistening muscular male bodies and on the men's triumphant embraces, slaps, and hand claps as they score points. Charlie is thus punished for her earlier refusal to "drop right down on the floor and go for it" in the ladies' room of the bar where Maverick has followed her on the first night he sees her—the ladies' room being the place where, according to a joke made by Maverick's chief competitor in flight school, the plaque for Top Gun's runners-up is located. In this way the film suggests once again—and unwittingly, to be sure—that sexual and military conquest are somehow intimately related, and that the relationship has to do with the need to conquer femininity both within and without.

The character of Charlie represents one of popular culture's latest attempts to come to terms with feminism by appropriating it. Far from being the typical clinging, rather unintelligent heroine of so much contemporary film, Charlie possesses a Ph.D. in astrophysics and is in a position of authority over the hero. Her sexual capitulation begins when she learns that Maverick has actually done battle with a certain MIG fighter plane; she becomes more and more entranced as she submits to his superior authority gained from having experienced "the real thing" rather than deriving knowledge, as she has, solely through books. In the film's account, then, women desire men precisely in their capacity as warriors—a role to which they are shown continually to defer: thus, when his partner dies, Maverick goes to comfort the man's wife, who ends by consoling *him* and assuring him of how much his friend loved flying with him.

A much more elaborate example of popular film's cooptation of feminism, or at least of a liberal progressive attitude towards women and male/

female relationships, may be found in Clint Eastwood's film, *Heartbreak Ridge*. Judith Mayne has shown how Clint Eastwood films are of interest for the way they continually engage with the problem of woman—and this in contrast to most contemporary genre films which relegate women to an uninteresting periphery.[4] *Heartbreak Ridge* continues the pattern analyzed by Mayne, and, moreover, like Eastwood's previous film *Tightrope*, it helps us to shed light on the stakes of current male scholarship devoted to exploring male fantasies and of male feminism more generally.

In this film, Eastwood plays a hardened gunnery sergeant, Tom Highway, who undertakes the task of transforming a platoon of lazy, self-indulgent, undisciplined marines, whom he too calls "ladies," into a team of determined fighting men. As in *Full Metal Jacket*, the film's impact lies as much in the constant barrage of insults the sergeant hurls at his men as in the physical prowess they exhibit in their war games. Highway's conventional barracks language reveals a strong disgust associated with femininity—he speaks in his first lines of getting "the clap and the drip and the crabs and generally a poor attitude to the female of the species"; his speech contrasts ludicrously with the women's magazines that he takes to reading in an effort to find a means of communicating with his ex-wife Aggie (Marsha Mason) to win her back. In fact, it is precisely through the clash of two languages, two competing discourses, that the tension between maleness and femaleness is played out in the film—albeit in a somewhat humorous vein.

Early on, Highway tells the waitress at the local bar that he and his wife had divorced because "marriage and the Marine Corps weren't too compatible," and she responds, "Panther Piss. Some of the best years of my life were spent with a marine." Later, Highway waits for Aggie to get off work and sits in his car reading the magazines and muttering phrases like "sensitive dialogue," "meaningful communication in the relationship," and so on. Suddenly he gets angry and exclaims, "Panther Piss," whereupon Aggie, overhearing the last words, comes up and says sarcastically, "Well, I'm glad some things don't change; you still know what a woman loves to hear." The irony, of course, is that Highway has in fact used the words of another *woman*—words that functioned initially to discount the notion that marriage and war might be incompatible, and which now deny that a woman might want to hear and speak a language different from the language used by man to objectify and degrade her. Soon after this exchange, Highway and Aggie seem on the verge of reconciling, and he says, "Tell me something, did we mutually nurture each other? . . . Did we communicate in a meaningful way in our relationship?" Aggie looks surprised and then laughs, "Relationship? Hell, I thought we were married." Thus, the heroine herself is made to invalidate the language the man is using to try to communicate in her terms. The film also employs an editing strategy which works almost subliminally to suggest that women positively enjoy the pornographic language prevailing among military comrades: on several different occasions, when Highway and/or his men say something particularly obscene—as when one extemporizes the chant, "Model A Ford, and a tank full of gas/Handful of pussy and a mouthful of ass"—the camera cuts to very brief reaction shots of women, who have no narrative purpose other than to look titillated and amused by the obscenity. The subversion of any possible independent female viewpoint culminates in the final sequence of the film in which Aggie is seen wearing a white dress and waving a little American flag to greet the conquering heroes on their return from the successful invasion of Grenada. *Heartbreak Ridge* reveals itself to be a film very much of the moment in that, despite a few bows to the lessons of feminism, the film purveys a profoundly misogynist vision which it works to get women to share.

One might hope that views of women such as those found in mass cultural texts like *Heartbreak Ridge* would be seriously challenged by male critics wanting to take feminism seriously and trying to come to terms with the misogyny at the heart of the warrior mentality. And in fact, in his recently published book, *Man and Woman, War and Peace*, Anthony Wilden deplores the way mass media stereotypes women and thus helps to perpetuate "the colonization of women by men" that is one of the effects of war.[5] In drawing heavily on the work of Susan Brownmiller to expose the rapist mentality of men in war, Wilden is one of a number of male critics who are trying to see the woman's point of view and to incorporate it into the work they are undertaking on the subject of masculinity and war.

Nevertheless, there are problems: for example the sheer amount of quotation in Wilden's text—quotations from various sources that go into gruesome and excruciating detail about men's treatment of women in war and that are followed by little or no commentary—suggests a certain, no doubt unwitting, complicity with the material being exposed.[6] An even more serious problem occurs in the last part of Wilden's book, where he actually counsels women to learn the strategies of war. In doing so, he thereby replicates the tactics of a film like *Heartbreak Ridge*, which begins by appearing to take seriously the female viewpoint but only so as ultimately to secure women's assent to male discourse and the masculine perspective on war: "This is not to suggest," writes Wilden,

> that learning the practice of imperialism by following the strategy of male supremacy is in itself a good idea, but it is to insist that without the command of that ever-dominant strategy women can neither defeat it, control it, nor go beyond it—and thus never successfully declare their independence of men. (p. 232)

Feminism has now paradoxically become the last alibi for the liberal male's fascination with war. Wilden's strategy enables him to maintain a position of authority in relation to feminism and to instruct women in military tactics by rehearsing some of history's most famous battles, all the while denouncing the victimization of women that occurs in war. Indeed, Wilden goes so far as to contend that war is an appropriate "metaphor for everyday life" and that each person in a democracy should become a strategist—although a feminist might counter that the very language of war as the embodiment of patriarchal, imperialistic desires needs to be contested if the world is ever to be transformed along feminist lines.

Man and Woman, War and Peace vividly illustrates the fact that even today and even among men with feminist sympathies war is a condition that is felt to endow men with superior truth and insight. The truth of war may indeed be that it is hell, but for all that, it provides the ultimate authoritative experience. In Gustav Hasford's book *The Short-Timers*, on which *Full Metal Jacket* is based, a phrase is used throughout the novel by both the narrator and the other men whenever something especially telling or ironic is said about war: "There it is."[7] Nothing more, it is implied, needs to be said, or indeed can be said. War is the ultimate male referent: that state of affairs which, in Wilden's view, provides a language enabling us to understand all human events, or, in Hasford's, makes all other experiences pale into insignificance by contrast. Such an attitude, it should not need to be said, threatens to erode the gains made by feminists like

66

Brownmiller, who insisted on the need to adopt not just the perspective of the warrior but also that of the *victims* or potential victims of war and of the rapist mentality that reigns in wartime.

While the widely acknowledged first volume of Klaus Theweleit's book, *Male Fantasies*, shares some of the problems of Wilden's study—in particular, the reliance on a superabundance of evidence to "speak for itself"—Theweleit attempts to analyze more extensively the warrior's hostility towards women. As other of his left-wing compatriots have done before him (in particular, of course, the members of the Frankfurt School), Theweleit turns to a discussion of psychoanalysis to understand how this hostility finds root in the male subject, and he insists on the importance of taking into account the male's relationship with the mother. Thus after discussing the way in which Freikorps soldiers' fantasies exhibit "a desire for, and fear of fusion, explosion"—a dynamic we have seen to be at work in *Top Gun*—Theweleit concludes that, contrary to what some psychoanalytic critics would maintain, what is at stake is not so much castration anxiety, as "a fear of total annihilation and dismemberment," which has its sources in the early, pre-oedipal mother-child symbiosis and the separation-individuation processes (p. 205).

Theweleit's argument recalls that of Julia Kristeva, who, in analyzing "rituals of defilement"—among which we can surely count many of the practices of war, particularly with regard to women—displaces castration anxiety to emphasize the mother/child dyad. Kristeva claims that these rituals have to do with overcoming a "threat to the subject: that of being swamped by the dual relationship, thereby risking the loss not of a part (castration) but of the totality of his living being. The function of these . . . rituals is to ward off the subject's fear of his very own identity sinking irretrievably into the mother."[8] Theweleit, however, is less cautious than Kristeva, and the section entitled "Floods, Bodies, History" at the end of his volume becomes a virtual paean to the "swamp" of female sexuality. Noting that "in the eyes of men who fear streams (because they seem 'unclean'), the bodies of erotic women, especially proletarian women, become so much wet dirt," Theweleit proceeds to wax lyrical about dirt, mire, the morass, slime, pulp, shit, rain, and floods, each of which has a separate heading in the book (p. 421). However, this excessive language in praise of floods, which it would seem to be the business of feminism to challenge, clearly contains the potential of a severe backlash. As the work of Kristeva both discusses and exemplifies, such a powerful evocation of an image of the maternal/feminine as that which threatens the integrity of the subject only leads man to yearn all the more strongly for the paternal law that will rescue him.[9] Indeed, this is the purport of Dorothy Dinnerstein's influential study, *The Mermaid and the Minotaur*, which argues that man's need to separate himself from the powerful mother—"the dirty goddess"—results in the subjugation of women and the desire to embrace what seems to be a less arbitrary authority, paternal authority.[10]

However, not only does Theweleit minimize the importance of the paternal law by stressing the individual's pre-oedipal relation with the mother, he actually draws heavily on the book *Anti-Oedipus*, by Gilles Deleuze and Felix Guattari in order to mount an all-out attack on the theory of the Oedipus complex. Now, while it is no doubt true that Oedipus is a historically-specific rather than a universal phenomenon (and it is certainly in the interests of feminism to continue to insist on this historical specificity), there is, nevertheless, something peculiar in Theweleit's choosing to do battle with Oedipus in a study examining the fascist mentality of men who were prepared to die for their "fatherland." Nor is Theweleit's approach an isolated phenomenon, although it may be more extreme than that of other contemporary "male feminists"; on the contrary, his book may be seen as part of a general trend in contemporary theory to refuse to concede to castration and the father a central and determining role; the point of this refusal seems related to the desire to complicate the question of male sexuality and so move beyond the notion that masculinity is always about achieving a phallic identity and finding a secure place in the patriarchal order. But as laudable as this desire may be in some respects it is not without its problems. An earlier text of Deleuze on the subject of masochism is, I think, more useful than the *Anti-Oedipus* in illuminating these problems and in revealing what is at stake for some men like Theweleit who are currently entering into feminist debate.

In *Masochism: An Interpretation of Coldness and Cruelty*, Deleuze points to the importance of the pre-oedipal phase in the development of the masochistic personality, and describes the alliance between mother and son in terms that are strikingly relevant to a certain strain of contemporary "male feminist" discourse: "[What] seems to us the essence of the formal process [is] the transference of the law on to the mother and the identification of the law with the image of the mother."[11] And elsewhere, reversing Freud's interpretation of the childhood beating fantasy, in which the father seemed to be beating the child, Deleuze writes, "Where is the father hidden? Could it not be in the person who is being beaten?" (p. 53). Thus in masochism, according to Deleuze, the male child allies himself with the mother against the law of the father, which it is the function of the mother to beat out of the son, whereas sadism involves an alliance with the father against the mother.

Not only is a masochistic alliance as it is described by Deleuze operative in theories like Theweleit's that emphasize the role of the mother to the point of virtually excluding the father, but it can be argued that a similar alliance is being attempted today by some male theorists in relation to feminism: that is, feminism itself has come to occupy the position of the mother who is identified with the law. Thus, in *Men in Feminism*, the volume he edited with Alice Jardine, Paul Smith warns feminists of the dangers attending the "legalization" of their discourse, and he writes:

> But one question which needs to be considered, I think, is the normative, even legalistic aspect of feminist theory itself, and the ensuing culpability of the male breaker and enterer. The question—in any context—of who is allowed to say or do what, to whom and about whom, is ultimately a legal question: it can be raised only where any given discourse is forming or has formed a mode of pragmatic legislation, when it is legalizing itself, defining its outside, naming potential and actual transgressors.[12]

Interestingly, Smith's ironic remarks not only place him in a position similar to that of Deleuze's masochist, insofar as they transfer the law onto women, but they actually produce the effect desired by the masochist—that is, they result in a great deal of abuse being heaped upon him by the various feminist respondents in the volume. Smith—or the would be "breaker and enterer," the rapist/soldier/father *in* Smith—is publicly chastised and humiliated.

According to Deleuze—who, to be sure, is unconcerned about feminism—the equation of woman with the law has the effect not of empowering women, but of throwing the law itself into question and crisis, by deriding it. This is clear enough in Paul Smith's article, with its plays on the notion of men "breaking and entering, entering and breaking" feminist discourse and feminist theory, but it is even more evident in the exchange with Derrida in the same volume.[13] In regard to the question of integrating feminist studies into the curriculum, that is, of making it part of the law that presides in the academy, one of the discussants speaks in terms recalling the rhetoric analyzed in the previous chapter:

> Feminizing the curriculum . . . is trivializing it, is dismantling it, is displacing it; it is making it as trivial as women, and I wonder if it isn't our real strategy: that we work from the base of an operation such as this in order to trivialize philosophy, to trivialize history, to trivialize economics.[14]

Aside from the obvious need for feminists to refuse to allow themselves to be used in one man's war on Western metaphysics, the point that needs to be stressed about all this is that man's alliance with the mothers, formed in order to beat out (or write out) the fathers, is doomed to failure, from a feminist point of view, unless the father is frankly confronted and the entire dialectic of abjection and the law worked through; otherwise, as Deleuze's analysis confirms, the father will always remain in force as the major, if hidden, point of reference—and he may in fact be expected at any time to emerge from hiding with a vengeance.

He has certainly emerged as a strong force on other fronts. While male theorists have been busy disavowing the father, he has made his return via the channels of mass communication—rather like Jack Nicholson at the end of *The Witches of Eastwick*, who, having failed to ingratiate himself with the women by avowing his feminist sympathies, his "admiration" for them, communicates with his three sons from the television screen.[15] And the father is nowhere more visible than in contemporary war films. In *Top Gun*, for example, the entire narrative works to vindicate the father who had served as a pilot in Vietnam and whose career seems to have been shadowed by a major disgrace, the particulars of which are obscure until the end of the film. At the beginning, Maverick's superior officer reprimands him for his reckless flying and says, "Your family name ain't the best in the Navy—you need to be doing it better and cleaner than anyone else." Interestingly, the reason for the reproach is that Maverick, instead of landing his plane, has gone back to rescue another pilot, who has lost

70

his nerve as a result of "holding on too tight" to his family, becoming paralyzed at the thought of making his children "orphans." Later, Maverick's partner, Goose, dies shortly after his wife and child come to visit him, so that he too would seem to be doomed as a consequence of his divided loyalties, to the Navy and Maverick, on the one hand, and to his family, on the other.

Maverick, by contrast, being an orphan as well as a single man, would seem to be the ideal warrior; however, his foolhardy acts, which are continually said to endanger the group, are attributed to the shame the father has visited on the son: as one of the other pilots says, "You always seem to be flying against a ghost up there." After the death of Goose, "the only family" Maverick says he has, Maverick loses his nerve since he is unable "to let him go." Maverick is so inconsolable over the loss of Goose that he ignores Charlie, who goes off to Washington to a new and more prestigious job. All the personal and professional turmoil is set to rights, however, the homosocial and heterosexual bonds renewed in a more moderate way, when Maverick finds out from Top Gun's commander that his father "did do it right," that he died performing feats of incredible bravery.

The desire to rewrite the history of Vietnam to prove that we were not cowardly losers but merely unacknowledged winners—true heroes, in fact—may be seen in many forms of popular culture today; what *Top Gun* makes especially clear is how this rewriting frequently expresses a yearning for a strong paternal figure who will enable young men to go off and "do it right" too, to become heroic soldiers in the new wars to come. *Heartbreak Ridge* offers further testimonial to this desire and indeed at one point has the Clint Eastwood character, a veteran of Vietnam, remark that we won all the battles, we just lost the war. In contrast to *Top Gun*, which is told from the point of view of the son, *Heartbreak Ridge* adopts the point of view of the "father," Tom Highway, who is continually referred to as an anachronism, a "relic," someone who should be "locked in a case that reads, 'Break glass only in the event of war.' " The glass *is* broken, of course, and Highway goes off to Grenada with his refurbished platoon of marines and at the end hands the warrior's mantle over to the surrogate son, Stitch Jones, the young black male, who in the racist homosocial tradition of American letters occupies a subordinate role to the white hero.

Both *Top Gun* and *Heartbreak* Ridge are clearly "entertainment films"

71

designed to exploit American chauvinism and the warmongering that has prevailed since the beginning of the Reagan years. One might expect that a film like *Platoon*, which is said to be critical of our participation in the Vietnam war, and perhaps critical of war in general, would call into question the hierarchical and authoritarian structure of the military that a film like *Heartbreak Ridge* promotes and celebrates. Far from doing so, however, the film awards its hero with a surplus of authority figures. Thus at the end of the film the protagonist, who has been writing to his grandmother in letters presented to us through voice-over, discovers that he is the spiritual son of *two* fathers—an evil one and a good one. Moreover, after the good one is shot by the evil one, the film ludicrously shows the dying man holding out his arms in imitation of Christ on the cross, thereby sententiously bringing in God the father to add extra authority to the weighty proceedings.

It is important to note as well that in *Platoon* the discovery of so many fathers goes hand in hand with a meliorist position in relation to war. The film's young hero, a Harvard student who joined the army to encounter reality, gets to go through the ultimate authoritative experience, war, and to learn, precisely, a lesson about his relation to authority—i.e., that he *is* the son of two fathers. Far from being critical of war, the film shows it to be capable of providing its sons with crucial insights (about good and evil, etc.) and to be the primary agency of their oedipalization. Now, it is understandable that men who must undergo the dangers and deprivations of war would want desperately to extract some meaning from their experience.

"The deepest fear of my war years," writes J. Glenn Gray, who is also concerned to bring his readers to an awareness of God, "is that these happenings had no real purpose. . . . This conclusion I am unwilling to accept without a struggle; indeed, I cannot accept it at all except as a counsel of despair. How often I wrote in my war journals that unless that day had some positive significance for my future life, it could not possibly be worth the pain it cost" (p. xii).

Perhaps, drawing a very different conclusion from Gray's meditation, we could claim that the supreme and necessary act of courage would be to admit that in fact there often is no higher purpose in war, that the pain it costs is *not* worth it. This, at least, seems to be Stanley Kubrick's view,

72

and more than any of the other films I have discussed, his is concerned to reveal the meaninglessness and absurdity of the Vietnam War in particular and of militarism in general. Interestingly, in direct contrast to a film like *Top Gun*, which is concerned with validating the military father of the orphan/hero, or a film like *Platoon*, in which the hero discovers his true military paternity in two fathers, *Full Metal Jacket* begins by depicting the most exaggerated kind of military father possible, the gunnery sergeant in boot camp, and then killing him off halfway through the film, thus orphaning the men of Parris Island, who subsequently find themselves lost in Vietnam. At one point, in fact, they become literally lost since the leader, nicknamed "Cowboy," has misread the map—the implication being that the authoritarian nature of military training is positively disabling. (Hence, the disjunction between the two halves of the film, which even its supporters consider a flaw, is hardly a problem, but precisely the point.) The critique of authority is sustained right to the end of the film, where, in the last shot, we see the soldiers on the march and hear them softly singing the Mickey Mouse Club song: "Who's the leader of the gang that's made for you and me? M-I-C-K-E-Y M-O-U-S-E."

After getting rid of the father, who is killed as an enemy by the one man who has had the most difficulty learning the masculine behavior and rituals of Boot Camp, the film substitutes for the face of "the enemy" that of a very young woman. In doing so it brings to a logical conclusion the treatment of the Vietnamese women in the film, who are there as prostitutes, commodified objects for the soldiers' use, and it also, interestingly, corresponds to the practice of some of the "male feminists" discussed earlier: in replacing the sergeant/father, who represents traditional military and patriarchal authority, with a woman, the film seems to be pointing to the absurdity of authority itself. In contrast to Wilden, who proposes in all seriousness that women learn military strategy and tactics, Kubrick's black humor and satirical vision find their culmination in this substitution, just as the masochists analyzed by Deleuze deride the law by placing women in the role traditionally occupied by men. As Deleuze notes, "In the contractual relation the woman typically figures as an object in the patriarchal system," but in masochism the situation is reversed, and the woman is made into the "master and torturer" rather than the object, with the result that the entire system is exposed as a mockery (p. 80).

73

Thus Kubrick extensively undermines male authority; the father is not resurrected after he is killed off; neither is war itself seen to confer on its participants any special wisdom. This is not, however, to say that *all* authority has been undermined; it is, of course, recuperated in the signature of the filmmaker himself, the man who has the power to undertake the critique of authority in the first place. In one of the essays in *Men in Feminism*, Cary Nelson, writing about another "male feminist," notes that an essay indicting patriarchy and its institutions and practices will read "differently depending on whether we take it as coming from a man or a woman. [If from the man], then, despite his elaborate efforts at self-effacement, we will hear him . . . as producing his own masochistic subordination, as possessing certainty about where it is he is speaking from, as occupying the site of a phallic truth, however veiled."[16] Deleuze too, in writing about the masochistic position, notes that it is a juridical one and that the masochist, paradoxically, has the power to persuade woman to take up the role of master, the power to "fashion the woman into a despot" (p. 20). Indeed, Deleuze goes so far as to write, "The weakness of the [masochist's] ego is a strategy by which the masochist manipulates the woman into the ideal state for the performance of the role he has assigned to her" (p. 107). Thus, for all the recent theoretical emphasis on the primacy of masochism, a trend motivated in part by the desire to counter the tendency of some feminisms to ascribe a monolithic power to the phallocratic order, it is crucial to understand that no necessary shift in power dynamics accompanies such a move.[17]

In addition, then, to being skeptical of a position that protects male authority, while *appearing* to relinquish it, feminists also, obviously, have much reason to be suspicious of a strategy that uses them to "trivialize" war (or philosophy, or history, or economics, or anything else). For all the recent male concern to critique war, male sexuality, and male aggression, it remains for women to continue to claim the right to be taken *seriously* as authorities—and in fact there has recently been a surge of interest on the part of feminists in the issue of war.[18] In attempting to come to terms with the phenomenon of war such women are not trying to effect a simple reversal of roles, claiming now that they are the ultimate authorities on the subject. Rather, in denying men the prerogative of being the *sole* authorities on the subject, they deny the "aperspectivity" of the male view and insist

74

on the perspective of women as *a* valid, and necessary, perspective. Despite the heavy fortifications of this last bastion of male comradeship, then, women seem determined not to be barred from it, insisting that men learn to respect them as subjects in their own right and no longer to view them as "the enemy."

CHAPTER FIVE

Three Men and Baby M

While some of the films in the current boom of baby boom movies suggest that woman's primary role is to be a mother, others show men taking over this role. In fact, a whole host of comedies are participating in the trend, also noted in the previous chapter, of redeeming and celebrating fatherhood. Two of the most popular such comedies are the enormously popular French film, *Three Men and a Cradle*, and the American remake, *Three Men and a Baby*, which are about an infant named Mary who is left on the doorstep of the infant's father and his two male housemates. These films are especially interesting manifestations of the concern about father's rights that intensified with the controversy over surrogate motherhood. Indeed, what we might call the American "Baby M" film could be seen as the "theory" of contemporary fathering, while surrogate motherhood is, or at least seemed for a time to be, the practice. This is a practice that involves, as Katha Pollitt has argued, women signing away one of the rights that, until the twentieth century, they rarely possessed: "the right to legal custody of their children."[1] It is in *this* historical context, in which women's rights as mothers have been virtually nonexistent, that a film like *Three Men and a Baby* must be seen, rather than being considered the product of a historically unprecedented, feminist-inspired, and altogether contemporary reconceptualization of the paternal role. To be sure, although *Three Men and a Baby* does its utmost to invest desire in the humorous and sentimental vision of a collective male fatherhood, it is a relatively benign version of a father's rights scenario, since it does in fact "make room for Mommy" at the very end of the film. Nevertheless, by keeping the mother from the audience's sight until this point, the film effectively de-realizes her—just as, in Pollitt's argument, the term "surrogate mother" renders the woman's role "as notional as possible," thereby suggesting that since the (biological) mother is the surrogate, the father must be "the real thing" (p. 683). Moreover, even though the men in the film do ultimately incorporate the mother, her return is experienced by the audience as an unfair intrusion and the men's inclusion of her in their ménage a generous (if also pragmatic) gesture.

Even in some of its small details the film surreally evokes, while comically displacing, paternal anxieties about men's relatively minimal role in the process of generation, a role that the very language used in the Baby M case worked to expand. For example, it employs a comic gag involving that infamous do-it-yourself inseminator: a turkey baster. In the men's initial fumbling attempts to give the baby a bath, they use the baster to squirt water at her vaginal and anal areas so as to avoid touching "where the poop was." As this image suggests, the film's popularity may in part be attributed to the way it arouses and contains, in a highly condensed manner, a whole host of male fears not only about fathering, but about female sexuality itself. I would like to look at some of these fears as well as to situate the film within the context of an older myth, embodied in John Ford's 1948 film *3 Godfathers*, a story which has been filmed so many times it is impossible to escape the conclusion that it touches on some very powerful cultural themes. The fact that Ford's film involves a male child, however, will give us an opportunity to analyze how different the stakes are when the sex of the child is female.

The most striking aspect of *Three Men and a Baby*, on first viewing, is the explicitness with which the film reveals men's desire to usurp women's procreative function. In the scene where the three men, having become unwittingly involved with drug dealers, attempt to capture the criminals for the police, the baby's father, Jack (Ted Danson), disguises himself as a pregnant woman. We first see him in a long-shot side-view walking down the dark street, and then the camera switches to a frontal view, as he opens up his coat to reveal little Mary being carried in a sling. The image is a disturbing and unsettling one, reminiscent of those medieval icons of the virgin whose body opens up to display scenes of the holy family. Later, after Mary has been taken away by her mother and the men are mourning the baby's loss, Jack puts a pillow under his sweater and poses in front of a mirror. What are we to make of such scenes? It would appear that "womb envy" and male hysteria are no longer latent thematics to be teased out by the psychoanalytically oriented feminist critic; such envy *is* the manifest content of the film. Are we to conclude that, *pace* Freud, femininity in man is no longer something to be denied and repressed, no longer the object of "normal" male "contempt," but rather a condition that man desires for himself? Are men now prepared openly to avow their bisexuality?

There are two points to be made here: first, that envy of woman can coexist with castration anxiety and with the profoundest misogyny—that men can want to *be* women and still hate and fear them—and, second, that this envy is in fact concomitant with a fear of feminization, even though existing in logical contradiction to it, so that male identification with woman is hedged about with many varieties of "masculine protest."

Indeed, the pedophilic aspects of both the French and American versions of the film point to a kind of revulsion on the part of the men against mature womanhood. That Walt Disney should produce, and audiences receive as "heartwarming," a film laden with jokes about a female baby as an adequate object of sexual desire for three aging bachelors is perhaps not surprising, but it is certainly disturbing, given statistics that show female children to be the chief victims of sexual abuse and males to comprise the overwhelming majority of perpetrators. In both films the men lose interest in sleeping around after Mary becomes part of their lives—a development we're clearly supposed to approve, since it shows the men learning to commit to someone. (As the theme song has it, "Something happened, baby, in my life / The minute I saw you / All the others faded from my life / The minute I saw you.") The fact that this someone is less than a year old, the fact that, as regards the rest of the sex, the men have thrown out the woman with the bath water—i.e., in giving up philandering, they virtually give up interest in women—may perhaps be easily overlooked. Indeed, the ending of the French film points to the kind of comic inversion at the heart of both films, suggesting the infantilization of woman and the sexualization of babyhood that is part of the film wish. At the end of that film, the mother, exhausted from trying to care for the baby alone, is shown *asleep in her baby's crib*, while the baby, walking for the first time, advances toward the camera, and is caught in a freeze frame—a device that, originating in the French New Wave, has become a cliché of film and television, but is entirely appropriate to the pedophilic impulse to freeze the life process so that the object will not outgrow the desire. Even the baby's name, "Mary," points

78

to this reversal of mother/child roles since "Mary," Christianity's mythical mother, becomes Mary the magical foundling—and it also, in a related ideological inversion, expresses a *male* desire to undergo virgin birth, to dispense with the woman's part in conception altogether.

It is clear that in this film fear of woman, along with the castration anxiety her sight provokes, are not less pronounced than in older classical narrative film, but are, in fact, rather more so. In the film's opening sequence, Peter (played by Tom Selleck, whose television character, Magnum, is also part of a trio of male buddies) is being given a birthday party, during which many jokes are made about the men's prowess (or lack of it) with women. Michael (Steve Guttenberg), carrying a video camera, conducts a mock interview of Rebecca, the woman with whom Peter has an "open" relationship, and he asks her why she finds Peter attractive. She responds that he has an "amazing . . ." and substitutes a knee in the groin for the word. The anxiety about castration, conjured up everywhere in the text, is even projected onto the *mise-en-scène*: in the hallway the walls are painted with pictures of chorus girls whose legs are high in the air, their genital areas emphasized by a lamp that hangs on a level with their crotches.

When the baby arrives, shortly after Peter's birthday party (where Peter is shown to be more interested in retreating to a room with a group of men to watch videotapes of himself playing basketball than he is in mingling with the heterosexual crowd), this event elicits a hysterical reaction from Michael and Peter (Jack, the father, is out of the country). While Peter runs in his jogging clothes to buy food and diapers, Michael is left to care for the baby, and he tries desperately to entertain it so it will stop crying, at one point pulling open his shirt to show the baby a hairy chest, at another turning on the television, and then turning it off again quickly when Dr. Ruth appears on the screen saying, "Women are wondering, are they having orgasms; men are worried about their penises." The comic anxiety about bodies, the urge to put masculinity on display (Michael's hairy chest; Peter/Tom Selleck's muscular arms and legs, the famous "thighs and whiskers"[2]), are provoked by the arrival of this tiny incarnation of sexual difference, and build up to a gag in which the men try to diaper the baby, emitting sounds of disgust because she has "doodled," while the camera in some shockingly voyeuristic shots focuses on the baby's genitals. The confusion between genitality and anality exhibited here in the conflict between sound and image is symptomatic of the psychosexual dynamics of the text as a whole—a confusion, which, as we shall see, amounts to a regression to a childhood phantasy that denies what Freud calls "the clear-cut distinction between anal and genital processes" insisted upon in adult sexuality.[3]

In fact, one of the main sources of the film's humor lies in its play on the meanings of the word shit. When Jack goes away, he asks his housemates to receive a package that he has agreed to hold for a friend, and when the baby arrives, the men mistakenly believe her to be the package. They are so preoccupied by the baby that when the real package, containing heroin, arrives, it goes unnoticed. A few days later, two men come by to pick up the heroin, and they converse with Michael at cross purposes about "the shit." Michael says, "There's been shit all over this place for days," and the men ask, "Well, did you put the shit back?" The film becomes virtually obsessed with the fact of shit: a policeman's horse "befouls" the sidewalk in front of the house; Michael plants the heroin in the baby's diaper, and the head of the narcotic's squad assumes when he holds her that she needs to be changed; the heroin is subsequently hidden in the "garbage pail with the other dirty diapers"; and, finally, the three men almost fail in their efforts to entrap the criminals because Jack goes back to the car at a crucial moment to change the baby, who has once again "doodled."

The equation of feces with baby (the baby mistaken for the "shit," the heroine for the heroin), which is *the* central joke of the film is, as we know from Freud, a common phantasy dating from childhood; the child first views the feces as a "gift" and later they "come to acquire the meaning of 'baby'—for babies, according to one of the sexual theories of children, are acquired by eating and are born through the bowels."[4] The "cloacal theory," which is at least as old as Dante (according to a traditional mythology, the devil gives birth to babies by shitting them out), is particularly suited to facilitate the phantasy, expressed so forthrightly in the film, of male usurpation of women's reproductive function. We might even speculate that the necessity imposed on the child early in life of relinquishing anal eroticism and its attendant fantasies results in a feeling of deprivation that aggravates male envy of women for possessing certain pleasures and privileges (few and equivocal as they may be) denied to men. As Lou Andreas Salomé, whom Freud cites, points out, "From that time on, what is 'anal' remains

the symbol of everything that is to be repudiated and excluded from life."
And this is so because

> the prohibition against getting pleasure from anal activity and its products is
> the first occasion on which the infant has a glimpse of an environment hostile
> to his instinctual impulses, on which he learns to separate his own entity
> from this alien one and on which he carries out the first "repression" of his
> possibilities for pleasure.[5]

As this passage helps us to understand, however—and this point cannot
be stressed enough at a time when feminists are increasingly becoming
preoccupied with masculinity, searching for ways to displace the primacy
of castration in film theory and in psychoanalysis, and affirming as tacitly
feminist the "nonphallic" values of male subjectivity—the regressive phantasy involving babies and bowels in no way precludes castration anxiety,
but, on the contrary, exacerbates it: it is, in fact, a prototype of it. " 'Feces,'
'child,' and 'penis,' " writes Freud, "form a unity, an unconscious concept
. . . —the concept, namely, of a little thing that can become separated
from one's body"[6] (what Lacan calls *objets petit à*). Further, in his case
history "The 'Wolf Man,' " Freud explicitly addresses himself to the question of how castration anxiety may coexist with "an identification with
women by means of the bowel." Admitting that this state of affairs is a
logical contradiction, Freud adds that this "is not saying much," since the
unconscious is in fact characterized by conflict and contradiction. Analyzing
the "Wolf Man," Freud shows how the identification actually *gives rise* to
the dread; for not only does the substitution of the bowel for the womb
phantasmatically empower men by enabling them to appropriate women's
reproductive function, but, in being associated with the female genitalia,
the bowel itself comes to signify castration—"the necessary condition of
femininity."[7]

Given that the baby in the film signifies castration in an overdetermined
way—both because of her genitals and because, as "shit," she is psychically
associated with the male desire to become woman—she not surprisingly is
made into the comically fetishized object of disavowal, and is masculinized
in a variety of ways. For example, when Peter, the architect, takes the baby
on the construction site of one of his jobs, she wears a little pink hardhat

that later becomes the object over which he mourns after Mary's mother takes her away. At another point, he reads to her in a tender, soothing voice an account of a bloody boxing match from the newspaper. He says to Michael, who, it will be remembered, did *not* allow Mary to listen to Dr. Ruth talking about women's orgasms, that it's not "what you say but how you say it."

Remarking further on the significance of the anal zone, the organ by which the "Wolf Man" phantasmatically achieved an identification with women, Freud tells us that this organ was also the means by which a "passive homosexual attitude to men was able to express itself."[8] We can speculate that the popularity of a film like *Three Men and a Baby* is partly attributable to its successful negotiation of homosocial desire—male bonding in this case being effected through the agency of a baby girl, rather than through the exchange of women, as has usually been the case. Father's rights, male appropriation of femininity, and male homoeroticism fuse perfectly in a film that nearly squeezes woman out of the picture altogether, just as the mother is squeezed to one side of the frame in the last shot of the film.

In this final shot, as the four push the baby stroller off screen, we are left facing the picture of the three men whose caricatures have been painted on the elevator doors. Only now, in addition to a picture of the mother painted in on one side, a picture of the baby has been added, exactly at crotch level of the men. We are presented with a perfect image of disavowal: the baby, whose arrival had given rise to the men's feminine identification and whose genitals had signified castration anxiety and induced hysteria, is equated with the endangered penises. All of those little objects that may be separated from the body are, the image assures us, intact. In the contemporary version of "Superman," he is the one who "has it all"—penis *and* baby: in fact, the perfect penis-baby.

That the men have gotten away with something, have, indeed, subverted the law, is suggested by the film's criminal subplot, involving the heroin package. Given that the men are involved in an "unlawful," "unnatural" appropriation of femininity, it is highly significant that the package containing an illegal substance arrives at the same time as the baby and is confused with it. The narcotics officer assigned to the case is revealed to be a family man and at one point he asks to hold the baby, whose diaper is loaded with heroin. While Michael tries to refuse, Peter, unaware of the presence of the incriminating diaper, forces Michael to hand the baby over to the inspector. Later, the men manage to appease the law by entrapping the real criminals—a plot that, as we have seen, actually involves the baby's father dressing up as a pregnant woman. When the police arrive on the scene, the narcotics officer thanks the men and then asks again to hold the baby, but at this point the men triumphantly refuse, each saying "no" in turn. Unlike the trajectory of many older Hollywood films, which involves the heroes' accepting the father and the castration he represents, in this film the men ultimately reject paternal authority and continue to disavow castration: in short, while they embrace the state of fatherhood, they refuse to grow up.

Three Men and a Baby is a profoundly regressive film on many levels. On the psychic level, as I have tried to demonstrate by analyzing the central joke as if it were a highly condensed, overdetermined dream image, it involves a regression to the anal stage. On the social and narrative levels, it involves a desire to reject the symbolic father and to refuse castration. This Peter Pan fantasy (*about* a man named Peter, and brought to us by Walt Disney) even incorporates a kind of Wendy figure at the end, a woman who is not (or not any longer) the object of any man's desire but part of the group that gets to play perpetually with the baby. (There is even a scene in which Peter tastes the milk from the nipple of the bottle, and then pours it into his coffee.) That mass art involves "the infantilizing of culture" has been remarked upon often—by Ariel Dorfman, for example, who points not only to the adult values that are projected onto children and their culture but to "the infantilization that the mass media seem to radiate onto adults."[9] Long before Dorfman, T. W. Adorno noted the same process of infantilization when he analyzed the lyrics of popular songs, but Adorno could not have anticipated the latest postmodern twist to the process given by the film, in which song lyrics addressed to one's "baby" would *literally* refer to a baby ("Little baby want to hold you tight / I don't ever want to say goodnight"), although retaining, of course, the sexual charge they have gained from years of metaphoricity.[10]

It becomes apparent that the film is centered around a paradox: in order for the men to be the kind of fathers they want to be (fathers who also take on the role of mothers, of nurturers), the men actually have to deny the father who represents the law (although, as we have seen, not without hedging their bets). In this respect it is interesting to compare the film to its antecedent, John Ford's *3 Godfathers*, which deals with three outlaws who inherit a male baby from a woman they encounter in the desert while they are hiding out. Shortly before dying, the woman names the baby Robert William Pedro Hightower, after the three men (John Wayne is Robert Hightower, a name whose phallic connotations scarcely require commentary). From the moment they receive the baby, the men are re-formed characters, and their sole mission is to get him out of the desert and into New Jerusalem (the film draws explicitly on the myth of the Christ child), a journey in which they find themselves increasingly guided by the Bible. Two of the men—William and Pedro—die in the course of the journey, but come back as ghosts to encourage Hightower when he is on the verge of succumbing to exhaustion.

Preoccupied with sacrifice, redemption and the scriptural law of the father, *3 Godfathers* suggests precisely how the narrative dramatically shifts when the baby is male and Oedipus is at stake. But even in this film there are moments of narrative instability and turbulence, provoked, I would argue, by the very fact that the men are in some sense taking over the role of the mother, and hence in danger of being "unmanned." Many of the jokes of the film are related to the men's inability to perform certain feminine tasks, like breastfeeding. The sense of uneasiness instigated by the film's very premise may also be detected in the other main source of humor in the film, which has to do with the problem of names. Early in the film, the men encounter the town marshall (Ward Bond), on whose shingle is written the name "B. Sweet." Hightower laughs uproariously at this name, and then laughs again when he discovers that Sweet's wife calls her husband by the feminine name of Pearly, although Sweet calls *himself* Buck. Later the joke is on Hightower, when at his trial the judge reveals his middle name to be Marmaduke. Finally, throughout the middle part of the film, a running gag has the men arguing about the baby's name: Hightower keeps referring to him as "Little Robert," whereupon the second man insists, "Robert *William*," and the third, "Robert William *Pedro*." (We might compare *Three Men and a Baby*'s use of the generic female name "Mary"). This is a film, then, that is obsessed with the idea of passing on the name of the "father"—a concern that obviously could be expressed only in relation to a male child—while at the same time revealing through its comical play with names an insecurity about masculine identity and a discomfort with the close homosocial relationship of the three men whose "marriage" is suggested by the composite name given the son.

One moment of *3 Godfathers* is particularly notable for the hysteria of its comedy: when the men are first learning to care for the baby, they read in a book that its body should be rubbed with oil. In a rather lengthy close-up Hightower's hand is shown greasing the baby's backsides, while the men's laughter fills the soundtrack, its prolonged hilarity far exceeding the response justified by the image. The sight of an exposed, naked and vulnerable body in the midst of the repressive world of Ford's West provokes this hysterical reaction because it would seem to violate several strong taboos—taboos relating to pedophilia, homosexuality, and even sensuality itself, i.e., the very intimate pleasure of the parent's bodily contact with the child. According to one of the most famous articles on John Ford, the landmark essay *Young Mr. Lincoln* written by the *Cahiers du Cinema* collective, such moments of comedy in Ford's films are signs "of a constant disorder of the universe," a disorder that subverts the "castrating action" of the Ideal Law, and are thus to be affirmed precisely because they point to a desire capable of undermining the patriarchal order.[11]

It would appear that now, in the 1980s, we have precisely the (fully comic) film the *Cahiers* editors might have approved, a film that rescues the father from his repressive, castrating function and admits his desire for the child. It is important, of course, to recognize that such an illicit desire may be most easily embodied in the genre of comedy, which facilitates disavowal by allowing us to deny the seriousness of its concerns. Thus, comedy, as the realm of the carnivalesque, has always permitted a certain freedom of expression in relation to our collective anxieties, fears, and wishes (a fact that is often ignored by auteurist critics who tend to neglect issues of genre—thus, for instance, Howard Hawks's comedies are considered unique for their inversions of the all-male world of adventure films; Pee-wee Herman and Jerry Lewis are viewed as exemplary male hysterics; etc.). Nevertheless, despite the notorious problems inherent in claims for the subversiveness of comedy as a genre, feminists themselves have found the realm of comedy and carnival to be an important arena both for the working out of utopian desire and for ideological and psychical subversions of the dominant regime. Critics like Juliet Mitchell and Laura Mulvey, drawing on the work of Julia Kristeva (the latter indebted to Mikhail Bakhtin), have discussed the relation of carnival to the pre-oedipal—the traditional province of the maternal—and the way in which it semiotically disrupts the symbolic order, challenging norms, hierarchies, and established systems.[12] In some ways *Three Men and a Baby*, with its carnivalesque defiance of psychic and social categories (related to gender, age, etc.), its refusal to renounce the pleasures proscribed by the symbolic order, seems to confirm the insights of these theorists. But while the film may indeed be said to situate itself in the pre-oedipal, it is clearly very far from engaging in a utopian celebration of the maternal; on the contrary, it constitutes a flagrant encroachment of the (ever multiplying) fathers onto the mother's traditional domain.

The desire expressed by the film for what we might see as a kind of pre-oedipal father/child relation corresponds, interestingly, to a development in contemporary critical theory. A lecture on the myth of Oedipus Rex with which feminist film theorist Laura Mulvey toured the United States, drew on the work of Marie Balmary, whose *Psychoanalyzing Psychoanalysis* searches for a profounder understanding of the lessons Oedipus Rex holds for psychoanalysis and finds the key in the story of Lauis, father of Oedipus (see especially Balmary's chapter rather ominously entitled "Oedipus Has Still More to Teach Us").[13] Mulvey expressed the desire to use Balmary's insights to find a way of importing the father into the pre-oedipal relation, a move that has in fact already been theorized by Julia Kristeva. In the first chapter of her book *Tales of Love*, Kristeva waxes lyrical about the concept of "imaginary paternity," speaking of "a warm but dazzling, domesticated paternity," one that while it guarantees the subject's entry into an oedipal disposition, "can also be playful and sublimational." Kristeva writes eloquently of the desire for such an entity:

> Maintaining against the winds and high tides of our modern civilization the requirement of a stern father who, through his Name, brings about separation, judgment, and identity, constitutes a necessity, a more or less pious wish. But we can only note that jarring such sternness, far from leaving us orphaned or inexorably psychotic, reveals multiple and varied destinies for paternity—notably archaic, imaginary paternity.[14]

One might note that in the Baby M case a similar desire to jar such "sternness" led many feminists to support Mr. Stern himself, and to reject the claims of the biological mother of the child, Mary Beth Whitehead. Women like Mary Gordon in her essay in *Ms.* magazine wrote compellingly about men's need to nurture—an argument that, as Janice Doane and Devon Hodges point out, ironically allied her with both nature and the symbolic order—with, that is, "a judge who argues in favor of men's driving need to procreate."[15]

While the desire to find alternatives to harsh notions of phallic paternity is entirely understandable, feminists need to be very clear about whether in endorsing these alternatives they are undermining patriarchal structures or, on the contrary, shoring up patriarchy against its ruins—in this case, ironically, by relocating it *in* the ruins of a more ancient civilization. Freud, it will be recalled, likened the discovery of the girl's pre-oedipal relation with the mother to the discovery in archaeology of an older civilization buried beneath a more modern one.[16] Now, along with the mother, Kristeva would place an "archaic father" who "introduces the Third Party as a condition of psychic life, to the extent that it is a loving life (34)." Although woman in Kristeva's scheme still has a place (which would seem, however, to be dispensable since Kristeva says this father is the same as both parents), it is a very traditional one—the place of the female whose desire for the male Other initiates the child into "the loving life." (In a more recent work, however, Kristeva's ever escalating misogyny leads her to call for the psychic obliteration of the mother—"matricide is our vital necessity," she declares—and for the psychic extension of the father's reign, via the importation of the paternal figure into the realm of the Imaginary.[17]) But even the role Kristeva occasionally grants woman—that of the desiring female guiding the child into the "loving life"—is a role that men may, as we see from the film, play for themselves and each other. Indeed, the men in the film show themselves to be continually preoccupied with, desirous of, the image of themselves *as* fathers: in a swimming pool, surrounded by mothers and babies, they take pictures of themselves playing with Mary, and when the child is taken away, one of them whiles away the lonely hours looking at videotapes of himself and the baby.

Nevertheless, while optional, women are not altogether absent from the picture; rather, they serve further to legitimate and guarantee the men's appropriation of the maternal. In a montage showing the men performing various activities with their baby, they are surrounded by women who are charmed not just, it would appear, by the baby herself but by this "warm" and "dazzling" incarnation of one of the "varied destinies" of paternity. In short, the women occupy a role similar to that taken up by Kristeva—and consistent with the one she herself theorizes: that of the woman who so desires the father, so desires to save the father (from himself, as it were) that she authorizes the widening of the patriarchal sphere and underwrites the diminishment of her function within this sphere.

Such is also the role of the female audience of the film. Although, as I have tried to show, the film is entirely preoccupied with male fantasies and fears, it seems clear that the women in the audience are as amused and deeply touched by the film as men are—probably more so. No doubt the reasons for this appeal are complex. In my experience of different audiences, much of the laughter at the beginning of the film was aimed at the men for the incompetence they displayed in dealing with the child, although, by the end, the pathos of the situation had clearly overwhelmed all other response. No doubt, too, the film speaks to a legitimate desire on the part of women for men to become more involved in interpersonal relationships, to be more nurturant as individuals, and to assume greater responsibility for childcare. At the same time, it suggests the limits and problems of this aspect of the feminist agenda. Some years ago, both Dorothy Dinnerstein and Nancy Chodorow wrote forcefully of the need for men to contribute more extensively to parenting arrangements—a development they believed would lead to the psychic and social recognition of women as full human beings. However, *Three Men and a Baby* demonstrates the insufficiency of this solution to the problem of misogyny: it is possible, the film shows, for men to respond to the feminist demand for their increased participation in childrearing in such a way as to make women more marginal than ever. In the final analysis, the effect of films like *Three Men and a Baby* and *Three Men and a Cradle* and of television programs like *My Two Dads* (about a girl who lives with two men, either of whom could be her father) and *Full House* (about three men and *three* little girls) is simply to give men more options than they already have in patriarchy: they can be real fathers, "imaginary" fathers, godfathers, *and*, in the older sense of the term, surrogate mothers. The fact that in every one of these cases the children reared exclusively by men are female suggests that the daughters are being seduced *away* from feminism and into a world where they may become so "dazzled" by the proliferating varieties of paternity that they are unable to see whose interests are really being served.

CHAPTER SIX

The Incredible Shrinking He(r)man

Male Regression, the Male Body, and Film

Even in this age of female liberation, the pressures on men in our society are immense—to perform, to succeed, to "score" with women, to hold up an image that is illusory and usually leads to an early demise. Who needs it? An ever-growing number of red-blooded males are turning on to the ultimate escape from such pressure: babyhood.

> —*The porn magazine,* Swank, *discussing diaper fetishists (men who like to be diapered by women), quoted in* Barbara Ehrenreich, The Hearts of Men

Asked in an interview about his sexuality, Boy George replied, "I am just like everyone else in that I like sex, food, and love. I just don't believe in male or female: I'm not particularly masculine, and I'm certainly not feminine. But I don't think it matters".[1] In a perfectly postfeminist statement Boy George thus affirms sexual difference *and* the male/female hierarchy in the very act of denying them, just as we saw in the last chapter a man may hold femininity in contempt at the same time that he appropriates it. Insofar as such attitudes assume the character of the fetish, and operate according to a strategy of disavowal, they form part of the larger "postmodern" culture as this culture has been theorized by various critics. The disavowal often involves the illusion that one can not only have it all, but also *be* it all—male and female, father and mother, adult and child—without altering the power structure in which men rule over women and

90

adults over children. We might recall, in this connection, that for Lacan the very definition of sexual difference is the distinction between "being" and "having" (the phallus), a choice on which our culture no longer seems prepared to insist—at least as far as the male subject is concerned.

Of course, one of Lacan's main lessons is that nobody really possesses the "phallus," a term that refers to an idea of paternal potency and power unrealizable by any single individual, female *or* male. To be sure, as Kaja Silverman notes, the male subject has greater access than the female subject to the symbolic order signified by the phallus and hence to "the cultural privileges and positive values which define male subjectivity within patriarchal society";[2] nevertheless, Lacanian feminists have found it valuable to insist on the discrepancy between phallus and penis and, in their critical practice, to expose or "unveil" the lack at the heart of patriarchal representations, thereby attempting to undermine the stability of the power structure appearing to sustain them.[3] Since Hollywood Cinema, easily the largest and most influential such system of representation, has been massively and continually devoted to perpetuating myths of phallic potency—in, for example, its portrayal of he-men from John Wayne to Sylvester Stallone—it was probably all too predictable that when a "her-man" came along and seemed openly to refuse to take a position on one side of the divide of sexual difference and, moreover, flaunted his lack of phallic potency, he would find champions among these feminists.

Indeed, although it is Pee-wee Herman's television show that has elicited most interest among cultural critics, an episode from the film *Big Top Pee-wee* illustrates perfectly the way Paul Reubens's character resists traditional notions of masculinity and in fact sends up the traditional oedipal narrative of classic Hollywood Cinema. In the film, Pee-wee falls in love with an Italian trapeze artist, Gina, who just before they sleep together for the first time gives him her (dead) father's costume so Pee-wee may join the circus. After the kiss, the camera cuts to a shot of a train entering a tunnel, another of fireworks, another of female mudwrestlers, then fades to black; the next morning a jubilant Pee-wee, who has been experimenting with growing huge vegetables on his farm, enters his greenhouse wearing the father's costume and proceeds to feed his hotdog tree a special solution he has concocted; instead of growing larger, however, the hotdogs shrivel into cocktail wieners. Meanwhile, the nasty and mostly elderly townspeople have refused to allow the circus to be performed in their town, but Pee-wee saves the day by offering them the wieners, whereupon the adults shrink into children and excitedly run off to see the circus.

Pee-wee's rejection of a fully oedipalized masculinity, as well as of more fantastic notions of phallic sexuality purveyed in much popular culture, may be seen as the comic equivalent of certain concerns expressed in contemporary "gender studies." For example, not unlike Pee-wee with his tiny wieners, film critic Peter Lehman in a recent issue of *Genders* argues against phallic notions of masculinity, asserting the need for feminists in both their criticism and their fantasies to separate the penis from the phallus—and, implicitly, to appreciate the former while renouncing the latter. Lehman's essay compares Oshima's film *In the Realm of the Senses* with hard-core pornography, arguing that the former "speaks to a female desire about which pornography cares nothing."[4] This desire, it turns out, "centers almost exclusively on [the man's] penis," which is represented in a way feminists ought to approve since, unlike the pornographic imagination, it eschews "exaggeratedly large penises" (p. 99). In concluding, Lehman laments the fact that some women are still unregenerately attracted to a phallic masculinity, and in particular he chides the women who appear on the videotape *Dick Talk* for not questioning "the way in which they are drawn to powerfully dominating and controlling male bodies" and for "constantly" expressing their "desire for large penises and hard thrusting" (p. 108). Putting aside the (typically postfeminist) incongruity of Lehman's insinuation that the women need Oshima to teach them about what constitutes female desire, and putting aside too his tendency to confuse the symbolic with the anatomical in discussing the phallus, we can at least credit Lehman with having begun to talk about the male body, and in this essay I want to take up his challenge and ask: what difference does size make? Also, why has the theme of male regression, the refusal to *get* "big" or the desire to return to childhood, become so popular recently, and what's in this development for feminism? In general, then, I want to continue questioning along the lines of the previous two chapters, considering how various representations of masculinity that resist traditional patriarchal images and plots either contribute to or, on the contrary, undermine the feminist project.

Before beginning an analysis of the contemporary films, I would like to discuss as a backdrop to the issues I will be raising in this chapter a film from the 1950s, the period toward which the regressive fantasies of much contemporary culture yearn. The film, *The Incredible Shrinking Man*, may seem humorous to us now, but the script is a heavily existential tragedy of male diminishment, a scenario which will be rewritten—this time as farce— by that essentially 80s figure of masculinity, Pee-wee Herman.

If the 1950s may be seen not only as the era of the feminine mystique, but also as a time when "the domestic mystique" became part of the reigning ideology, a time when what Barbara Ehrenreich calls "the breadwinner ethic" was being urged on men, who were encouraged to display their "maturity" by holding down a secure job, supporting a family, and inter- acting with that family as much as possible, then the film *The Incredible Shrinking Man* may be seen as an angst-ridden response to the narrowing of the masculine role and the foreclosure of possibilities for adventure so dear to the fantasy life of the American male.[5] The film begins with Scott Carey and his wife on vacation, lounging on a boat. He asks her to get him a beer, and at first she playfully refuses, but eventually she gives in. While she is in the cabin, the boat sails into an ominous mist, which will eventually prove to be the cause of the man's condition. In a sense, the film may be seen as a response to the questioning of male authority within the domestic unit initiated in this light-hearted opening sequence (although a feminist critic is tempted to point out that had the man gotten his own beer his tragedy would have been averted and the *wife* would have been the victim; as it is, the world would have to wait nearly twenty-five years for woman's role to seem large enough that the possibility of an "incredible shrinking woman" could be entertained).

Soon after, Carey begins to grow smaller and is eventually forced to take up residence in a dollhouse, where one day he is spied by his cat named Butch (!) and chased around the house. We might say that the film is centrally concerned with posing a question most pertinent to the insecurities of the 50s male—a question usually uttered by the stereotypical "castrating wife": "Are you a man or a mouse?" Indeed, the film makes this analogy between hero and mouse into a veritable motif: for example, after the cat causes him to fall down the stairs into the basement, Carey tries to spring a mousetrap to obtain the bit of cheese that will provide the sustenance he needs for survival in the wilds of the basement. In the basement—that quintessential 50s space where Dad could escape the routine of family life to pursue the solitary hobbies that would bolster his flagging masculinity— Carey faces numerous adventures, including one of the most common suburban disasters, the flooded basement. A very striking shot in the film occurs before the fade following the flood and shows Scott Carey lying exhausted on the storm drain in the middle of the floor—a piece of flotsam tossed about by the tide of banal middle-class 50's existence.

Ultimately, however, Carey manages to regain his manhood as he progressively learns to make use of what he calls "the resources in my basement universe": a leak provides his water supply before the flood; a matchbox affords a dwelling place; a pin from a pincushion is transmuted into a weapon.[6] "With these bits of metal," says Carey of his arsenal, "I was a man again." The final battle comes when Carey uses the "weapon" he has fashioned out of a feminine domestic tool to vanquish the dreaded spider, the creature that so commonly figures as an image of feminine entrapment (as we saw in Puig's novel). "My enemy seemed immortal, every fear forced into one hideous night black horror." After Carey succeeds in impaling the monster, he approaches the piece of cake in its web—"the prize I had won," he comments. But, like Gregor Samsa in Kafka's "The Metamorphosis," he discovers that he is no longer hungry—"It was as if my body had ceased to exist"—and that he has lost "the terrible fear of shrinking," even though he continues to dwindle. "To become what?" he ponders. "The infinitesimal." In a final epiphany, as he disappears into the cosmos, he exults:

> So close: the infinitesimal and the infinite. But suddenly I knew that they were really the two ends of the same concept. The unbelievably small and the unbelievably vast eventually meet like the closing of a gigantic circle. Yes, smaller than the smallest I meant something too. To God there is no zero. I still exist.

And yet if we continue for a moment to compare the film to Kafka's text "The Metamorphosis," we note some crucial distinctions. In the Kafka story, Gregor *himself* becomes the grotesque body and ultimately sacrifices himself by yielding to starvation and decay, thus ensuring the revivification of the bourgeois family. Hence the poignancy of the text's final statement

94

following on the parents' realization that (Gregor's death having emphatically reinstated the incest taboo) Gregor's sister has blossomed into a lovely young woman and is now marriageable: "And it was like a confirmation of their new dreams and good intentions when at the end of the ride their daughter got up first and stretched her young body."[7] In *The Incredible Shrinking Man*, by contrast, Carey destroys the monstrous body, which remains Other to himself, and simultaneously manages to transcend—actually to sublate—his bourgeois existence. In the very process of disappearing, of becoming disembodied, he is able to affirm his tragic grandeur, thereby confirming what Kaja Silverman has so ably demonstrated in her book on voice in the cinema, that whereas narrative cinema often disempowers woman by reducing her to the body, the power of the male is enhanced the more his presence moves out of the regime of the visible and tends toward pure voice. In this respect the voice-over is a privileged cinematic device, conferring a kind of godlike (i.e., phallic) authority on the male protagonist who remains firmly in control of the narrative.[8]

The incredible shrinking man's affirmation of existence as he undergoes disembodiment might serve as a caution to feminists who argue that characters like Pee-wee Herman are helping us to redefine "sexual roles and sexed identities." For if, indeed, "the unbelievably small and the unbelievably vast" are the "two ends of the same concept," are actually both part of the same, eminently masculine, preoccupation with size (consider the very titles of the films *Pee-wee's Big Adventure* and *Big Top Pee-wee*), we cannot necessarily conclude that characters like Pee-wee Herman are genuine alternatives to the he-man types so popular during our decade. In fact, it might be noted that the miniature and the gigantic *do* meet in, for example, a film like *Twins*, starring Arnold Schwarzenegger and Danny Devito, which thus closes the circle of the divergent images of masculinity characterizing contemporary popular culture.

These two extremes in the representation of masculinity meet for a variety of reasons: not only is it the case that both the phallic male and the pee-wee male may avail themselves of the "cultural privileges" denied women in patriarchal society, but also, and more surprisingly, that the macho posturing of the phallic male may actually seem to feminize him as much as the shrinking man's diminishing stature threatened to emasculate him. As Lacan has written, "The fact that femininity takes refuge in [the] mask,

95

because of the *Verdrängung* inherent to the phallic mark of desire, has the strange consequence that, in the human being, virile display itself appears as feminine."[9] Thus it is possible to see in a film like *Twins* and in some of the other films I am analyzing here a problematization of the male body, which has usually been taken as a natural given. Such a development is of great interest for feminism but, as I will suggest, entails many forms of disavowal enabling the spectator to evade its consequences.

That masculinity may, as the quotation from Lacan suggests, function as a mask is an idea made popular by sociologists, who speak of the "male role," although the concept has not received corresponding attention among psychoanalytic critics despite their having taken up the notion of "femininity as masquerade" with great enthusiasm.[10] That the male "role" is associated with attributes the ordinary man might like to repudiate—perhaps without giving up his cultural privileges—is made comically clear in the quotation I have taken as the epigraph to this chapter. Men are turning on to babyhood. The work of Ehrenreich gives this phenomenon a historical context, showing the extent to which masculinity in the last thirty years has been characterized by a flight from commitment, responsibility, and adulthood; in short, men have been engaged in a revolt, or, in our terms, have increasingly tended to evacuate the middle ground between the two extremes of masculinity—extremes that frequently meet in their common rejection of women and domesticity.

The hit film *Big*, which appears at first to follow the opposite trajectory from *The Incredible Shrinking Man* only to have its hero abandon growth once he has achieved it, corroborates the notion that men may be seeking the ultimate escape in a phantasmatic retreat into childhood or "babyhood." The protagonist of the film is a boy named Josh who is thirteen years old, the age at which males begin to experience major bodily changes. In the beginning of the film, Josh wishes to be big because he is denied admission to a carnival ride with a girl taller than he, and he soon finds himself inhabiting the body of a thirty-year-old man. Significantly, his first experience on assuming his adult body is to be chased around the house by his mother as she brandishes a carving knife (again the mouse motif), having mistaken him for an intruder (the same actress played the "ballbusting" wife of the gangster in *Married to the Mob*). With the help of his young friend Billy, Josh goes to the city to find the carnival machine that had granted his wish, and in the meantime he lands a job at a toy company, where, under the benign eye of the paternalist boss, he becomes an executive utilizing his boyish knowledge of toys for commercial purposes. Susan, a female executive, falls in love with Josh, explaining his attraction to her jealous lover by observing that Josh is "a grown-up." Much of the humor of the film derives from this reversal, whereby childhood is made to seem more mature than adulthood, and also from the discrepancy between the euphemistic, evasive, and complex language of the grown-ups and the literal understanding of this language on the part of Josh (Susan speaks about spending the night with Josh, and he asks, "You mean, sleep over?"). Such a device is by no means new: it is the structuring principle of the classic text of American boyhood, *Huckleberry Finn*, which pitted the innocence and literal-mindedness of the child and the slave against the corruption and hypocrisy of repressive adult society. The effectiveness of this century-old device depended on a highly ideological notion of child-hood innocence and purity that seemed to have been replaced for a time— notably in the 1970s—by an obsession with demonic children. But it is no doubt true, to paraphrase the shrinking man, that the angelic and the demonic are two ends of the same concept, and so the sentimentalized version of childhood has returned with a vengeance.

Josh and Susan begin to have sex together: the first time, she removes her blouse, and Josh is shown to be utterly captivated by the sight of her breast. The turning point of the film, however, comes at the moment when Susan confuses Josh by asking him to reflect on their relationship. In the very next scene, Josh and Billy quarrel because Josh no longer has any time for his friend; for the first time Josh is shown to be caught up in the responsibilities of his job, on his way to becoming as callous and boring as many of the other adult males in the corporate world. Realizing the danger and hence determining to shed the adult body that brings with it messy complications, Josh resolves to return to childhood. Thus, just as his adventures began with his being chased by a "castrating" woman, so do the demands of a woman for commitment and complexity precipitate the flight back into childhood—and into a homosocial relation that can seem all the more innocent because it has the alibi of the literal: when Josh confesses to Susan that he's a child, and she responds angrily, "Who isn't? Don't you think there's a frightened child in all of us?" he says, "You don't

97

understand, I'm *really* thirteen years old." Therefore, it is not, as it might appear, a question of Josh's choosing a male companion over a female lover; he's simply thirteen years old and wants to be with his pals. Soon after this conversation, Billy and Susan cross paths at the elevator, the episode clearly marking the exchange of woman for boy.

It should also be noted that the alibi of the literal enables the film's *viewers* to disavow the unpleasantness of its sexual politics. After all, since the film is *really* about a thirteen year-old boy trapped in a man's body, it is beside the point to criticize the crassness of its conception of masculinity, announced in the very baldness of its title. Hence the film, which is about the desirability of escaping adult responsibility, manages *itself* to escape accountability, while nevertheless delivering its message that Josh is the model of what it means to be a "grown-up."

In the final scene of the film, Susan takes Josh back to his boyhood home and, watching him walk away from the car, smiles benignly as he shrinks to childsize and walks into his house. Resembling the shrinking man in that he is no longer visible to the spectator, Josh is heard to say, "Mom, I've missed you so much." In denying time and change, Josh returns to the enclosed space of the house, the kind of space Jurij Lotman in his study of narrative sees as identical to "woman." In this regard part of the interest of the film may be said to lie in the way it so clearly bares an aspect of narrative structure usually kept more hidden and thus in need of the interpretive work of sophisticated narratologists to uncover it: the ending signifies return, which is equated with going back to the womb, to the mother.[11]

That the female love interest colludes with the mother in desiring the male's regression is seen in the final sequence in which Susan looks on approvingly as the male walks away from her (one might think of Kim Basinger/Vicki Vale's beatific smile at the end of *Batman* when she is told that Bruce Wayne *won't* be joining her for a while). The shot is in an important respect emblematic of the film's production itself, since *Big* was actually directed by a woman, Penny Marshall, who as a former character in the television program *Happy Days* and, later, in *Laverne and Shirley*, is closely linked to America's obsession with its own imagined innocent past, the 1950s. Thus once again we see woman presiding over her own marginalization, participating in a nostalgia for a time in which human

98

relationships are felt to have been relatively uncomplicated, although the cost of this simplicity is her own repression.

This is a role, as I have shown before, that the feminist critic has played as well. An important instance of this is the recent special issue on "Masculinity" published by *Camera Obscura*, which includes a "dossier" on Pee-wee Herman, the child/man, woman/man hybrid being of which postmodern culture is so fond.[12] The articles argue that (unlike *Big*, which relies on a notion of adolescent innocence that negates female and gay sexuality) Pee-wee Herman's appeal lies in the way the camp gay subtext subverts the idea of adolescent innocence and "re-presents masculinity right at the edge of the territory of the child, that morally quarantined and protected area" (p. 151). Whereas in *Big*, the alibi of the literal helped render the film's homoerotic subtext innocent, Pee-wee Herman's films and television show supposedly subvert literal meaning and invest language and behavior with a sexualized double meaning. Hence Constance Penley detects in Pee-wee Herman's work an implicitly feminist deconstruction of masculinity:

> the adult fantasy of childhood simplicity and happiness is a founding fantasy, one that offers the possibility of innocence to those who need to retain the idea of innocence itself. As long as this fantasy remains unexamined, so too will the fantasy of masculinity. (p. 151)

This argument seems to me extremely problematic from a feminist point of view, in part because it ignores the extent to which masculinity itself, i.e., heterosexual masculinity, has *often* been constructed, in American society, "at the edge of the territory of the child," the very territory Huck Finn "lit out" for, while women have typically represented the repressive forces of civilized, adult society—that which man rejects in order to live out his perpetual youth. It is this tradition, in which the film *Big* is situated, that Pee-wee Herman's work draws on in constructing its supposedly gay text. For example, describing an episode from the television program in which Pee-wee resists being Daddy when the other characters play house and ends the game when he has to kiss a woman, one commentator asks:

> Is Pee-wee . . . the little macho boy grossed out by the prospect of consorting with girls, or is he rather another sort of boy, one who simply isn't interested

in girls? The film *Pee-wee's Big Adventure* features a scene in which Pee-wee resists the advances of Dotty and explains to her that there are some things about Pee-wee that she "couldn't understand, shouldn't understand."[13]

And Penley, describing the program's references to homosexuality, cites an episode in which Pee-wee rejects Miss Yvonne to dance with a male wrestler and comments that such scenes are probably taken by children "as no more than a perfectly adequate representation of their own dismissal of the opposite sex and all that 'icky stuff,' " whereas adults are supposedly capable of tapping into the program's gay subtext (p. 136). But it is precisely this aspect of the show, celebrated by Penley and others, that seems to me problematic both for women *and* gays—for the latter because it perpetuates the idea, conveyed over and over again by the American psychiatric institution as well as in popular myths, that homosexuality is a result of arrested development and involves man's turning away from the "mature" object choice, woman. As for her lighthearted remark about children's "dismissal of the opposite sex and all that 'icky stuff,' " Penley here falls victim to the very myth of childhood innocence she criticizes, ignoring the fact that this dismissive attitude—stronger in boys than in girls—is congruent with the misogyny of patriarchal ideology and reveals the contempt for females Freud saw as characteristic of "normal" masculinity. Little boys are indeed "grossed out" by little girls.

If Pee-wee can hardly be affirmed from a feminist point of view simply for its refusal of adult masculinity, a more persuasive case might be made for Pee-wee's subversive transgression of male/female boundaries. For the pee-wee body is not only part boy and part man, but also part male and part female. Like Jerry Lewis, but without the latter's anxiety, Pee-wee, we are told, presents an image of the hystericized male body, oscillating between masculine and feminine identifications in such a way as to destabilize the fixity of gender categories. Insofar as Pee-wee plays at being feminine, dressing up as a woman, affecting feminine gestures, etc., he participates in a long tradition of female impersonation central to gay camp, the category most frequently invoked by Pee-wee enthusiasts. Camp, according to one commentator, "is a way of poking fun at the whole cosmology of restrictive sex roles and sexual identifications which our society uses to oppress its women and repress its men." Camp provides "the shock of recognition," the "idea of seeing . . . the absurdity of those roles that each of us is urged to play with such a deadly seriousness."[14] Thus we might say that if a film like *Big* manages to escape accountability by relying on the alibi of the literal, a camp text like Pee-wee Herman manages to escape accountability by relying on the alibi of the figurative— indeed on the alibi of the alibi: nothing is what it seems or where it seems; nothing is to be taken seriously.[15] At its extreme, camp abolishes the category of the literal altogether; hence, its proponents emphasize the way style replaces substance: camp "signifies performance rather than existence; . . . the emphasis shifts from what a thing *is* to what it *looks* like; from *what* is being done to *how* it is being done."[16] In this respect, as has been noted, camp coincides with postmodern aesthetics in general—the latter having been famously characterized as concerned with parody and pastiche, and as representing the triumph of image and spectacle over meaning and "the real."[17]

The emphasis on "performance rather than existence" in both camp and postmodern aesthetics has coincided with a tendency to privilege "the feminine" in theories of representation. This should not be surprising if one remembers the (il)logic of contamination operating, for example, in Lacan's observation, quoted earlier: since femininity is associated with masquerade, masquerade—the figurative, textuality, etc.—comes to seem feminine. Femininity would thus appear to have lost its terrors, to have settled, like magic dust, over the terrain of culture generally, and in the process to have transformed masculinity itself: from he-man to her-man. Everyone may, in Deleuze and Guattari's phrase, "become woman"—although in their view this is coincident with becoming "a body without organs."[18]

The postmodern rejection of the specifically sexed body no doubt has an appeal for some feminists, especially the radical anti-essentialists, who, like Monique Wittig, have argued that because the biological category of woman has been the source of patriarchal oppression of females, feminists must strive to render the category obsolete.[19] The filmmaker Valie Export has argued along similar lines, maintaining that feminists "cannot refuse disembodiment," for "the abandonment of the body is the way out for the feminine Self."[20] Like certain French feminists, who have celebrated the hysteric's revolt against patriarchy,[21] Export argues that anorexia is one of "the great feminine forms of rebellion," in which woman attempts to break away from the body and from the very patriarchal images of women to which she seems, even in exaggerated ways, to conform (p. 22).

This privileging of anorexia is interesting to consider in the light of a phenomenon like Pee-wee, the "her-man" who appeals to some women, I would speculate, not just because he seems to constitute an alternative type of masculinity but because, as eternal adolescent, he provides a model of androgyny with which women, often uncomfortable with their own bodies, may identify and thus imaginatively escape the myriad images of ultrafemininity constantly held up to them by our culture. That Pee-wee may function to reinforce an anorexic mentality (we may think of the many scenes of animated food in *Pee-wee's Playhouse*) is strikingly revealed in a segment from one of the television shows. On this particular program, Pee-wee finds out that the secret word of the day—which, when uttered, elicits shouts and applause from everyone in the playhouse—is "little." Soon after, he performs a magic act and renders himself invisible, whereupon the fat lady enters and sees a chocolate cake. Cutting herself a piece (in fact, taking most of the cake), she starts to sit down to eat it, but the invisible Pee-wee has placed it on the chair and so she sits on it. Unable to find the cake and unaware of what has happened, she walks out the door, a chocolate mess dripping from the back of her skirt.

Referring to the regrettable retention of "one of camp's most dubious characters," the fat lady, Penley parenthetically wags a finger at *Pee-wee's Playhouse*: "(*Pee-wee's Playhouse*, fattist to the core, still has a ways to go here: Mrs. Steve is nasty and stupid, Mrs. René is a ditz [sic]") (p. 149). But if fat is in fact a feminist issue, because it represents a hyperbolization of woman's "mature" body pushed to the point of the grotesque, then such representations cannot be as easily detached from the "body" of the text as Penley's parenthesis would have us believe; indeed, it is possible to argue that the character of the fat lady is constitutive of the program's meaning, insofar as this character exists in opposition to and as the antithesis of the adolescent male—what one feminist critic, using Jungian terminology to describe the anorexic's ideal image, calls the *puer aeternus*, the "pure male adolescent spirit"—the "boy forever."[22]

Interestingly, the episode continues with Pee-wee, still invisible, attempting to look up the dress of another female character ("I see London,

I see France"). Citing not only this episode, but a cartoon in which the narrator notes, "girls grow to maturity faster than boys," Penley contends that such material is progressive for a children's show, since it admits sexual difference as an area of concern and interest. But I find less cause for optimism in this unequal distribution of differences. While the male, Pee-wee—always at the very least "a body without organs"—is able to disembody himself completely, it is the female who grows to "maturity," who possesses a body *with* organs (which males are always trying to "see"), and who, finally, is presented as a Rabelaisian figure of fleshly excess, dripping as excrement the very food she would greedily devour, body and organs out of control.

Despite, then, the celebrated "oscillation" of Pee-wee between femininity and masculinity, *both* modes entail a certain degree of misogyny. Insofar as Pee-wee draws on a tradition of escapist fantasy—even if its function is to serve as a cover story for a hidden gay text—*and does not put into question the contempt for women that has been central to this tradition*, feminism must be skeptical of claims for the character's emancipatory potential. And insofar as Pee-wee can "become woman" and at the same time revile through comic exaggeration the very traits that constitute "womanliness," he reveals how the desire to appropriate and the need to denigrate can easily coexist in male attitudes toward femininity. Above all, what an analysis of Pee-wee Herman can help feminists to see is the double bind in which women are placed with regard to the body. Obliged—not only by Pee-wee, but by camp and certain postmodern tendencies in general—to represent literality and the body (e.g., the fat lady) *and* the figurative, the body's transcendence (through impersonation, performance, masquerade, rhetoric, etc.—all of which in the era of poststructuralism have been theoretically and imaginatively linked to femininity), woman becomes at once only body and no-body. Another camp staple, the aging actress, would seem to be paradigmatic of this double bind, signifying decaying flesh and intimations of mortality, on the one hand, and muting their terrors through hysterical excess and parody, on the other.

If the icon of the aging actress represents the flesh and its denial from the side of the grotesque, another figure representing the same paradox assumes a more benign fantasy-form and has recently appeared in two seemingly very different, yet in some respects uncannily similar, films: *Big*

Top Pee-wee and *Wings of Desire*. I am referring to the trapeze artist, a figure that should have special resonance for feminists since it is presented at the end of the landmark film *Riddles of the Sphinx* as an augury of female desire in a possible feminist future.

If, following the film *Pee-wee's Big Adventure* with its resolute refusal of heterosexuality, *Big Top Pee-wee* created much disappointment by caving in to convention and featuring a love story, it must be stressed that the romance only minimally qualifies as such. To fall in love with a trapeze artist comes as close as possible to falling in love with a disembodied woman, one whose body, at any rate, appears to defy the physical laws that tie us to earth and wed us to mortality. We have already seen that the implied sex scene precipitates a move *backward* into childhood (with all the elderly people restored to youth) and, by inference, a negation of maturation and death. To the extent that Gina represents the sexual body, then, she is, in a manner of speaking, rejected. (Reinforcing a sense of disgust at female animal functions, incidentally, is a subplot in which Pee-wee's pet male pig is hotly pursued by a love-starved female hippopotamus.) To the extent, however, that Gina represents transcendence, this quality is usurped by Pee-wee, who once again "becomes woman" at the expense of woman: in the opening sequence, Pee-wee is performing in a Las Vegas nightclub, crooning on stage the song "Girl on the Flying Trapeze," as hysterical female fans scream and swoon below him in the audience; when he leaves the club his fans swarm around him, but suddenly he rises above the threatening female mob and finds *himself* flying through the air with the greatest of ease, thus suggesting the desire to escape the very romance plot the film will proceed to invoke.

The male fantasy of falling in love with a trapeze artist is certainly one of the most banal fantasies, and Pee-wee is surely in some measure making fun of it as well as appropriating the image for himself. In this respect, then, it is interesting to compare the treatment of the fantasy in *Big Top Pee-wee* to that found in the critically acclaimed high-art film, *Wings of Desire*, by Wim Wenders, a German director whose intense love for America seems now to be reciprocated. Indeed, what is striking at first view is how much *Big Top Pee-wee* reads like a comic version of *Wings of Desire*. Both films, for example, feature the circus; both are about the desirability of becoming (like) children again; both have plots centrally concerned with regression (from adult to child and, in one case, from angel to man); and both feature protagonists who fall in love with young, female trapeze artists from Latin countries. Above all, both seem concerned with rethinking what it means to be a man: Wenders especially appears to want to fashion what might be called a "kinder, gentler" masculinity, as he himself hints in an interview in *Film Quarterly*, where he also credits himself with having created a nonsexist image of an autonomous woman.

Wings of Desire, yet one more of the myriad variations on the buddy film, is about two male angels, Damiel and Cassiel, who travel around Berlin observing daily life, listening in on people's thoughts, and reporting to each other from time to time on the day's events. One of the angels, Damiel, played by Bruno Ganz, falls in love with Marion, a French trapeze artist in the circus, and eventually determines to become mortal so that he may know what it is like to possess a body—to experience, as Wenders puts it in an interview, "the taste of a steaming cup of coffee and feel the feel of cold hands over eternity and truth."[23] Meanwhile, Peter Falk, playing himself, is in town making a documentary about World War II, and, being a former angel (as it turns out), strikes up a little acquaintanceship with Damiel—"I can't see you, but I know you're there," he says when in the presence of angels. After assuming his mortal body, Damiel embarks on a search for Marion, who after the circus disbands stays on in Berlin. Eventually the two find each other in a bar, where Marion delivers a lengthy speech about love, destiny, choice ("Now at last, no more coincidence. I don't know if destiny exists, but decision exists"), and heterosexuality ("There's no greater story than ours, that of man and woman"—a sentiment Damiel echoes in the final scene: "Only the amazement about the two of us, the amazement about man and woman—only that made a human being of me").

In some respects following the opposite trajectory of *The Incredible Shrinking Man*, since the hero goes not from man to "spirit," but from spirit to mortal man and from invisibility to visibility, *Wings of Desire* might at first seem to represent an alternative to the films we have been discussing. Unlike *Big*, for example, *Wings of Desire* seems to present a protagonist in the act of coming to terms with time, mortality, and finitude. However, I would argue that this film too is postfeminist (and perhaps more insidiously so, since it carries the aura of European art cinema) in that its revisionary treatment of questions of masculinity, femininity, mortality, and the body is entirely superficial and masks what is in fact a reactionary position. In this respect, it is fitting that Peter Falk, who is continually referred to as Columbo in the film, is given such a prominent role. For, Lieutenant Columbo, we remember, assumed the image of a bumbling, soft-hearted, even somewhat soft-headed investigator, a guise that disarmed his adversaries and enabled him to move remorselessly in on his quarry all the while we watched the guilty party, initially arrogant and disdainful, reduced to a state of anxiety and fear. To use the terms we invoked earlier, Columbo appeared *not* to possess the phallus, but in the end, of course, always revealed that he did.

Now, just as Columbo only seemed to be "human" and fallible, but really was infallible and unflinching in upholding the law, so too do Wenders's men/angels appear to depart from traditional concepts of masculinity but really assume and even expand prerogatives reserved for men in patriarchy. In a stunning analysis of the film as exemplary of white male filmmaking, bell hooks observes, "Through much of the film male angels use their bodies in ways that subvert traditionally masculine physicality; their movements suggest tenderness and gentleness, never aggressiveness or brutality." But she goes on to situate the angel's freedom of movement in the context of "the reality of white male disregard [for] and violation of other people's body space."[24] As spirits (whom we register as white and male and human even while we know them to be innocent angels) the men have the perfect alibi for the colonization and occupation of "people's body space"—and so, we might add, does the camera, which continually moves in the same kind of prying manner (frequently from high above, craning down to a particularized view) that Hitchcock would often use—only Hitchcock would manage in the process to suggest the moral dubiousness of such voyeurism. Wenders, in contrast, boasts of the increased capacity to penetrate space and the body that his plot premise allows: "So," he says, "there was a whole new range of entering into people's heads and into many different stories all the time" (p. 7).

Of course, despite the fact that much of our pleasure throughout the greater part of the film derives from the transcendent position in which the camera places us as it glides through Berlin, the point is that one of the angels ultimately relinquishes his omniscience and in doing so and becoming mortal, accepts a limited point of view (as does the camera, which, once Damiel is human, also becomes more earthbound, less mobile). But the question then becomes: to what extent can Damiel actually be said to accept the full implications of embodiment and mortality, including its limitations, which is what the film appears to be all about? And here it must be stressed that the film is hedged about with many sorts of disavowals.

In particular we can note the same desire to regress into childhood and the past that we've noted in the other films. We might, for example, consider the function of Homer the storyteller, who serves as mankind's memory (so that when he appears on screen, Wenders often incorporates newsreel footage of the war); throughout the film Homer searches for Potsdammer Platz, a haunt of his youth before the war; and he meditates on the possibility of writing an epic of peace. An aged man, he is obsessed with childhood, an obsession shared by the film—its constant refrain in voice over, "when the child was a child . . . ," its ideal image, the child experiencing wonder at the circus. Being an artist Homer is able to console himself with thoughts of eternal life: "When mankind loses me it loses its storyteller," and at the end he nominates himself man's spiritual guide and confidently asserts that people "need me more than any other thing in the world." Thus the storyteller affirms the banal notion of the immortality of art and thereby wards off the need to confront death. It seems plausible to suppose that the storyteller is a representative of Wenders himself—and in light of Homer's preoccupation with childhood it is interesting to consider how Wenders justifies his *own* return to conventional narrative or "storytelling":

> It [storytelling] is one of the most reassuring things. It seems its very basis is that it reassures you that there is a sense to things. Like the fact that children want to hear stories when they go to sleep. I mean not so much that they want to know this or that, but that they want it as it gives them a security. The story creates a form and the form reassures them so that you can almost tell them any story—which you can actually do. So there is something very powerful in stories, something that gives you security and a sense of identity and meaning. (p. 6)

But, of course, this is exactly what a politicized avant-garde group of filmmakers and theorists who wished to change the world and not just reflect on it had *condemned* in narrative not so very long ago: in a world that desperately needs active, responsible, adult engagement on the part of its inhabitants, a world in which the very notion of a stable "identity" functions as part of an oppressive ideology, the regressive, falsely reassuring qualities of narrative were condemned precisely because they lulled us into complacency, suturing us into a spurious sense of identity and wholeness.

In considering the narrative structure of Wenders's story, it is not irrelevant to think again of *Columbo*, which was famed for its departure from the classic structure of the detective story in that the viewer knew from the outset "who done it" and could concentrate entirely on Columbo's brilliant solving of the crime: thus the very format of the program conveyed a sense of destiny, with Columbo the incarnation of fatality. So too does *Wings of Desire* enshrine a notion of fate in the miraculous meeting of male and female, which happens solely through narrative fiat: the woman walks into the bar and without ever having seen the man knows he is, literally, the man of her dreams (specifically, the dream she had the previous night). Despite the film's affirmation of openendedness (the final words on the screen: "to be continued," the storyteller proclaiming "*nous sommes embarqués*"), it eliminates in its very structure the terrors of mortality, which are, precisely, the terrors of contingency. "No more coincidence," says the woman, and "Look: my eyes they are the picture of necessity, of the future of everyone on the plaza."

That woman functions in an entirely conventional way in the film not only as mankind's "future," but the place of return, the locus of nostalgia, is revealed in the final speech of Damiel, after he has slept with Marion (the physical act of love having occurred, significantly, offscreen). As she performs on the rope above, Damiel stands below, holding the rope and looking up, and he meditates: "I was in her, she was around me; . . . No mortal child was created but an immortal common image. I learned amazement last night. She took me home, and I found my home. It happened once. It happened once, and so it will be forever." And thus we return to *Big* with *its* return to Mother and the womb. Throughout *Wings of Desire*, the woman's body has functioned as object of desire/object of the look, and as we listen in on her thoughts we hear that she is actually desiring the look of men ("I only need to be ready and all the world's men will look at me. Longing. Longing for a wave of love that will stir in me"), and she herself evokes such longing that the image periodically turns from black and white to color. It is because of his intense desire for the body of this surrogate angel (of a woman approximately twenty-five years younger than he: so much for accepting mortality) that the angel becomes man, but by the end the woman in her capacity as womb-bearer comes to stand as a guarantee of *im*mortality—of a "forever" that mitigates the terror of Damiel's subsequent declaration that the "immortal" image the two created the night before will be with him when he dies.

As a figure of contradiction, the trapeze artist is emblematic of this film's desire to have it both ways: while purporting to be undertaking the painful work of remembering the horrors of the past, revising concepts of masculinity and femininity, coming to terms with the body and its mortality, and holding out an ideal of freedom and hence of responsibility ("it's time to choose," says Marion, "the picture of necessity"), it consoles itself with nostalgia—for simple stories and mother's womb—and a hackneyed notion of "destiny" embedded in the "happily ever after," greatest-story-ever-told narrative of a man and a woman. Given that Wenders chose to cast his young girlfriend opposite the aging Ganz, it is tempting to speculate that the film documents the midlife crisis of a director who is no longer a young maverick but a worldly success and wants to assure himself that despite this success and his craving for mass appeal and artistic immortality, his rigorous standards are still intact, the questions he poses still difficult, and his social conscience still keenly alive. And indeed it may be that in the final analysis, the appeal of this film and so many others dealing with regression is that they express the collective midlife crisis of the entire baby-boom generation.

All of the films I have discussed in this chapter have at their core the male desire to escape the human limits of the body. For all their apparent concern with revealing the penis behind the phallus—the vulnerable, finite male behind the image of omnipotent superhero (and we might note the contemporary reworking of superhero stories like *Batman* and *The Last Temptation of Christ* to emphasize precisely the hero's humanity and vulnerability)—the films are as evasive as the older ones and certainly just as oppressive to women, who are made to bear, as always, the burdens of masculine ambivalence about the body.

Recently Jean-François Lyotard has posed the philosophical question, "Can Thought Go On Without A Body?" and, taking a position opposed to the shrinking man, answers in the negative. According to Lyotard, thinking involves a pain that comes not from outside, but from within the body. The "pain is thought itself resolving to be irresolute, deciding to be patient. . . . So that the suffering of thinking is a suffering of time, of what happens"— of, then, mortality.[25] Interestingly, Lyotard divides his essay into two parts—the first, concerned with the philosopher's dream of bodiless thought, he entitles "He"; the second, entitled "She," discusses the importance of the *gendered* body. Thought, according to Lyotard, begins only when a lack is perceived, a lack "present deep inside, in the body, in the mind. . . . Elusive, impossible to grasp"—a state Lyotard calls "transcendence in immanence" (p. 85). What Lyotard is suggesting (but also reproducing in the very division of the essay) is the fact that it is the female body alone which is gendered (as Monique Wittig has argued in her essay, "The Mark of Gender"), which serves as the site for the projection of "lack" and, indeed, as the very figure of "transcendence in immanence"—a phrase that perfectly captures the signification of the female trapeze artist and of Woman as she is generally represented in art.

In the same issue of the journal in which Lyotard's essay appears is the essay I discussed earlier by Valie Export who, in contrast to Lyotard, foregrounds the problem of the violence done to the female body in patriarchal systems of representation, calling for an end to the gendered body celebrated by Lyotard, and, as we have seen, finding in anorexia a laudable feminine rejection of this body. But feminists must, I think, refuse the romantic impulse to celebrate a disease that only reflects patriarchy's paradoxical image of woman ("transcendence in immanence") back to itself: on the one hand the anorexic views "the self" "concretely, as a body," but on the other hand desires "to escape the body entirely as a way of escaping [the] funnel of alien desires."[26] Instead, we need to understand that the anorexic refusal of "the suffering of time," the resistance to growth and maturity, are really characteristic of some *masculinities* today—as well as of postmodernism itself, insofar as it has been theorized as concerned with cultivating the image of the body *as* image, and with seeking to halt the passage of time—of history itself.

Of course, this refusal of history has been discussed by Fredric Jameson,

110

who has pointed to the nostalgia pervading contemporary culture.[27] Indeed, in the works we have examined, nostalgia has been explicitly thematized, for in a peculiarly postmodern move, the films hollow out the Freudian dictum that art always involves regressive fantasies and center on the fantasy of regression itself. That—despite postmodernists' tendency to proclaim the death of narrative—nostalgia would eventually come to focus on narrative itself, on the desire expressed by Wenders for the lost art of storytelling, was probably all too predictable. That woman would return along with narrative to figure in her traditional place—exactly, a *place*, matter and matrix, where man could retreat to stop the flow of time—was also predictable. But, as we have seen, the situation is hardly better for woman even in parodic, anti-narrative pastiches like Pee-wee Herman films and *Pee-wee's Playhouse*, in which woman's body is made to bear the burdens of time that the eternally adolescent male would refuse. So, regardless of whether the text in question is a narrative or the kind of anti-narratives considered by many to characterize postmodern art, nostalgia is bound up with sexual difference in ways that many male theorists have not considered.[28]

Feminists, however, are not only calling on men to come to terms with the male body, but are continuing to study the ways in which their own bodies have functioned in patriarchy. Work like this—on the aging body, the grotesque body, the anorexic body, etc.—is part of a general refusal on the part of women to allow patriarchal scapegoatings to continue.[29] As an ongoing project of female coming-to-consciousness, this work suggests that an analysis of the manipulations of the female body in and through representation is one of the most urgent tasks facing feminism today. And that an end to such extreme manipulations would seem to be, precisely, a matter of time.

PART III

Race, Gender, and Sexuality

CHAPTER SEVEN

Cinema and the Dark Continent

Race and Gender in Popular Film

Issues of race, gender, and ethnicity come together in an especially bizarre manner in one of the earliest sound films, *The Jazz Singer*, at the end of which the Jewish son, played by Al Jolson, donning black face for a theatrical performance, hears "the call of the ages—the cry of my race," sings "Mammy" to his mother, and rushes home to his dying father, promising to take up momentarily the father's role as cantor. Subsequently—and the coda is added to the film version of the stage play—the son returns to his show-business career, thus being permitted the best of both worlds, old and new. Here, of course, are the familiar oedipal themes of Hollywood cinema: the son's accession to the role of the father entails a modification of the stern and unyielding patriarchal attitude, thereby, in the case of *The Jazz Singer*, accommodating the assimilationist ideologies of the period. The mother is a key figure in the process of the hero's growth and acculturation, since in her unconditional love for her child she can serve as the mediating force between father and son, old world and new, the desire for cultural difference and the desire for cultural integration.[1]

But the mother in the film is not the only mediator, not the only person whose sole significance lies in the meaning she holds for the white man and *his* drama; the other such figure is, of course, the black man, metonymically summoned to represent the unalterable fact of "race," and thus to form one pole of the assimilationist continuum, at the other end of which stands the Jolson character's *shiksa* girlfriend. It is ironic, if utterly characteristic, that the essentialist notion of race the film draws upon is asserted through masquerade and in a space of illusionism, i.e., the theater. That is to say,

115

the jazz singer recognizes his supposed racial *authenticity* as a Semite in the process of *miming* another race—assuming black skin and black voice— so that the film is situated squarely in the realm of the fetish, whereby the notion of ineradicable racial difference (one which defies history and calls out across "the ages") is simultaneously affirmed and negated.

Recent work by Homi Bhabha has shown how colonialist discourse as a whole involves a process of mimicry that is related psychoanalytically to the mechanism of fetishization, the play of presence and absence. By mimicry, I take Bhabha to be referring to an imposition by one nation of its structures, values, and language upon the colonized nation, an imposition that rather than completely obliterating difference speaks of "a desire for a subject of a difference that is almost the same, but not quite" and hence is, Bhabha continually emphasizes, *ambivalent*.[2] Although Bhabha's terms of reference concern the British Empire, they apply equally to the American situation, for, as Thomas Cripps points out in his somewhat dated but still useful study of blacks in American film, the position of blacks in relation to the dominant culture and its representations has been an "ambivalent" one: blacks had "absorbed American culture but could not expect to be absorbed by it."[3] Moreover, Cripps himself points out that the British colonial system "resembled American racial arrangements" in the way "it encouraged cultural assimilation while denying social integration" (p. 313). One fairly ludicrous result of such "arrangements" was that, for example, in cinema what used to be called "race movies" often had to do without white people. "Without whites, the requirements of dramatic construction created a world in which black characters acceded to the white ideal of segregation, and unreal black cops, crooks, judges, and juries interacted in such a way as to blame black victims for their social plight." But the lack of versimilitude, which Cripps sees as a problem, can cut two ways: for it is easy to see how how such copies of white cinema could easily reflect back on the model itself, mocking it, defamiliarizing it, casting doubt upon its accuracy as, in the words of one film concerned with the perennial theme of "passing," an "imitation of life" (p. 322–23).

Eddie Murphy's *Coming to America* furnishes a contemporary example of a movie in which black mimicry of whites is both a source of humor and a fundamental structuring principle of the text. In this movie, Price Akeem leaves Africa to come to America—to Queens—in order to find a queen of his own choosing, one with a "mind of her own" rather than the woman destined and trained from birth to be his wife. Alhough on his arrival Prince Akeem discovers a world where black poverty seems to be the rule, the film rapidly moves beyond this world to enter middle-class black society, represented by the owner of a hamburger stand called McDowell's. The owner, whose daughter becomes Akeem's choice for a wife, explains the differences between his business and the McDonald's franchise: "they have golden arches, we have golden arcs. . . . Their rolls have sesame seeds, ours don't, etc."—distinctions, in other words, without a difference. The joke here, in which mimicry itself is foregrounded, may be said to cut a variety of ways, potentially mocking the white model for black middle-class ambitions but also, at least in the eyes of prejudiced white audiences, affirming white capitalism as the "real thing" and appearing to expose black aspirations as ridiculous and pathetic.

There is also another sense in which mimicry operates throughout the text. Insofar as the film may be said to belong to a recognizable genre, the screwball comedy, the film participates in, mimes, a fantasy unreal enough when it concerns whites and doubly so in relation to blacks. In a gesture reminiscent of the classic screwball hero Godfrey of *My Man Godfrey*, Akeem disguises himself as a penniless floor-washer in order to win over the father of the (motherless) woman he loves. As the barber advises, "If you want to get in good with the daughter, you got to get in good with the father." The film is clearly situated squarely within the bounds of the oedipal drama, the only twist being that the arrival of Akeem's real father is the decisive event in winning over the future father-in-law, who is bowled over on discovering the richness and royalty of his daughter's suitor. The film's major conflict thus turns out to be not an interracial or class conflict but one between the wealthy black Americans and the even wealthier Africans. That the film resolves its conflict according to the traditional dictates of the genre by ending with a wedding (between Burger Queen and future African king) that promises the harmonious union of two worlds—a black imitation of white corporate America, represented by McDowell's, and a black African nation represented by its royal family—takes on a particularly sinister irony in light of the role played by American corporations in the destruction of the environment of Third World peoples.

117

The ending of *Coming to America* may be seen as an attempt to resolve at the level of fantasy the ambivalence or doubleness Bhabha sees operating in representations of race: the black man as alien, African other (an otherness always already denied because it is the familiar, Americanized Eddie Murphy who plays the lead role) and the black man as assimilated dreamer of the American dream. Such an ambivalence, according to Bhabha, is explosive; there is an incipient menace in mimicry, and from "a difference that is almost nothing but not quite" it is but a step to a "difference that is almost total but not quite."[4] Switching genres, from comedy to horror, we may note that the film, *Alien Nation*, provides a vivid illustration of the thesis. In this film a group of aliens from another planet have been residing in Los Angeles as an oppressed minority, clearly meant to serve as allegorical figures for blacks. (Here we see vividly illustrated the dominant culture's tendency to collapse all racial groups into one undifferentiated mass which serves as the "Other" of white society. For, clearly, the notion of an alien nation draws on the existence of the Latino population of illegal "aliens.") The aliens are almost like whites but "not quite" (they get drunk on sour milk; the males have larger penises than the Americans; their heads are strangely shaped, hairless, and mottled[5]), and in the liberal surface text, the bigoted white cop must learn to accept his new alien partner, Sam Francisco, as someone whose differences are in fact insignificant in the face of the men's overriding common humanity. The two are involved in tracing down a deadly drug that has nearly destroyed the people on the alien planet, and at one point Sam forces his partner to witness the hideous physical transformation of a victim who has overdosed so that he may see "just how monstrous" his people "are capable of becoming." Yet, plot details aside, is it not the case that the threat of monstrosity—that is, of black monstrosity—has been present all along in the film as a consequence of the decision to make it an allegory rather than to treat the situation of blacks directly? And has not the tendency of films from the very early days of cinema to cast white people in black face served a similar function— i.e., to suggest that blackness may be so monstrous it can only be signified but not directly represented? When in *Birth of a Nation* we watch the lecherous man in blackface pursuing the young white girl to her death, do we need to know about, in order to feel the force of, Griffith's reason for

118

casting mostly white actors in the film: i.e., to protect the purity of white womanhood on the set?[6]

We need, then, not just to analyze the function of mimicry on the part of the colonized people, but to understand its role in the life and art of the *colonizer*—to understand, that is, the function of minstrelsy. Bhabha writes of the way the "not quite/not white" element of difference displayed by colonized races is related to the psychoanalytic notion of the fetish: "black skin splits under the racist gaze, displaced into signs of bestiality, genitalia, grotesquerie, which reveal the phobic myth of the undifferentiated whole white skin."[7] Minstrelsy would be a method by which the white man may disavow—acknowledge and at the same time deny—difference at the level of the body; as a process of fetishism, it seeks, like all fetishes, to restore the wholeness and unity threatened by the sight of difference, yet because it enters into the game of mimicry it is condemned to keep alive the possibility that there may be "no presence or identity behind the mask."[8] The concept of fetishism enables us to understand why minstrelsy has never really died out—why it lives in a different form in the "trading places" and "black like me" plots with which Hollywood is enamored, the most recent example being Paul Mazursky's *Moon Over Parador* (actually an instance of "brownface"), in which the Richard Dreyfus character, an unemployed Hollywood actor, is pressed into masquerading as the leader of a Central American country and in effect winds up playing the "Tootsie" of Latin American dictators.

Some of Bhabha's discussion covers familiar territory for a feminist reader, since he draws on material elaborated in feminist theory. The problematics of difference and sameness have, for example, been brilliantly analyzed by Luce Irigaray in her readings of Freud's essay "On Femininity" and Plato's *Republic*. Irigaray shows that for all Western culture's emphasis on the difference between the sexes, there is an underlying negation of the difference—and the threat—posed by the female sex, a negation evidenced for example in Freud's theorizing of the woman as an inferior man, as bearer of the "lack."[9] In Freudian theory, of course, the fetish is precisely the means whereby "lack" and difference are disavowed—accepted and negated simultaneously. It is the means, in other words, whereby "a multiple belief" may be maintained and hence serves to support the wildly divergent stereotypical associations that accrue around the fetishized body. For it is not just the black who is marked in the dominant discourse as, in Homi Bhabha's words, "both savage . . . and yet the most obedient and dignified of servants; . . . the embodiment of rampant sexuality and yet innocent as a child; . . . mystical, primitive, simple-minded and yet the most worldly and accomplished liar, and manipulator of social forces."[10] Much of this description also applies to the representation of woman, who in the male Imaginary undergoes a primal splitting into virgin and whore.

The importance of Bhabha's work, like Fanon's before him, lies partly, for me, in the way it insists on understanding the psychosocial dynamics of colonialism and racism, bringing psychoanalysis to bear on questions that have unfortunately all too often been viewed as not susceptible to a psychoanalytic understanding. Yet, unaccountably, although Bhabha utilizes the very concepts originally developed in the theorization of sexual difference, he almost entirely neglects the issue of gender and slights feminist work. In virtually ignoring the "woman question," while retaining the terms in which it has been posed, Bhabha commits the same kind of error for which Freud can be and has been criticized. The latter was undoubtedly being both racist and sexist in designating "woman" as the dark continent. But the answer is surely not to reverse the proposition and implicitly posit the "dark continent" as woman—not, at the very least, without carefully theorizing the relation.

Alhough he does not examine how race and gender intersect, Bhabha nevertheless notes at one point, "Darkness signifies at once both birth and death; it is in all cases a desire to return to the fullness of the mother, a desire for an unbroken and undifferentiated line of vision and origin."[11] For the heart of the matter, the heart of darkness, is, after all, "Mammy"—she who, absent in her own right, is spoken by man as guarantor of his origin and identity. In the face of the male desire to collapse sexual and racial difference into oceanic plenitude, feminism needs to insist on the complex, "multiple and cross-cutting" nature of identity and to ask: how do we rid ourselves of the desire for a "line of origin," how avoid positing either sexuality or race as theoretically primary, while we at the same time undertake to understand the vicious circularity of patriarchal thought whereby darkness signifies femininity and femininity darkness? I would

120

like in this chapter to address this question by examining first the way our culture through its representations explores the highly charged taboo relationships between black men and white women (specifically focusing on *Gorillas in the Mist* and a scene from an early film, *Blonde Venus*) and then to focus on the representations of black women in popular film, looking especially at the ways in which the black woman functions as the site of the displacement of white culture's (including white women's) fears and anxieties.

In *Gorillas in the Mist*, the question of origins is posed at the outset by, of course, a white man—in this case the anthropologist Dr. Louis Leakey, who is seen in a large hall lecturing about gorillas: "I want to know who I am, and what it was that made me that way." As if conjured up by his words, Dian Fossey appears, the woman who will journey alone to the heart of darkest Africa and whose story may be viewed as a phantasmatic answer to the white man's question.

It is an old story, an updated, middlebrow version of the King Kong tale, which itself is part of a tradition of animal movies that have functioned as thinly disguised "allegories for black brutes."[12] Of the perennial popularity of the film *King Kong*, for example, X. J. Kennedy wrote:

> A Negro friend from Atlanta tells me that in movies houses in colored neighbor-
> hoods throughout the South, *Kong* does a constant business. They show the
> thing in Atlanta at least every year, presumably to the same audiences. Perhaps
> this popularity may simply be due to the fact that *Kong* is one of the most
> watchable movies ever constructed, but I wonder whether Negro audiences
> may not find some archetypical appeal in this serio-comic tale of a huge black
> powerful free spirit whom all the hardworking white policemen are out to
> kill.[13]

Putting aside the way this passage provides a textbook example of how white racism gets projected into the psyches of the black audience, we may note that Kennedy's remarks are paradoxically couched in a liberal frame which tacitly acknowledges the legitimacy of black political grievances while employing an ahistorical notion of "archetype," which would deny the humanity of blacks (imaged as beasts) and so function to prevent them from achieving social and political equality. This is not to say that

Kennedy's response is idiosyncratic: on the contrary, films like *King Kong*, made by whites in a racist society, lend themselves to this kind of interpretation, which is situated in the space of disavowal characteristic of colonialist discourse (the fetish indeed being a means by which two apparently opposed beliefs, "one archaic and one progressive," may simultaneously be held). This is a space, as we shall see, increasingly occupied in a post feminist, post-civil rights era by a mass culture that must on one level acknowledge the political struggles of the last few decades and on another, deeper level would ward off the threat these struggles pose to the white male power structure.

Thus, for example, *Gorillas in the Mist* seems to respect the notion of a woman sacrificing the opportunity for a husband and family in order to pursue a career, a career that, indeed, involves her living the sort of adventurous and dangerous life usually reserved for men in popular films and that also accords her the kind of single-minded dedication to a cause typically attributed to the *male* scientific investigator. But the film takes it all back, as it were, by "deprofessionalizing" Fossey, neglecting to mention her growth as a scientist who in the course of her research in the mountains of Rwanda earned a Ph.D. from Harvard. The film further subverts its apparently liberal attitude to woman's independence by suggesting that Dian is merely channeling and sublimating (or should it be *de*sublimating, since she goes "back" to the apes?) her sexual desires and maternal instincts into her cause. In the last scene, for example, after her death, the image track shows the son of the slaughtered gorilla swinging in the trees—clearly *Fossey*'s son, since her tryst with its father, the gorilla Digit (in which the romantic music swells as Dian lies on her back, smiling blissfully when the gorilla slowly takes her hand, leaving a precious little deposit of dirt in her palm) is followed by her coupling with the *National Geographic* photographer. The soundtrack records a conversation between her and Roz Carr, the plantation owner, in which Fossey remarks, "I expected to get married and have children," and her friend replies, "Instead there's a mountain full of gorillas who wouldn't be alive if it weren't for you." The titles at the end tell us that Fossey's work "contributed significantly to the survival of the species"—woman's function, after all, even if it isn't quite the right species.

The transfer of Fossey's affection from her fiancé to Digit and his "group" is visually marked by the film through its replacement of the photo of the fiancé, which we see early in the film placed on a little typing table outside Dian's hut, with photos of the gorillas ("gorilla porn," as one of my friends remarked) that she passionately kisses right before her murder, while a song of Peggy Lee's ("I'd take a million trips to your lips") plays on the phonograph. But perverse as all this may sound—and in my view *is*—the most remarkable aspect of the film is the way in which it manages to make its psychosexual dynamics seem innocent. Indeed, the very title of the film points to a kind of disavowal, suggesting a tamed, romanticized, "misty" view of beasts and bestiality: a film whose *own* sublimating efforts work on every level to deny the perversity of the gorilla/woman sexual coupling it continually evokes.

Black skin "splits" in this film, to recall Homi Bhabha's words, into images of monstrosity and bestiality on the one hand and of nobility and wisdom on the other. Fossey's tracker, Sembagare, represents the latter option; he is presented as a man whose family has been wiped out along with their tribe and thus, having no story or plot of his own, he is free to live a life of self-sacrificing devotion to the white woman. It is impossible to overestimate the importance of this character—a common type in Hollywood cinema—in serving as a guide to the audience's interpretation and judgment of events, and it is interesting to reflect on the fact that such a character's possession of the gaze may be concomitant with a radical *dis*possession in relation to the narrative. Throughout the film, the camera continually cuts to shots of Sembagare, usually gazing approvingly on some action performed by the heroine, but also, occasionally, registering disapproval and dismay. Mostly what Sembagare cares about is that the heroine's sexual and romantic needs be fulfilled, and this is made clear from the very outset when he first sees and comments on the picture of the fiancé. By attributing a kind of maternal concern to the black male as well as granting him a degree of moral authority, the film can appear to be, in liberal fashion, empowering the character while at the same time relieving the audiences' anxieties about the proximity of white womanhood and black manhood.

That fears about the threat posed by the black male to white woman are *not* far beneath the surface can be seen in the film's treatment of all the other black men, who are usually shown in menacing groups, surrounding our heroine, gesturing and muttering in their "savage" languages, and touching her hair in awe. Early in the film, some black soldiers come to Fossey's hut, destroy her possessions, and evict her from their country. The film treats African civil wars as nothing more than a nuisance impeding Fossey's crusade—a crusade aligned with the film's project of substituting a timeless, pastoral "gorilla nation" for the eminently less important struggles of emerging black nations. Significantly, as the men attempt to force her to leave, Fossey furiously tells them not to touch her, to get their hands off her. Now, given that the big love scene with the gorilla involves Fossey holding hands with him, and indeed that the love interest is given the name "Digit" by Fossey because of the webbing of his fingers, and finally that the film is most horrified by the castration of the gorillas' heads and hands, the latter made into curio ashtrays for rich Americans, we might be justified in seeing in this motif of the hand a condensation of the film's basic conflict: a pitting of animals *against* black men, with the former ultimately viewed as less physically and morally repellent than the latter. Here we might note that we come full circle to Griffith's film *Birth of a Nation*, which had intercut shots of Flora being stalked by Gus with ones of squirrels framed in an iris. The black man thus becomes, as Cripps observes, "a predator about to pounce upon a harmless animal" (p. 48). Thus it is that in *Gorillas in the Mist*, the machete-wielding black men who earn their living destroying gorillas are depicted as *less* truly and movingly human than the tragic and noble gorillas—as was the case in *King Kong*, as well.

Of course, at the level of its script, the film suggests a more complicated view, and at one point the photographer Bob cautions an angry Fossey that the black men are simply pawns in an economic power game that chiefly benefits rich Americans. In this respect too, then, the film operates in the realm of disavowal, verbally disputing its own visual scapegoating of the black men *and*, moreover, projecting the scapegoating onto the character of Fossey, who at one point terrorizes a little black boy by pretending to be a witch and at another point conducts a mock lynching of a black male poacher.

It is the white man, then, who in the end seems to be the most fully human character, while the black men are either self-sacrificing servants or threatening monsters, and the white woman is at the same time both a noble savior of innocent creatures and a witch whose unholy alliance with the beasts of the forests turns her into a raving monomaniac. In other words, into the space hollowed out by the film's fetishistic splittings steps the white man, equipped with the photographic apparatus which apparently enables him to establish the proper voyeuristic distance from the perversity that surrounds him. Interestingly, since this is Dian Fossey's story, and most of the film is from her point of view, the film gives the point of view over to Bob on several occasions. I have already referred to one instance—when Bob stares in fascination at Dian's "mating" with Digit, the camera cutting to tight close-ups of him as he crouches near his photographic equipment and stares intently at the coming together of woman and ape. Another such moment occurs when he first arrives on the scene, and we see Dian squatting on the floor, imitating the gorillas' movements and noises. So vertiginous does the film's play with mimicry become that the woman is constantly shown copying the gorillas, aping the anthropomorphized apes; like the blacks, she seems to occupy a position one step below the animals, to be not quite capable of achieving the same degree of humanity attained by the beasts.

But while an analysis of the point-of-view structure of *Gorillas in the Mist* suggests that, like most Hollywood films, and despite its biographical claims, this one is largely concerned with white male fears and fantasies and seems designed to assure the white man of his full humanity in relation to the animals, the female sex, and other races, it is important to understand that the voyeuristic distance between the white male and his "others" ultimately collapses. Bob, it turns out, is drawn to gorillas too, and he gets to act out his bestial lusts vicariously when he and Dian become lovers after he sees her with Digit and during an elaborate verbal play in which references to the beauty of the animals serve as double entendres applying to Fossey herself. Here we encounter the perennial thematics of homosocial desire, according to which the woman functions in a triangular relationship between two males, the woman becoming attractive to the second male as a result of being sought after or possessed by the first: a matter of, in René Girard's words, *mimetic* desire—of, in the film's case, man imitating beast.[14] Thus, we might say, by the end of the twentieth century, homosocial desire, long the cornerstone of patriarchal society, has expanded to include the entire order of Primates.

In *Gorillas in the Mist*, then, woman serves to initiate man into the secrets of his origin, whereupon he goes off to a new job in the wider world, escaping the carnage and destruction visited on the other players. Such violence is made to seem an appropriate ending to a film that touches on so many taboo areas, situating itself at the shifting borders between man and woman, whites and blacks, humans and animals, nature and society. One might expect that because of its unsettling obsession with these taboos, its nearly uncontrollable play of iteration, audiences would be troubled by the film's perversity. Seldom, however, did reviewers even mention the film's bizarre psychosocial dynamics; instead, the main "controversy" surrounding *Gorillas in the Mist* had to do with its accuracy as representation of Fossey's life—a question, once again, of mimicry, or mimesis. It is tempting to speculate that this question arises as a response to the disturbances created *by* the film at a phantasmatic level, instilling in us a longing for an authentic human life to serve as ground and source of the film's meaning, just as the film itself attempts to foreclose the historical process and establish a natural, pastoral space which would pre-exist the struggles of feminists and black nationalists. Such a question would take on a special urgency precisely because the lines toed by the film are so thin that it comes perilously close to mocking its own quest, making monkeys of us all.

In his book, *The Signifying Monkey: A Theory of Afro-American Literary Criticism*, Henry Louis Gates praises Jean Renoir's silent film *Sur un air de Charleston* for its parody of the literature of discovery popular in Renaissance and Enlightenment Europe. In the film, a black man in blackface discovers a post-holocaust Europe and its only survivors, "a scantily clad white Wild Woman . . . and her lascivious companion, an ape." Gates sees in this scenario a "master trope of irony," which operates a "fairly straightforward . . . reversal . . . of common European allegations of the propensity of African women to prefer the company of male apes." That Gates can see nothing dubious in Renoir's "surrealistic critique of . . . fundamental conventions of Western discourse on the black" and can entirely neglect to consider the potency of myths like *King Kong* (which long precede the 1933 film) suggests a very large blind spot indeed—blind, that is, to the way the female Other, regardless of race, has been frequently consigned to categories that put her outside the pale of the fully human.[15]

126

(Why, we might inquire, did it not occur to the "master" ironist to depict a scantily clad white man lewdly gyrating with his pet ape?)

Most pertinently we need to ask if, given the fetishistic nature of discourses on race and gender, a politically effective representational strategy can ever operate via "reversal." Gates's own lucid discussion of the complexity of black American "signifying," which he argues both participates in and subtly undermines white discourse, implicitly repudiates the viability of "straightforward reversal" as political critique. If, as Gates argues, blacks have developed a double-edged discourse capable of responding to what W.E.B. DuBois called the "twoness" of their existence in American culture, how much more pertinent is the theorization of such a discourse for anyone concerned with understanding the complex articulations of race *and* gender in American life and with avoiding the "reversals" that keep us continually veering between the Scylla of racism and the Charybdis of sexism.

To illustrate this point, I want to return to a scene in a film by a director whose presence is strongly felt at the "originary" moment of feminist psychoanalytic film theory: namely, Josef von Sternberg, the auteur who was the focus of Laura Mulvey's comments on the way popular narrative cinema tends to fetishize the female body.[16] The film—*Blonde Venus*—has been as riveting to contemporary theorists of cinema as the sight of Dian Fossey lying among the apes was to the character Bob in *Gorillas in the Mist*.[17] A still from the scene to which I am referring graces the cover of an issue of *Cinema Journal* which includes an article about the subversiveness of the film's treatment of female sexuality.[18] In the plot leading up to this scene, the heroine Helen, played by Marlene Dietrich, has recently left her humble home and her husband and son to return to a career on the stage; in the still, she has just emerged from an ape costume, although hairy bits of the costume remain around her genital area, her shoulders, and her derrière, and she is about to sing "Hot Voodoo." On her head is a blonde Afro wig and behind her stand a group of women in blackface holding spears and giant masks painted with large mouths and teeth.

Nowhere does Sternberg more forcefully reveal himself to be the master fetishist of the female body than in this scene, which for an adequate reading requires us to apply the insights of *both* a Homi Bhabha and a Laura Mulvey. Too often feminist film critics have alluded only parenthetically to the film's racism while devoting themselves chiefly to considering

127

whether the film is "progressive" in its emphasis on performance and spectacle, its subtle visual undermining of the domestic ideal that the narrative purports to uphold. Yet the racism is not an incidental, "odd" moment to be bracketed off in order to pursue more pressing concerns, but is, in fact, central to the evocation and manipulation of desire that begins with the Hot Voodoo number and continues up to and beyond Helen's flight south to increasingly exotic locales, the last of which is a Louisiana boarding house run by a black woman.

In the Hot Voodoo sequence, the fetishistic working of presence and absence, difference and sameness, depends, as it does in *Gorillas in the Mist*, on the interplay of the elements of white woman, ape, and blacks. If it can be said that the film draws on the stereotypical association, referred to by Gates, of apes and black women, it can also be that said the white woman *is* the ape. But then again, of course, she is not the ape. Part of the sexual charge of the spectacle derives from the disavowal, the doubleness, the contradictory belief structure whereby she is posited as *simultaneously* animal and human, as well as simultaneously white and not white (suggested by the blonde Afro wig). Similarly, the white women in blackface and black Afro wigs who stand behind Dietrich are also affirmed and denied as African "savages" (and are fetishized further in that the war-paint on their faces resembles the painting on the masks they carry in front of the lower halves of their bodies—the teeth on these masks clearly symbolizing the *vagina dentata*). I think we can take this fully theatricalized image as emblematic of some of the complex interrelations of gender and race in popular representation.[19]

In doing so, however, we are forced to recognize that while everyone in this scenario (except for the white male, played by Cary Grant, who is looking on) is relegated to "the ideologically appointed place of the stereotype"[20]), the black women in the film are in the *most* marginalized position. If it is true, to cite Claire Johnston's famous formulation, woman as woman has largely been absent from patriarchal cinema, this has obviously been much more literally the case for black women than for whites.[21] And if the white woman has usually served as the signifier of male desire (which is what Johnston meant when she spoke of the absence of woman *as* woman), the black woman, when present at all, has served as a signifier of (white) female sexuality or of the maternal ("Mammy"). In the last part of this essay I would like to explore the way in which black women in contemporary popular film are reduced to being the signifiers of signifiers.

The use of the black woman to signify sexuality is vividly illustrated in one of the most recent films in the tradition of *The Jazz Singer*. In this case, however, the protagonist is a *woman* who finds herself going back to her Jewish roots. In *Crossing Delancey*, directed by Joan Micklin Silver, Amy Irving plays Izzy, a thirty-three year-old white woman who lives alone in Manhattan, works in a prestigious bookstore organizing readings by the literati, and, vehement disclaimers to the contrary notwithstanding, is clearly desperate to find a man. Indeed, she is so desperate that after ridding herself of an infatuation with a self-absorbed and pretentious writer, she overcomes a strong distaste for a Jewish pickle salesman, who has been chosen for her by a marriage-broker in collusion with Izzy's grandmother. In a brief scene occurring rather early in the film, Izzy is trying to decide whether or not to call the writer to ask him out, and she asks the advice of a friend as the two relax in the sauna after a workout in the gym. While the women recline in their towels, the camera pans down to reveal two black women, one of whom, a very large woman whose ample flesh spills out of a tight bathing-suit, loudly recounts to her friend an anecdote about love making in which while performing fellatio ("I'm licking it, I'm kissing it, he's moaning") she discovers a long—"I mean long"—blonde hair, which the man rather lamely tries to explain away. The camera tilts back up, as Izzy, having listened intently to the conversation, thoughtfully remarks, "Maybe I *will* call him."

Clearly the black woman, small as her role is, represents sexuality and "embodiment" in a film that never mentions sex at any other time (to be sure, the fact of sex is hinted at when Izzy spends an occasional night with a married male friend, but it is never shown or discussed). Even the framing of the scene we have been discussing suggests in amazingly exemplary fashion the hierarchical division between black and white women, with the uptown Manhattanite princess-"on-her-high-horse" (to quote the grandmother), who will be forced to accept as a lover a Jewish man from lower Manhattan, placed in the upper part of the frame and the sexualized black females situated, as always, on the bottom (a spatial metaphor with both social and psychic dimensions). The black woman's story not only hints at the threat of miscegenation—for, just as this woman's lover has strayed, so too is Izzy straying from her roots—but represents directly all those desires that this postfeminist film is disavowing: both a voracious sexuality and a voracious hunger in general, resulting from the deprivations suffered by single middle-class white women in the modern world. Thus the fact that the one sexual act mentioned in the film (which is about a woman's love for a pickle salesman, no less) is the act of fellatio is not surprising given the ubiquitous presence of food in the film (scenes of Izzy and her friend eating hotdogs on Izzy's birthday after she lies to her boss about going to a fancy restaurant [obviously women cannot nurture themselves or each other]; of lonely women picking at food in salad bars and eating Chinese takeout while watching television; of a baby nursing at his mother's breast while the heroine looks on in envy—envy *not*, it is quite clear, of the mother but of the suckling child; and finally, of the [as the film portrays her] obnoxiously loud female marriage broker continually gobbling down other people's food, eating with greasy fingers and talking with her mouth crammed full).

In the previous chapter I talked about the horror of the body expressed in contemporary culture, the anorexic mentality to which this horror gives rise, and the tendency on the part of men to deal with these fears by displacing them onto the body of the female; what we need to note here is the special role played by the woman of color as receptacle of these fears. The function of the fat, sexually voracious black woman in *Crossing Delancey* is to enable the white Jewish subculture, through its heterosexual love story, to represent itself in a highly sentimentalized, romanticized, and sublimated light, while disavowing the desires and discontents underlying the civilization it is promoting. (Once again, then, we see the need for feminist analysis to consider the ways in which ethnic and racial groups are played off against—and play themselves off against—one another.[22])

If in *Crossing Delancey*—a film written and directed by *women*—the black female body is the sexualized body, in other films the black woman functions not only as the sexual other, but as the maternal body, as psychic surrogate for the white mother—in short, as "Mammy." Recent feminist theory has shown that the nursery maid in Freud's own time played an important, although largely unacknowledged, role in initiating the child into sexual knowledge.[23] In America, as black feminists have pointed out,

130

the black woman has more often than not served a similar function in the acculturation of white children. *Clara's Heart*, starring Whoopi Goldberg, provides an unusually stark illustration of the process whereby the young white male achieves maturity through penetrating the mystery of the black woman—"her wisdom, her warmth, her secret," as the poster proclaims. That (returning to the metaphor of the dark continent) we are dealing here almost literally with the "heart of darkness" is suggested by Clara's last name, which *is* "Heart"—an organ that turns out to be a euphemism for a more libidinally cathected body part.

For Clara's secret, which her young charge David, suffering from neglect at the hands of his narcissistic parents, attempts to discover, is that she has been raped by her own son. The horror, the horror, indeed. The black male thus literalizes the psychic reality of the bourgeois male, for the rape is in fact the logical result of the *white* boy's—and the narrative's—probing. At one point, for example, David sits at Clara's knee and begins slowly and sensually to feel her leg, moving inexorably upward until Clara screams at him—an "overreaction" explained when we learn of the son's rape. Moreover, David not only continually badgers Clara to reveal her story but reads in secret the letters he finds in a suitcase under her bed. Again, Clara reacts furiously, saying he has ruined their friendship, although at other times she says he can never do anything to destroy her affection. The intense aggression aroused by the promise and withholding of unconditional love ultimately finds expression in the revelation of incest and rape—a rape that is enacted by the sexually monstrous black male, who is presumably incapable of sublimating such feelings and thus destined to remain forever a casualty of Oedipus, while the recognition of his own desires in the mirror provided by the black male enables the white boy to rechannel his hostilities and become a man: previously unathletic, we now see him win a swimming championship under the approving eye of his father! Thus the black man comes to serve as as the white male's oedipal scapegoat, and the black woman is positioned, as in so many popular representations (like Spielberg's *The Color Purple*), as sexual victim—not of the white man, of course, the historical record notwithstanding—but of black men, including even their own sons.[24] And black people in general are once again consigned to the level of bestiality.

A more recent, enormously popular film in which Whoopi Goldberg again has a major role shows yet another way the black woman serves the function of embodiment. In *Ghost*, Whoopi Goldberg plays a spiritual medium, Oda Mae Brown, who stands in for the body of the white *male*, Sam, played by Patrick Swayze. Sam has died as a result of a mugging, which turns out to have been engineered by a coworker embezzling funds. When he learns of the plot and of his wife's danger at the hands of the mugger, he seeks out Oda Mae to help him communicate to his wife. After a great deal of mutual mistrust between the wife and Oda Mae, climaxed by a scene in which Oda Mae stands outside the door trying to convince the wife of her "authenticity," as it were, she is allowed inside the house, and the wife expresses a great longing to be able to touch her husband one last time. Oda Mae offers up her body up for the purpose, and Sam enters into it. The camera shows a close-up of the black woman's hands as they reach out to take those of the white woman, and then it cuts to a shot not of Oda Mae but of Sam, who in taking over her body has obliterated her presence entirely.

This sequence, in which Goldberg turns *into* a man may be seen as a kind of logical extension of all her comedic roles, for she is always coded in the comedies as more masculine than feminine. For example, there is a scene in *Jumping Jack Flash* in which she dresses up in a sexy evening dress that nearly gets chewed up by a shredding machine, and, as she climbs the stairs to her apartment at the end of the evening, she is heard muttering in anger because the taxi cab driver mistook her for a male transvestite. In *Fatal Beauty*, too, Goldberg's donning of women's clothes is seen to be a form of drag—of black female mimicry of (white) femininity, and when she dresses in such clothes she walks in an exaggeratedly awkward fashion like a man unaccustomed to female accoutrements.

Two important points need to be made here. First, the kind of "gender trouble" advocated by Judith Butler and others in which gender, anatomy, and performance are at odds with one another does not necessarily result in the subversive effects often claimed for it (we will return to this point in the next chapter); on the contrary, in certain cases, such as those involving the woman of color who has often been considered, in Bhabha's words, "not quite" a woman, this kind of "play" may have extremely conservative implications. Second, when both extremes of the Whoopi Goldberg persona are considered together—those in which she represents the maternal/female

132

body (as in *Clara's Heart*) and those in which she is coded as more or less male—we see that we are not all that far from the situation addressed by Sojourner Truth, whose speech I discussed in the first chapter. The black woman is seen either as too literally a woman (reduced to her biology and her biological functions) or in crucial ways not really a woman at all.

I must acknowledge, however, although it places me in an uncomfortable position, that I personally find the Goldberg character in the comedies both attractive and empowering (and I know some young white girls who have made Goldberg a kind of cult heroine), and that part of this attraction for me lies in the way she represents a liberating departure from the stifling conventions of femininity. Yet I have to recognize as a white woman the extent to which these images are at least in part the creation of a racist mentality and to acknowledge how such images and my own reaction to them may serve to keep me and black women at odds (although I would also argue strongly that Goldberg's powerful acting allows her frequently to transcend some of the limitations of her material or else to bring out the subversive potential buried within the text).

It is urgent that white women come to understand the ways in which they themselves participate in racist structures not only of patriarchal cinema— as in *Crossing Delancey*—but also of contemporary criticism and theory. In an important article surveying the work of white women newly addressing issues of race, Valerie Smith points out that some white feminist theorists may be participating in an old tradition of forcing the black woman to serve the function of embodiment:

> [It] is striking that at precisely the moment when Anglo-American feminists and male Afro-Americanists begin to reconsider the material ground of their enterprise, they demonstrate their return to earth, as it were, by invoking the specific experiences of black women and the writings of black women. This association of black women with reembodiment resembles rather closely the association, in classic Western philosophy and in nineteenth-century cultural constructions of womanhood, of women of color with the body and therefore with animal passions and slave labor.[25]

What Smith's remarks clearly suggest is the black woman's need to refuse to function as either the man's *or* the white woman's bodily scapegoat, just as some white women are refusing any longer to function this way in male discourse.

I would like to end, however, with a fantasy, which involves reading the scene I have discussed in *Ghost* against the grain. This may be a fantasy that for many reasons black woman will not fully share, since it points in a utopian direction and wishes away some of the contradictions I have been analyzing. Without for a moment *forgetting* these contradictions, without denying the force of Hazel Carby's observation that feminist criticism (to say nothing of a "woman's film" like *Crossing Delancey*) has too often ignored "the hierarchical structuring of the relations between black and white women and often takes the concerns of middle-class, articulate white women as the norm," I nevertheless want to point to an alternative to the dominant fantasy expressed in *Ghost*.[26] If in the film the black woman exists solely to facilitate the white heterosexual romance, there is a sense in which we can shift our focus to read the white male as, precisely, the obstacle to the union of the two women, a union tentatively suggested in the image of the black and white hands as they reach toward one another. I like to think that despite the disturbing contradictions I have pointed out in this chapter, a time will come when we eliminate the locked door (to recall an image from *Ghost*) that separates women (a door, as we see in the film, easily penetrated by the white man), a time when we may join together to overthrow the ideology that, after all, primarily serves the interests of white heterosexual masculinity and is *ultimately* responsible for the persecutions suffered by people on account of their race, class, and gender. But since it is white women who in many cases have locked the door, it is their responsibility to open it up.

CHAPTER EIGHT

Lethal Bodies

Thoughts on Sex, Gender and Representation, from the Main Stream to the Margins

ANTI-ANTI-ANTI-PORN

If there ever was a quintessential postfeminist issue, pornography is it. Feminists have been largely responsible for theorizing and politicizing the question of sexual representations, and they now find their "point of view" being used as the means by which men may affirm their interest in pornography and claim it as a "realm of empowerment."[1] That men *do* feel disempowered by the anti-pornography feminists becomes clear when, for example, in his book *No Respect*, Andrew Ross discusses the problem faced by "straight male intellectuals," even "reconstructed" ones, when asked by feminists about their interest in pornography: such a man, Ross laments, is "bound to fail to explain why he likes pornography."[2] Ross himself finds a way around the dilemma by rehearsing the pornography debates that have occurred within feminist intellectual circles. He champions women like the lesbian sadomasochist Gayle Rubin, who has defended pornography on behalf of sexual minorities and, for reasons we will be exploring, has stressed the importance of separating sexuality from gender; of course, once sexuality is liberated in this way, the straight male is empowered to speak with as much authority on the subject as anybody else.

By now there is an entire genre of "anti-anti-porn writings," to use Ross's term (p. 190) (does this mean we should be "pro-porn"? the double negative seems symptomatic). Typically, anti-anti-porn essays isolate the writings of Andrea Dworkin and Catharine MacKinnon (admitting perhaps that the field of anti-pornography criticism is not a unified one, but then proceeding to ignore this fact), chastising the stand taken by these two women on censorship and pointing out that the distinctions made by earlier feminists between pornography and erotica are ultimately untenable because sexuality can probably never be uninflected by issues of power and violence. It is argued, with considerable justification, that the anti-pornography stand often does most damage to sexual minorities (insofar as it stresses censorship) and, further, may work in various ways to repress women whose sexuality has traditionally been inhibited through their socialization as females.

My sense is that among intellectuals the "anti-anti-porn" position has pretty much won the day, although no one seems to admit this is the case; thus Andrea Dworkin, for example, continues to be berated as if she weren't already sufficiently discredited by the majority of intellectuals. However, a recent, fascinating essay by Leo Bersani, "Is the Rectum a Grave?" which appeared in a special issue on AIDS in *October*, reopens the case argued by Dworkin and MacKinnon, finding in their writings much that is useful for a gay male critique of sexuality and sexual representations. Among other accomplishments, Bersani's essay presents a welcome respite from the standard tirades against the radical feminists, and I would like to consider it here in the context of a larger discussion of sex, gender, and representation. My aim in this chapter is twofold. First, I want to look at recent attempts by feminists to abolish the category of gender altogether or at least to separate it from the category of sexuality. Second, I would like to work out some of the points of conflict about the issue of representation between sexual minorities and women (some of whom are of course *members* of sexual minorities) as well as to elucidate problems and aims these groups share in common (thus this chapter continues in the spirit of the previous one). I will begin at the opposite pole from Ross, by considering "straight male" fantasy—in this case, as it is expressed in two mainstream films, *Dead Poets Society* and *Lethal Weapon* (also considering its sequel); I will then move to the margins of the discourse on sexuality, specifically considering gay male sexuality, and then to the margins of the margins, as it were, focusing on some writings of lesbian sadomasochists and considering the challenge they pose to feminist orthodoxies. My concern at that point, however, will also be to show that in a postfeminist age some of the *most* marginal positions may be unwittingly bringing us back to the center.

The films I would like to look at before turning to a consideration of

136

Bersani's attempted rapprochement between feminists and gay men are works which taken together indicate the range of response found in contemporary mass culture to male homoeroticism and homosexuality: the first seems to be one of sheer repression, the evocation of a desire to return to a supposedly presexual and pastoralized—yet really very disciplinary—past; while the second response takes male homoerotic impulses, embedded in homosexual panic, to their most murderous extreme.

DEAD WHITE MALE HETEROSEXUAL POETS SOCIETY

In an earlier chapter I examined contemporary films' preoccupation with male regression, and I considered various *kinds* of regression—physical, psychological and historical—connecting nostalgia for the past and for childhood with male fears of the body and with a search for literalness in language. Nowhere are these fears and this quest more evident than in the hit film *Dead Poets Society*, which is set in a boy's boarding school in 1959. Here the insistence on boyhood sexual innocence is so extreme that the film may be said to mark the return of the "hysterical" text, in which the weight of the not-said, that which is again rapidly becoming "unspeakable," threatens to capsize the work's literal meaning. According to Geoffrey Nowell-Smith, who uses the term in discussing the family melodramas of the 1950s, the "hysterical text" is one in which the repressed sexual content of a film, banished from the film's narrative, returns to manifest itself in various ways in the *mise-en-scène* and through textual incoherences.[3] In *Dead Poets*, the repressed content is related to homoeroticism and gay sexuality. It is interesting to speculate on how the film's meaning would have changed were it to have introduced one literary figure in particular—Oscar Wilde, whose writing is judged by some critics to be the first in which "it was generally recognized that a literary work had a meaning other than its face value," whose work, then, posed a threat to the transparency and innocence of language, seeming to contaminate it with duplicitous double meanings.[4] In Wilde's case, of course, as a result of the trials, this doubleness has been lost to us and it has become impossible not to perceive the "gay" meanings of the texts.

So it is not surprising that the film turns to Walt Whitman as a more sexually ambiguous figure through whom to work out its ideologically conservative projects: first, not only to deny the homosexuality of Whitman but more generally to evade its own relation to homoeroticism; second, to appear, in true post-gay rights fashion, to be endorsing rebellious anti-authoritarian modes of behavior, but, third, to be actually evoking a longing for a closeted world in which such behavior would only serve to perpetuate a power structure that would ceaselessly punish it. Thus, despite the fact that Whitman's sexuality has been contested throughout many decades of literary criticism, the film makes no references to the debates over Whitman's homosexuality, focusing only on Whitman as the good grey poet: the free-thinking English teacher Mr. Keating, played by Robin Williams, insists on being called "Captain" or "Oh Captain, My Captain," singling out the one poem that exhibits pious deference to male authority—the very authority the film pretends to be challenging. It is not, incidentally, without relevance and certainly not without irony that Whitman's "corporeal utopianism" has recently been seen by one gay critic as existing in opposition to the moral-purity writers of the nineteenth century who were especially alarmed by the possible depravity of such homosocial environments as the male boarding school.[5] Welton, the setting of *Dead Poets*, would have given these writers no cause for concern.

Although the film exists in a genre of boys' boarding school films, some of which (like *The Devil's Playground*) brilliantly explore the homoerotic tensions of such an environment, and although it is directed by Peter Weir, whose previous work (e.g., *Gallipoli*, *Picnic at Hanging Rock*) is suffused with a lyrical homoeroticism, *Dead Poets* denies this dimension of boarding school life so resolutely that its repression can be systematically traced, the duplicitous meanings emerging after all. For example, one of the characters is a kind of misfit and a loner, unable to articulate his feelings and hence marginal to the group forming around Keating: in fact, the character reveals many of the signs of a sexual identity crisis, and in a more honest version of the film might have been shown struggling to come to terms with being gay in a heterosexual, homosocial environment. That the possible "latent" homosexual theme is overdetermined is suggested in one rather amazing scene in which Keating instructs the boy to come to the front of the room and, since he has been unable to complete the poetry writing assignment, to stare at a picture of Walt Whitman and spew out poetic phrases, while

Keating spins him round and round, violently extracting the speech the boy has been withholding.

As for Keating, whose presence spawns the boys' secret society, lest anyone suspect his motives in returning to the repressive boys' school in which he had been a student, we see him in a carefully staged scene writing a letter to his fiancée whose picture is conspicuously propped on the desk. (Performing similar roles as "disclaimers" are the girls whom the boys entertain at one point in their cave, reciting poems that one of them claims to be original compositions.[6]) Asked by a student why he stays in such a stifling place, Keating responds that he loves teaching more than anything in the world; he gives no explanation of why he left the school in England, where his fiancée still lives, or why he has ruled out teaching in the public schools—clearly a more congenial place for his democratic, free-thinking sympathies. Such "disclaimers" as the photo (as well as a banal subplot in which a boy falls in love with a cheerleader and becomes rivals with a football hero in one of the public schools) and such narrative incoherences might be taken as indicators of the film's repressed homoerotic content— the symptoms in the "hysterical text."

At the end of the film one boy, whose father has forbidden him to act in a play, defies his father by playing the role of Puck in a student production of *A Midsummer Night's Dream*, and then ends up killing himself because his father forbids him to continue in the role. Of all the roles to have chosen, this one seems most filled with latent—and because latent, homophobic— meaning, as if the struggle between a boy and his father were over the boy's right to "pose as a fairy." In the investigation that follows the suicide, John Keating becomes the scapegoat and is forced to leave the school, and the boys are called individually up to the principal, who orders them to "assume the position," and then paddles them. Implausibly, Keating comes to collect his things in the middle of an English class, which the principal has taken over, and as he leaves, one boy stands up to voice his support of his former teacher and then climbs up on his desk, repeating an act Keating had earlier urged the students to perform in order to encourage nonconformity. The other class members, conforming, as it were, to the boy's gesture of nonconformity, follow suit. In the final shot of the film, the camera frames the student as he stands looking at John Keating, the legs of another student straddling the image in the shape of an inverted V—the sexualized body which has been so systematically denied throughout the narrative emerging here, in hysterical fashion, in the body of the film itself, its *mise-en-scène*.

Like the films discussed in some of the other chapters, *Dead Poets Society* is a profoundly regressive film, fixated on adolescence and a mythical moment in the past that it appears to repudiate but really longs for: a moment of repression and discipline and stable authority, represented by fathers, high school principals, and dead poets. By no means does the film anticipate the real rebellions that were shortly to erupt, even though it presupposes an audience that has lived through them. Thus the film: challenges the literary canon and the orthodoxies of the "discipline" of literary studies (represented, for Keating, by the "realists" and by the textbook's editor whose introduction Keating instructs the boys to tear out), but returns us to this canon via a sanitized image of one of our most heterodox and sexually explicit authors; pays lip service to feminist demands for an end to exclusionary male societies, but on the grounds that male sexual needs will be better served (i.e., as one of them jokes, so the boys won't have to masturbate); and encourages such marginalized people as gay youths to speak, but only in unintelligible language. Far from anticipating the specific struggles of the 1960s and 1970s, the film lyricizes life in the closet, yearning for the time just before these rebellions—a time when, for example, there were no dead women poets (not even Emily Dickinson) and live females apparently could not tell the difference between Shakespeare and a schoolboy's poetry, a time before gay men would aid in problematizing the very notion of adolescent sexual innocence and Whitman would be brought further out of the closet. Like Keating and despite its disclaimers, its bad-faith mockery of "tradition," the film chooses the particular chronotope of the 1950s boys' school because it *wants* to be there: at a time and place in which rebellion seemed entirely a white male heterosexual affair and could itself appear innocent, devoid of substance and body.

Lethal White and Black Male Homosocial Body/Machines

If *Dead Poets* deals with the fear of the sexualized male body by repressing it, other films deal with the fear very differently and increasingly seem to court the pleasures and dangers of homosexuality—with what explosive consequences we shall see.

In the film *Lethal Weapon* Detectives Riggs (Mel Gibson) and Murtaugh (Danny Glover) begin a criminal investigation by visiting the house of a prostitute to look for clues. As they approach the house they remark on the "thinness" of their conjectures about the crime, thus inaugurating a running joke in the film—for as they approach the house it explodes and bursts into flames, thereby spectacularly confirming the accuracy of their suspicions. As the men's speculations continued to be confirmed, Murtaugh at one point invokes the ritualistic line, "Thin, very thin," and Riggs replies, "Anorexic." That the concern with "thin" plots is linked with an idea of thin men—thus connecting us to the thesis of the chapter dealing with the anorexic mentality of certain contemporary masculinities—is suggested in a scene where the two detectives are at target practice. Discussing the thinness of their evidence, Murtaugh says, "Thin is my middle name," to which Riggs responds, "With your wife's cooking I'm not at all sur-prised"—thereby invoking the other running gag of the film regarding Trish Murtaugh's culinary incompetence.

In *Lethal Weapon 2*, the gag about the wife's cooking is reprised, this time in yet another scene involving explosion. The black partner, Roger Murtaugh, has been sitting on a toilet all night long, having become aware that a bomb has been placed underneath him, set to explode when he stands up. Riggs has discovered him in this position, alerted the bomb squad, and now sits holding his partner's hand in preparation for a leap into the bathtub, into which they have one second to jump before the bomb goes off. Murtaugh jokes that it's too bad the bomb wasn't placed in Trish's stove instead, and Riggs says, "Yeah, think of all the needless suffering that could've ended right there." Now, when a script calls for a bomb to be placed underneath the naked bottom of a black man sitting on a toilet (holding hands with his white partner) and has the man express the desire for that bomb to have been placed in his wife's *oven*, a feminist/psychoana-lytic critic is entitled to regard the ingredients of the film's formula as a heavily condensed mixture of racism, misogyny, homoeroticism, and heterosexual panic.

The joke about thinness seems related to a masculine fear about the body that is also central in *Dead Poets Society* (as well as, we saw, in the Pee-wee Herman films). In *Lethal Weapon* the fear is combated by turning the body into a machine: thus, in an exchange between the two detectives regarding Murtaugh's inferior gun, Murtaugh (who, as convention requires, is initially wary of his new partner and even suspects him of being psychotic) remarks, "They should register *you* as a lethal weapon." That the body as vulnerable object of aggression *and* as potential object of desire is at stake in these films becomes obvious from the opening scenes of *Lethal Weapon*. In the first sequence, a half-naked woman on drugs leaps from the balcony of a highrise building after some dizzying point-of-view shots; subsequently, Murtaugh is shown in the bathtub as his family enters the room with a cake and sings "Happy Birthday," whereupon his daughter teases him about getting old. In the next sequence, Riggs is shown in his trailer home getting out of bed naked and going to the refrigerator for a beer, the camera positioned from behind, discretely keeping its distance in a long shot. Once the male body as an exposed and vulnerable object is evoked, the fears associated with this vulnerability are displaced retroactively onto the body of the woman: first, we see Riggs making a drug deal undercover, and, shortly after that, he saves a man from jumping off a building by handcuffing himself to the man and leaping off the ledge into a safety net (which the audience does not know is there until the men have fallen). In effect, then, the film places the hero in a position similar to that of the woman—involved with drugs, taking a suicidal leap off a building—only it reveals him to have control over the conditions that destroyed her.

The question of control is in fact very much at stake in the film, and is posed over and over again in relation to the suicidal, almost maniacal hero's sanity, which is questioned by his fellow officers and the police department's female psychiatrist. As much as the film is engaged in the denial of the body's vulnerability, then, it is equally engaged in disavowing the realm of the psyche—the source of desire and inward-turning aggression (masochism) capable of undermining the subject's control. Thus the dis- avowal of the protagonist's insanity, viewed as part of the legacy of the Vietnam War, is accomplished in each film by having Riggs undergo a kind of psychiatric "cure," but one that is displaced from the register of psychiatry onto the crime story itself. At the climax of the first film, which, like its sequel, involves an elaborate drug-smuggling scheme, Riggs is hung up and tortured by an Asian man with an electroshock instrument he applies to Riggs's body until Riggs manages to fight him off by choking him in a leg lock (in this way the film also manages to suggest a defeat of the Asian enemy we were unable to accomplish twenty years ago). In the second film, Riggs is placed in a straight-jacket by the criminals and dumped into the ocean, but he escapes by dislocating his shoulder and slipping out of the jacket. The body in pain is thus turned into a manipulable machine, and in the process the films manage both to render the psyche its due (through the use of psychiatric techniques and mechanisms for controlling psychotic behavior) and to deny its force. Indeed, the films try very hard to render the body/machine and the psyche, as the realm of the irrational, into a binary pair: "Are you crazy," asks Murtaugh in awe of his partner's marksmanship and bravery, "or are you really that good?"

Yet despite or perhaps because of the denial of the psyche, the repressed returns in a kind of hysteria about a whole range of sexual and racial differences, figured as threats to the white male body/machine. Here another gag in *Lethal Weapon 2* is key. Riggs announces to everyone at the police station that Murtaugh's daughter is making her screen debut in a television commercial. As we watch the commercial along with the family and Riggs, who have gathered around the television set, we learn that the advertisement is for condoms. Murtaugh's humiliation is subsequently exacerbated when on two different occasions men tell him that his daughter's performance makes them "want to buy rubbers" and when his fellow officers present him with a "rubber tree." The joke here links together stereotypical notions of black male potency, black female licentiousness, and, of course, in the era of AIDS (the reason such ads are shown at all), homosexual promiscuity.

Moreover, just as the condom is designed to protect the body from the contamination threatened by contact with the other, so too does the narrative organization of the actants, serving as protectors, function to betray and help alleviate white male anxieties about the body and sexuality. The plot of the film has Murtaugh and Riggs engaged in exposing the drug dealings of corrupt South African diplomats (characters who, of course, enable viewers to congratulate themselves on the presumed racial equality in *this* country). As part of their investigation, the detectives are assigned the task of protecting a criminal, Leo (Joe Pesci), who is coded as gay (e.g., he fusses about Riggs's messiness and at one point is shown wearing an apron and vacuuming Riggs's floor). Now, this character, who is set up as

143

the "homosexual," is narratively placed in opposition to the heterosexual woman, the South African secretary—and, in fact, as the climax of the film begins, with the villains on the rampage killing off all the police officers, Murtaugh is revealed to be undercover protecting Leo, while Riggs is shown at his home in bed with the woman. The fact that Murtaugh is on assignment with Leo is what saves him from the fate of his poker-playing buddies, who are blown up, but Riggs's lovemaking with the secretary (intercut with, and thus symbolically and temporally linked to, shots of his fellow officers getting blown away) nearly destroys him: at one point, for example, the police are trying to warn Riggs of the danger he is in, but the woman inadvertently knocks the phone onto the floor. Interestingly, it is Riggs's *dog* who becomes alerted to the helicopters on their way to Riggs's trailer and who thus saves his master's life. The equation of the "gay" man with the dog, both protectors and "helpers" in the narrative, to use Proppian terminology, is much more than a fortuitous conjunction in the plot; throughout the film the detectives treat the man, literally, like a dog—a fact about which Leo himself complains when they keep commanding, "Stay!" as they leave to go off on their investigations. The most dispensable person, it turns out, is the woman, and because the rectangularity of the characterological arrangements tells us that either the dog or the woman will have to be sacrificed, it comes as no surprise that the woman is soon killed off.

Both heterosexuality and homoeroticism in the film are, then, clearly connected with male bodily fears—the former, to be sure, more overtly expressed through the cutting between the couple's lovemaking and the scenes of mass destruction involving the police officers—but the latter the subject of equally intense ambivalence, of both fascination *and* aversion. The fears arouse the need for "protection," as we have seen, and control: hence the relegation of the Others to the realm of the subhuman and the continual humiliation of the black man, who, at the same time, is evoked as an object of desire ("Give us a kiss," says the wounded Riggs to his partner at the end of *Lethal Weapon 2*; "Suck on this," says Murtaugh in *Lethal Weapon*, inserting his gun into Riggs's mouth in order to call the apparently suicidal man's bluff). Nevertheless, the film continually places its hero, along with the audience for whom he is surrogate, near an abyss where a masochistic "self-shattering" is always about to occur (hence the exploding windows, houses being pulled off their foundations, etc.) before it pulls back from the brink to reveal him as more firmly in charge than ever.

COMING TO POWERLESSNESS

I have chosen to discuss two films that would at first glance seem to represent the limits of mainstream culture's representation of male homosexuality—on the one hand, repression, as in *Dead Poets*, or, on the other hand, an astonishingly open *expression* of male/male desire that nevertheless is accompanied by phobic denial of homosexuality *per se*. Buddy films like *Lethal Weapon*, *48 Hours*, *Tequila Sunrise*, and, as discussed earlier, *Top Gun*, to name only a few examples from this burgeoning "genre," have become so explicitly and intensely homoerotic ("Why don't you just fuck him?" Michelle Pfeiffer in *Tequila Sunrise* says to outlaw Mel Gibson about Kurt Russell, the policeman on his trail) that one can only wonder at the public's seeming obliviousness to this dimension of much current popular culture. But for all *Dead Poet*'s apparent difference from films like *Lethal Weapon* which flaunt their homoerotic content, the two extremes represented by the two films might be said actually to converge in some very important respects. For in *Dead Poets* the censored "subtext" is so insistent, it renders the kind of interpretation I have offered—which discovers "latent" homosexuality everywhere—almost inescapable. In *both* films, homosexuality becomes, in D. A. Miller's words, a more or less "open secret" which thus depends on disavowal rather than negation.[7] Needless to say, however, the balance between openness and secretness is clearly threatened by gay male pornography which openly acknowledges the male body as object of desire, thereby flouting one of the strongest taboos in our culture. Thus, as has been frequently pointed out, Robert Mapplethorpe's homoerotic photographs were the first to be censored in the latest wave of repression coming from the Right; neither is it accidental that gay men have been nearly unanimous in their defense of pornography. For gay men, indeed, pornography is one of the primary means by which their identity *as* men who engage in sexual relations with other men is expressed, confirmed, and—to the extent that desire is mobilized in and through representation—constituted.

Gay men would thus appear to have very different stakes from women in the pornography debates initiated by the radical feminist wing of the woman's movement. To put the case somewhat baldly, the problem with regard to the representation of the male body as openly avowed object of desire is one of *under*representation, whereas, since the female body is most commonly figured as object of desire, the problem for women seems to be one of *over*representation. Despite such an obvious difference, however, radical feminists like Andrea Dworkin and Catharine MacKinnon have tended to condemn all forms of pornography, homosexual as well as heterosexual, and gay men who have attacked the radical feminist position on pornography have largely accepted the assumption that the stakes are the same for both groups.[8] Leo Bersani's essay, "Is the Rectum a Grave?," however, represents a marked departure from this tendency. In his essay Bersani actually credits the MacKinnon/Dworkin analysis with intelligence, and while he too ultimately elides the points of tension between gay men and feminists, rather perversely finding in these straw-women of so many "anti-anti-pornography" polemics arguments for actually *proliferating* both heterosexual and homosexual pornography, his forceful arguments open the way to rethinking the entire debate.

Bersani's essay, which is an attempt to reconsider the links between sex and politics, constitutes a serious challenge to some of the orthodox thinking on this subject by gay and lesbian theorists, who in Bersani's view exhibit the same unavowed "aversion" to sexuality as their straight counterparts and who, while insisting on the radical potential of their sexuality, tend to find this potential not in actual sexual practices but in the "gay-life style" or in gay parody of dominant male/female roles and images. According to Bersani, such writers—both those who stress the subversiveness of gay "mimicry" of straight roles as well as those who plead for a liberal tolerance of the diversity of human sexuality—are engaged in a project of "domesticating" or "pastoralizing" sexuality, and Bersani is remorseless in his criticism of these approaches: to make such arguments, he says, is "to be disingenuous about the relation between homosexual behavior and the revulsion it inspires. The revulsion, it turns out, is all a big mistake: what we're really up to is pluralism and diversity, and getting buggered is just one moment in the practice of those laudable humanistic virtues."[9]

In place of such liberal pluralism, Bersani theorizes a darker, more ambivalent view of sexuality and its relation to dominant sex roles. Ac-

146

cording to Bersani, for example, the gay man's emulation of the macho style is not simply a "defilement" of this style, but also a "worshipful tribute to it"—thus, for instance, the "leather queen," the macho man with the "sexually feminized body," exhibits a *"yearning* toward" the machismo that his very existence would seem to undermine (p. 207). Bersani concludes, "If, as [Jeffrey] Weeks puts it, gay men 'gnaw at the roots of a male heterosexual identity,' it is not because of the parodistic distance that they take from that identity, but rather because, from within their nearly mad identification with it, *they never cease to feel the appeal of its being violated*" (p. 209).

In mounting his attack on liberal approaches to the question of gay sexuality, Bersani finds unexpected allies in Andrea Dworkin and Catharine MacKinnon, who in their writings against pornography have in Bersani's view had the courage "to be explicit about the profound *moral revulsion* with sex" that inspires what he calls the "redemptive sex project"—a project that would insist on the natural antithesis between sex and violence, on the natural affinity of sex to "tenderness and love."[10] They have shown how sexuality and pornography, even when not obviously violent, eroticize hierarchy and gender inequalities, and thereby celebrate "the violence of inequality itself" (p. 213). As MacKinnon has written, pornography "institutionalizes the sexuality of male supremacy, fusing the eroticization of dominance and submission with the social construction of male and female" (p. 172). This insistence on the interrelatedness of sex and gender, sexuality and the social, will be contested, as we shall see, by lesbian sadomasochists, and it ultimately is an insight that Bersani will allow to lapse. But it is clear how up to this point it accords with his own discussion about the ambivalent nature of gay sexuality, which he sees to be in part *"constituted"* by the "internalization of an oppressive mentality" (p. 209). Bersani concurs with MacKinnon and Dworkin that pornography is "the most effective promotion" of gender inequality, despite its apparently marginal status in relation to mainstream representation. He refers to the "abominable and innumerable TV ads in which, as part of a sales pitch for cough medicine and bran cereals, women are portrayed as slaves to the normal functioning of their men's bronchial tubes and large intestines": "only pornography tells us why the bran ad is effective: the slavishness of women is erotically thrilling" (p. 214). By insisting on the pornographic nature of sexuality itself, MacKinnon and Dworkin have exposed the violence inherent in sexuality, a violence that they deplore but Bersani wants to *celebrate* for being "anticommunal, antiegalitarian, antinurturing, antiloving" (p. 215).

Part of Bersani's project is to align gay sexuality with femininity, an alignment that is, to be sure, at the heart of a homophobic *and* misogynistic phantasmatics in heterosexual patriarchal culture (he speaks of the "seductive and intolerable image of a grown man, legs high in the air, unable to refuse the suicidal ecstasy of being a woman" [p. 212]) but for that very reason dictates a common response from gays and feminists. This response, says Bersani, drawing on his previous work, begins by acknowledging the inevitability of "relations of mastery and subordination" in sex which is "grounded in the shifting experience that every human being has of his or her body's capacity, or failure, to control and to manipulate the world beyond the self" (p. 217). Here Bersani is close to the Marcusian doctrine of surplus repression—the "surplus" being the amount of repression, imposed by capitalism, over and above the repression necessary to the survival of every individual. For Bersani, relations of mastery and subordination are similarly requisite for species survival; but patriarchy erects a system in which surplus violence and fixed power imbalances guarantee male mastery over the female. But while admitting that an analysis of "the ideological exploitations" of the body's potential to control the world would involve a "history of male power" (p. 216), Bersani waives this discussion and turns to look at the subject from a different angle—a low angle, to use a film term—the view from the bottom as experienced by the individual subject in the sexual act itself. From the angle of the man, legs high in the air, enjoying the suicidal ecstasy of being a woman (what Bersani calls a "self-shattering *jouissance*"), the view is so spectacular that he can only wonder how it is that everyone doesn't seek it out. Phallocentrism must be, Bersani magisterially proclaims, "not primarily the denial of power to women . . . but above all the denial of the *value* of powerlessness in both men and women" (p. 217).

It is exactly at the point where Bersani declines to factor in the "history of male power," however, the point where he drops the main argument of MacKinnon about how the sexuality of male supremacy fuses with the *social* construction of male and female, that he loses the sympathy of a feminist reader. Phallocentrism has, of course, sought *continually* to instill in women a sense of the value—for them—of powerlessness and of masochism. The problem here (and this is where the gay male project as Bersani outlines it diverges from the feminist project) lies in the way the category of *gender*—the sum of all the practices through which bodies sexed as female are, to requote Bersani, "ideologically exploited" so as to restrict their "potential to control and to manipulate the world beyond the self"— gets elided in Bersani's account, which in the end focuses exclusively on sexuality and in the process loses its hold on the concept of ambivalence. We find ourselves back in the familiar territory of male masochism, a term Bersani uses as a synonym for powerlessness ("a radical disintegration and humiliation of the self" [p. 217]), but which we have seen to be not synonymous at all: masochism in the *guise* of powerlessness is, I have argued, frequently the luxury of empowered beings, and, as I discussed earlier, social power and sexual humiliation may coexist quite easily. That Bersani at this point loses the feminist edge to his argument becomes clear when he cautions gay men in the age of AIDS against "welcoming the return to monogamy"—against welcoming the degeneration of the sexual into a "relationship," which inevitably entails hierarchy—and encourages them to "resist being drawn into mimicking the unrelenting warfare between men and women" (p. 218). The "history of male power," summarily banished from the text, returns as an apolitical notion of the eternal battle of the sexes. And politics becomes primarily a bedroom, or bathhouse, affair.

It is clear that powerlessness *and* masochism have different ideological valences for women than for gay men. In an analysis of male masochism, Kaja Silverman, who, I think, overstates the case for the subversive potential of even *male* masochism, observes that since masochism is so close to the norm for women, it is unlikely to have the radical force it has for men. (I think of Gayle Rubin's essay in *Coming to Power* in which she claims that among heterosexual S/M groups, most appear to be male submissive/ female dominant. No doubt the institution of marriage renders female submissive groups redundant.[11]) Silverman writes:

> While [masochism] is a centrally structuring element of both male and female subjectivity, it is only in the latter that it can be safely acknowledged. It is an accepted—indeed a requisite—element of "normal" female subjectivity, providing a crucial mechanism for eroticizing lack and subordination. The male subject, on the contrary, cannot avow his masochism without calling

into question his identification with the masculine position, and aligning himself with femininity.[12]

Although it has been a major project of this book to insist on the fact that male alignment with femininity is not the same thing as—could even be diametrically opposed to—male alignment with *feminism*, it is at least conceivable that a man adopting a position typically associated with femininity is driving a wedge into the sex/gender system, whereas for women to continue to assume the position, as it were, is to shore up this system.

But I am not convinced that Bersani has made the most effective case even for the radical force of *gay* sexuality. For all his positive emphasis on the self-shattering *jouissance* inherent in sexuality, Bersani's solution to the complicated questions he raises is surprisingly individualistic—and indeed may in the end *ratify* the self as well as the social order being denounced. "It is possible," writes Bersani in terms that remind us of the dynamic of *Lethal Weapon* with its swings between self-shattering and self-mastery, "to think of the sexual as, precisely, moving between a hyperbolic sense of self and a loss of all consciousness of self." But "sex as self-hyperbole is perhaps a repression of sex as self-abolition" (p. 218). It is never clear, though, how, if loss of "self" is as eminently desirable as Bersani claims, the concept has ever taken hold in the first place: if it is only in order for the self to repeatedly experience its own shattering, then are we not doomed to reinvent the self and enact the dynamic in perpetuity? Similarly, is it not the case that for powerlessness to be a "value," it can be so only in relation to a notion of power, which we thus permanently install? And are we all that far, then, from *Dead Poets Society*, in which rebellion against authority seemed to be less about truly challenging that authority than about exacting its punishment and confirming its sway? Beginning his discussion with a "provisional acceptance" (p. 209) of a homophobic representation of gay sexuality, has not Bersani in the end come dangerously close to enshrining it?

SADISM IN THE POSITIVE SENSE

If Bersani's essay is not ultimately persuasive in its attempt to demonstrate that the stakes of representation are the same for women and gay men, perhaps we will find in the writings of *women* who defend sadomas-

ochism *among women* and who are militantly anti-anti-porn more compelling arguments against the MacKinnon/Dworkin line defended so eloquently (if finally abandoned) by Bersani.

While Bersani does not allude to this fact, there has long been a current
of antagonism between gay men and lesbians over just those issues most
crucial to his argument—in particular, the idea that sexuality is in its
essence "anticommunal, antiegalitarian, antinurturing, antiloving." Despite
Bersani's rather perverse attempt to infer this attitude from the work of
MacKinnon and Dworkin, whom he lauds for refusing to "prettify" or
"romanticize" "fucking" in any way, the fact is that feminists, including
lesbian feminists, have on the whole tended to emphasize the communal,
egalitarian, and nurturing aspects of sex and sexuality and have sometimes
explicitly condemned gay male sexual practices as dehumanizing. Thus
Adrienne Rich in her landmark essay "Compulsory Heterosexuality and
Lesbian Existence" compares lesbians favorably to gay men, and in an
infamous passage denounces "the prevalence of anonymous sex and the
justification of pederasty among male homosexuals, the pronounced ageism
in male homosexuality, etc." Rich continues:

> In defining and describing lesbian existence I would hope to move toward a
> dissociation of lesbian from male homosexual values and allegiances. I per-
> ceive the lesbian experience as being, like motherhood, a profoundly *female*
> experience, with particular oppressions, meanings, and potentialities we can-
> not comprehend as long as we simply bracket it with other sexually stigmatized
> existences.

And, finally: "As the term 'lesbian' has been held to limiting clinical
associations in its patriarchal definition, female friendship and comradeship
have been set apart from the erotic, thus limiting the erotic itself."[13] But in
opposing the clinical view of lesbianism, Rich, whose project is clearly
described in Bersani's language as "sex-redemptive," "pastoralizing," and
certainly, given the association between lesbianism and motherhood, "domesticating," has been criticized by other lesbians for erring too far in the
other direction and *expanding* the category of the erotic to the point of
eradicating the specificity of lesbian existence. In sum, Rich allows the
category of gender to overwhelm that of sexuality and ends by placing *all*
women (insofar as they have friendships with other women) on the lesbian
continuum: every woman is thus more or less lesbian.

Reacting against "the party line" of lesbian feminists like Rich, who condemns pornography and all manifestations and representations of sexuality that do not promote egalitarian and loving bonds between women, in bed and out, female sex radicals like the lesbian sadomasochist Gayle Rubin have sought to reclaim the specificity of their experience as women who sleep with other women. In order to do so, they have found it necessary to defend all forms of pornography and most sexual practices (including pedophilia), identifying more with other "stigmatized erotic populations" than with radical feminists, and calling for an absolute separation of the categories of sex and gender.[14] In marked contrast to feminists like MacKinnon and Rich, who stress the constraints on the notion of woman's "consent" in a society that enforces compulsory heterosexuality and female submission, the sex radicals tend to emphasize the individual's "free choice" in matters of sexual behavior, including such activities as lesbian sadomasochism, which many women denounce as acting out oppressive patriarchal relations of dominance and subordination.[15]

Ironically, in order to counter such charges, some of the sex radicals, even sadomasochists and their proponents, end up *themselves* engaged in the sex-redemptive project referred to by Bersani; they often minimize the issues of power and violence that one would have thought to be definitionally inherent in sadomasochistic practices, ultimately implying that whips, razors, and nipple clips are part of the panoply of devices to be used in furthering the practice of "laudable humanistic virtues." This kind of upbeat tone, for example, pervades Parveen Adams's assessment of lesbian sadomasochistic activity as it is described by the contributors to the anthology of lesbian S/M, *Coming to Power* by the SAMOIS collective. According to Adams, who has read a somewhat different book from the one I read, the lesbian sadomasochist "has separated sexuality from gender and is able to enact differences in the theatre where roles freely circulate." In place of the compulsiveness characteristic of male masochism, "there is choice and mobility, an experimentation with the sexual yield of consensual constraint; there is the construction of a sexuality between women; there is genital satisfaction as one among many pleasures of the body."[16] Similarly, Gayle Rubin stresses the happy pluralism of sexual diversity, with lesbian sadomasochism as just one of a variety of choices tempting the consumer. Invoking an analogy between

152

meals and sex, as she frequently does, Rubin writes, "Although people can be intolerant, silly, or pushy about what constitutes proper diet, differences in menu rarely provoke the kinds of rage, anxiety, and sheer terror that routinely accompany differences in erotic taste."[17] I think this statement is extraordinarily naive—and not just about sex. For, far from wanting to argue that sex is entirely different from food (as desire is from need), I would want to make the *opposite* claim: that both sex and food are much more fraught with taboo and forbidden desire than Rubin acknowledges. Thus, we could point to the increasingly common problem of anorexia, which testifies, precisely, to the "rage, anxiety, and sheer terror" the sexually maturing young girl associates with eating caloric foods; and we could also consider the genre of food pornography developed under consumer capitalism (see Rosalind Coward's discussion of this phenomenon in her book *Female Desire* which includes an illustration of an ad for cherry cake bearing the headline, "Take a Bite of the Cherry"[18]). In this respect consumer culture is simply capitalizing on a *widespread* cultural equation, noted by Lévi-Strauss, between sex and food (as in the phrase "consummating a marriage").[19]

With this link between sex and food we find ourselves back to the bran ads invoked by Bersani—and the erotic thrill of a woman's slavish devotion to her husband's intestines. We remember that Bersani used this example to illustrate what might be called the eroticization of domestic arrangements before he abandoned the problem to proselytize against the domestication of eros. But what if the woman is "slavishly" devoted not to her husband but another woman? Does the vexed problem of the erotics of gender inequality become irrelevant, as Adams maintains, or are such women reproducing oppressive gender relations, as their critics claim? In thinking about the question of the domestication of desire, I can't resist citing one of the essays in *Coming to Power* in which the writer, Susan Farr, refers to a happy by-product of her lesbian S/M relation:

> Another playful use of discipline in our relationship is as a motivator. It can convert drudgery into cheerful slavery: "You wash the kitchen floor today or else . . . " What was simply onerous is now erotic. And it can highlight the importance of doing some task long postponed: "I want you to renew your driver's license by the end of the week or you'll face a licking." What was a lonely burden is now shared. The expression of dominance is also an assump-

tion of responsibility. The acceptance of submission is also an agreement to act. (p. 186)

It seems obvious that in the context of a same-sex relationship the playful threats "enforcing" the completion of domestic duties, everyday tasks, etc., may take on a different meaning from the one they would possess in the context of most male/female relations where such threats, if uttered seriously, would have the weight of male physical and economic power behind them. It is striking that the exercise of dominance within a relationship of gender equals destabilizes the very meaning of the terms "dominance" and "submission," so that, as the writer suggests, each blurs into the other. Thus the continual emphasis in *Coming to Power* on the transformative nature of lesbian S/M practices is not the alibi we might at first suspect it to be. When the writers insist on the stark contrast between, say, their former existence as battered wives and their current contented, voluntarily assumed roles as "bottoms" in a lesbian S/M relationship; when they speak of sadism "in the bad sense," implying the existence of a qualitatively different *kind* of sadism, these claims must be taken very seriously. And it is no doubt because she felt the force of such claims that Adams is drawn to celebrate the freedom of choice and the playful "mobility" of meaning and desire in lesbian S/M.

The emphasis placed on freedom of choice, on "consent," by the SA-MOIS collective in distinguishing between good and bad sadism is understandable, given the women's perception that outsiders have seen *only* "the acting out of power, *never* the demonstration of consensuality" (p. 61, emphasis mine). Unfortunately, however, the correcting of this misperception has meant a neglect of some of the most important, indeed the defining, features of S/M—the infliction of pain and humiliation by one individual on another—features requiring explanation even if they *are* desired by all parties. For, despite the playfulness exhibited in the scenarios described above, in the actual S/M rituals described in the anthology playfulness and parody seem to be entirely lacking, perhaps because, as Bersani notes, parody is an erotic turn-off.

One of the pornographic stories included in the SAMOIS volume will, I hope, help us clarify what is at stake in at least some of these rituals of humiliation. The story, "Passion Play," by Martha Alexander, concerns the relationship of Meg and Carole, two strong women active in the feminist movement; it opens with Meg visiting her lover Carole upon returning from a feminist conference. Beginning their sexual ritual, Carole slowly costumes Meg in feminine "drag"—stockings, garters, spike heels, pink dress, electric-pink lipstick, rhinestone clip-on earrings, etc.—and Meg is both sexually excited and deeply enraged. Finally, Carole places around Meg's neck something that Meg mistakes for a necklace but turns out to be a collar. She then forces Meg to look in the mirror: "You make a great little poodle, don't you Meggie?" The story proceeds:

> It was a complex image for Meg to face. It was her and it wasn't her. In her way of thinking, she almost considered wearing women's clothing as a form of cross-dressing, it was so against her character. To confront this image, this real and unreal image looking back at her—that *was* her, for the moment at least—was shocking. (p. 239)

The emotionally complex affect of this scene is, I would suggest, best explained by reference to the Deleuzian account of masochism I discussed in another chapter. Deleuze, we recall, spoke of the humor of masochism, by which he certainly did not mean a playful, parodic, or camp kind of comedy, but rather a militantly explosive derision expressed toward that which is "being beaten." For Deleuze, it is the father whom the heterosexual male masochist desires to be beaten out of himself, and in this enterprise he enlists the aid of the "mother"—the humorous effect being achieved precisely by the incongruity of placing a woman in a position of authority, of substituting her presence for that of the law.

Similarly, the lesbian sadomasochistic ritual in my reading of lesbian stories and accounts contains a strongly derisory component, but what is being mocked and beaten out of the woman is, I think, most accurately described as the *law of gender* itself, in its patriarchal form—the law that dictates the subordination/humiliation of woman to be the very essence of her role. And as the mirror scene described above attests, the woman both sees herself in this role and yet separates herself from it. (This kind of ambivalence, needless to say, is entirely missing from mainstream porn and its favorite plot, in which the more the woman is subjugated and reduced to a slavering devotée of the phallus, the more she is seen to be discovering and liberating her *essential self*.) The ambivalent (mis)recognition expressed in the story we have been discussing resembles, although is not identical with, the ambivalence Bersani attributes to male homosexuality, which, he says, "never stops re-presenting the internalized phallic male as an infinitely loved object of sacrifice" (p. 222). For the lesbian sadomasochist in the scenarios we have examined, it is the internalized feminine woman who is constantly re-presented as a loved object of sacrifice. As another SAMOIS member observes in trying to account for her attraction to clothes she "would never, *ever* wear" of her own accord: "For me S/M is about emotion, the erotic tension between my impulse toward something and my resistance against it" (p. 107). Interestingly, the ambivalence these writers reveal to be at the heart of lesbian sadomasochism may be compared to the belief structure characteristic of fetishism ("I know very well . . . but all the same"). Dressed in heels, corsets, stockings, and garters, woman is constructed as fetish—and thus as phallus, for which the fetish is substitute—and both affirms and denies herself *in* this construction. In a way, we could say, a doubled belief structure is redoubled, so that the woman looking in the mirror at her fetishized self could say something like, "I know very well I am not the object patriarchy knows—but also seems not to know—I am not, but all the same . . ." In such a case the woman is no longer the *object* of male disavowal but the subject of disavowal in relation to the objectified self patriarchy wants her to be.

That the woman is constructed as fetish *by another woman* also seems crucial. It may be useful here to think of the concept of "entrustment through disparity," which Teresa de Lauretis has recently elaborated in a discussion of the work of Italian feminists.[20] The very phrase suggests a way to understand what seems like a hopeless contradiction in lesbian sadomasochistic writings, which simultaneously stress, on the one hand, painful and humiliating enactments of dominance and submission and, on the other hand, absolute trust as a condition and consequence of these enactments. The woman in the position of power in the lesbian sadomasochistic ritual would be what the Italian feminists call the "symbolic mother" (and here we are very close again to the Deleuzian model), a term that signifies "at once its power and capacity for recognition and affirmation of women as subjects in a female gendered frame of reference." As the woman standing behind the woman in the mirror (to recall "Passion Play" again), the "symbolic mother" serves an almost archetypal function, initiating the woman into symbolic order, but transferring and transforming a patriarchal system of gender inequities into a realm of difference presided over by women.

My analysis of one scenario within lesbian sadomasochistic activity is meant to show how lesbian sadomasochism enacts a complex dynamic in which existing gender arrangements are simultaneously contested and preserved—preserved partly in order to *be* contested. And this in turn suggests the one-sidedness of the usual positions in the debates over lesbian sadomasochism—both the position that sees lesbian sadomasochism as replicating existing gender inequalities and the more utopian position, argued by Parveen Adams, in which the lesbian sadomasochist has entirely succeeded in separating sexuality from gender.

Adams is only one of an increasingly vocal chorus of women who have been interested in moving beyond gender and who have spoken from or on behalf of a lesbian position. Another example of such an anti-essentialist critique can be found in *Gender Trouble* by Judith Butler, who criticizes from a lesbian perspective the category of gender and the notion of identity itself (in Butler's view the taking up of an identity is concomitant with taking a position on one side or the other of the gender divide). As a radical Foucauldian thinker, Butler brilliantly analyzes various systems of revolutionary thought to show how they are implicated in, and frequently the effect of, the systems they seek to undermine. (Thus, for example, the avant-garde artistic practices deriving from the semiotic/maternal realm that Julia Kristeva considers to be subversive of meaning and the symbolic/paternal order only have value in relation *to* the law of the father and so serve ultimately to consolidate his reign.) Curiously, however, Butler finds one practice to be exempt from the rule—gay camp parody:

> As much as drag creates a unified picture of "woman" (what its critics often oppose), it also reveals the distinctness of those aspects of gendered experience which are falsely naturalized as a unity through the regulatory fiction of heterosexual coherence. *In imitating gender, drag implicitly reveals the imitative structure of gender itself—as well as its contingency* (emphasis in original).[21]

While acknowledging that not all parodies are ultimately "truly subversive," and having stated early in her study that there can be no female

157

sexuality outside of power, that the only possibility of opposing the law is through "a repetition of the law which is not its consolidation but its displacement," Butler seems in the above quotation and elsewhere to envision such a thorough "displacement" that the female parodist ends up outside the law after all. Further, Butler's radical critique of identity (her radical anti-essentialism) leads her paradoxically to promote an extremely individualistic solution to the problem of women's oppression, one that takes place primarily at the level of "performance." So, for example, she speaks of a situation in which "the anatomy of the performer is . . . distinct from the gender of the performer, and both of these are distinct from the gender of the performance," which suggests a "dissonance . . . between sex and gender, and gender and performance" (p. 137). We have seen this dissonance operating in the highly theatricalized *mise-en-scène* of lesbian sadomasochism (where for example, a woman, not a man, fetishizes woman; where the woman experiences feminine apparel to be entirely alien to her everyday identity, etc.); indeed the dissonance, far from dissolving the category of gender, provides it with a sexual charge. Teresa de Lauretis, in a different essay, recognizes the *erotic* nature of this dissonance (a dimension mostly ignored by Butler, who nevertheless criticizes many theorists for negating lesbian sexuality); in a discussion of Sheila McLaughlin's film *She Must Be Seeing Things*, de Lauretis remarks: "The butch-femme role-playing is exciting not because it represents heterosexual desire, but because it doesn't; that is to say, in mimicking it, it shows the uncanny distance like an effect of ghosting, between desire (heterosexually represented as it is) and the representation."[22] While this notion of dissonance takes us beyond the sterile terms of some of the older debates about lesbian sexuality and its relation to dominant gender roles, I think there is a real danger of feminist theory's *fetishizing* this dissonance—and thereby preserving the structure that is supposedly being destabilized. This reservation aside, it seems important to stress here the way Butler and de Lauretis, both lesbian feminist theorists working on the issue of gender, are in most respects poles apart: the latter, far from denying gender or reducing it (solely) to the level of individual performance, is concerned to elaborate the terms under which women become "gendered and embodied" sources of empowerment for other women: a political and not *merely* a philosophical concern.

158

ANTI-ANTI-ANTI-FEMINISM

While lesbian sexuality cannot help but participate in patriarchal structures of domination, it is certainly in far less complicity with and often more threatening to such structures than many sexualities. I am fully persuaded by lesbian writings which argue that feminism has too often adopted the role of gender police by rebuking certain lesbians for engaging in politically incorrect forms of sexual activity and by enforcing gender stereotypes that actually work to deny their sexuality altogether (as in the passages I quoted earlier from Adrienne Rich). It does not surprise me, then, that lesbians have sometimes reacted by insisting on the emancipatory potential of all varieties of sexuality and all representations of sexuality, including pornography. Many heterosexual feminists have joined forces with them on this issue, relieved by the new libertarian view from having to examine the contradictions inherent in their own rather more insidious relation to the sex/gender system. And it is certainly true that for women to insist on sexuality and on their right to enjoy pornography may be a liberating release from a socialization process that denies these rights.

Yet, as my discussion of Bersani was meant to show, I think the radical feminist analysis, which considers much pornography demeaning to women because of its enforcement of the sex/gender system, its eroticizing of gender inequities, is a very compelling one. To be sure, the most articulate advocates of this position, Catharine MacKinnon and Andrea Dworkin, go wrong in two important respects. First, they in effect promote censorship. At a time when Safe Sex ads, tapes, and films are prohibited for allegedly "condoning" homosexuality, and when the federal government has become involved in censoring mostly gay and lesbian artists, we are once again reminded that when censorship begins to be condoned, minorities, especially sexual minorities, are usually the first to suffer repression. Second (and the first error is a consequence of this), the MacKinnon/Dworkin analysis, as many critics have pointed out, is so totalizing that it leaves no room for differences and so every image in both mainstream and marginal representations becomes a manifestation of the *same* phenomenon of "woman hating." As Pat Califia observes:

[The] definition of violence is [too] broad. It includes any kind of sex with a minor, consensual sadomasochism, bondage, watersports, prostitution, fist-

159

fucking, casual sex and anal sex, as well as rape and assault. After seeing [the] slide show [presented by members of Women Against Pornography] where this connection is allegedly explicated, my head started to swim. They made no distinction between a photograph of a woman's genitals, gang rape, an advertisement for spike heels, child abuse, a photograph of a woman who was tied up and wifebeating.[23]

And yet, if Women Against Pornography seem fanatic in their refusal to make important distinctions, there are, it must be said, women on the fringes of the "libertarian feminist" group whose views, ironically, lead to the same danger discussed by Califia.

To take a highly visible example, recently the lesbian editor of *On Our Backs*, Susie Bright, has been lecturing on pornography and showing film and video clips from her favorite pornographic works. She speaks to sell-out crowds and clearly represents an empowering presence for young lesbian feminists eager to find a position within feminism which will validate and not simply censure their sexuality.

Bright's program begins disarmingly by presenting us mostly with unusual, "gender-bending" scenes from mainstream porn (e.g., a man who dresses up in his female lover's clothes) or scenes from marginal pornography (one in which a woman burlesques as a man in a San Francisco cabaret—although it is doubtful whether this qualifies as pornography at all—another that depicts a lesbian sadomasochist encounter [which Bright says is her personal answer to Freud's question of what women want]; another in which a male porn star enlarges his penis with a bilge pump). Throughout, Susie Bright valiantly lives up to her name by ignoring any elements of perversion in the material she discusses and speaking most often of how the characters/actors are "getting in touch with their sexuality." In other words, she shows porn, but she talks eros. As a result of her matter-of-fact presentation and the novelty of the clips, we are encouraged to let down our guard and to forget the objections we might have had to more standard porn fare.

Thus, by the time we are shown the final porn clip—from *The Devil and Miss Jones, Part 3*—it is possible even for skeptical audience members to be receptive to what is represented: a black woman, her body wrapped in chains, being, as Bright cheerfully says, "gang banged" by an interracial group of men, who grunt savagely throughout the scene. Introducing the clip, Bright instructs the audience to notice how the woman *as actress* is in complete "control" of the situation! If feminists like Butler have seen in the theatrical play with gender (camp and impersonation) a deliberate undermining of the "reality" status of gender roles, Bright turns this kind of thinking inside out: i.e., by focusing on the control that the actress as actress must "really" wield in order to stage the *representation* of woman's enslavement to the phallus, we can ignore what that representation actually signifies. We might further note that if feminists like MacKinnon and Dworkin have been criticized by libertarian feminists for simplifying the notion of "consent" insofar as they needed a Linda Lovelace to claim to have been physically *compelled* to act in porn films, Susie Bright, taking an opposite perspective—that not only was the woman not compelled, she played an active role in staging the scene—operates within the same reductive logic.

One of the most unsettling aspects of the scene we have been discussing is the way the camera obsessively focuses on the black woman's unusually protuberant genitalia, which resemble a small penis. In the film from which the scene in question is taken (a film in which "Miss Jones" dies of a fractured skull when the man violently thrusts her against the headboard after his climax during sexual intercourse) this image is the culmination of a homoerotic, misogynistic hysteria pervading the movie. In most of the pornographic "numbers," to use Linda Williams's term, anal penetration dominates the sexual activity (in one scene, the woman plays a horse and is whipped repeatedly on the buttocks as the man violently thrusts his penis into her anus). Midway through the film there is a "number" in which two men have sex with a woman, one of whom penetrates her anus, the other her vagina, and the camera continually cuts to shots of the penises as they verge on touching each other. And finally, of course, there is the scene in which the supreme act of male homosocial bonding—the "gang bang"— occurs, carried out on a woman whose genitals become the site of disavowal, as if the male brutality we witness, extreme as it is, is even so not enough to control the dread aroused by the sight of sexual difference. Thus with these images, we find ourselves back to where feminism, as the saying goes, came in—back within the male phallogocentric economy "of the same": the very economy that the ideology of sexual diversity was supposed to disrupt.[24]

161

Beginning at the margins of representation, Susie Bright folds these margins over into the center and ends by confirming images of extreme woman-hating, homophobia, and racism—the same reactionary forces at work, more genially, to be sure, in mainstream representations like the *Lethal Weapon* films. We recall, for instance, the way the black woman's body aroused in men the need for protection (as in the refrain, "she makes me want to buy rubbers," an ambiguous phrase suggesting both the desire for and the threat of the sexualized body of the black woman); we recall too how at the center of the film was an intense homoerotics displaced into aggression, scapegoating of the Other (women, gays), and the humiliation of the black man (in *The Devil in Miss Jones, Part 3*, a black devil who serves as Miss Jones's guide in hell, is portrayed as a lustful, animalistic buffoon—and here we discover the antithesis to the white male angels of *Wings of Desire* discussed in an earlier chapter).

That we are back to the realm of the fetish, the fetish being the means by which otherness is acknowledged and simultaneously negated, becomes clear in the final clip shown by Susie Bright, which is not from a pornographic film at all, but an advertisement for the National Rifle Association. (We might say that if Bright's program began disarmingly, she ends with an image of rearmament.) Introducing the segment, she says that she hardly knows what to say about it, it seems both progressive and reactionary, outrageously sexist and feminist, horrifying and funny, etc. The ad shows a voluptuous woman, a bodybuilder, dressed in a bikini and firing an automatic rifle that the woman's voice-over describes in detail, interspersing her commentary with patriotic platitudes about the blessings of bearing arms. Susie Bright's indecision about the politics of all this is symptomatic: the inability to "decide" on the ideological slant of a given representation is endemic to *much* recent cultural criticism, which repeatedly fails to understand how it has disabled itself by accepting the limits imposed on it by fetishistic representations. To go beyond these limits means finding representations that complicate the mechanisms by which the dominant culture reaffirms itself and makes all otherness and difference into its own reflection. In terms of our analysis here, it would mean trying lucidly to elaborate and to respect the differences among gays and feminists, straight women and lesbians, gays and lesbians, whites and blacks (the chains around the body of a black woman in a pornographic image, for example,

162

clearly have an additional significance to the one identified by anti-porn feminists like Susan Griffin as implicit in every sexualized image of woman: "[The] model in a pornographic magazine . . . is chattel. When she is chained her chains are redundant, for we know she is not a free being").[25] It means, then, not working for censorship, but nevertheless making necessary judgments about various kinds of representation—between, say, the lesbian pornography discussed earlier, which makes of the fetish a contested practice, and the kinds of representation, pornographic or not, that operate squarely within the realm of the fetish. And it means continuing to strive for solidarity in the face of our common oppression (for we saw in *Lethal Weapon* and in *The Devil and Miss Jones, Part 3* what we also saw in the previous chapter that all "others" are dehumanized so as to assure the superior humanity of the white man).

Above all it means, *pace* the enemies of the category of woman, continuing to organize around the issue of gender—perhaps with the ultimate goal of moving beyond it, but realizing that we have not yet arrived at the "beyond." Indeed, part of the project of this book has been to show the myriad ways the desire to deny gender, to break free of restrictive gender roles, to realize a "transgender" ideal in the here and now, laudable as these desires may be, can if we are not careful end up benefiting the interests of a "hommosexual" economy (to use Luce Irigaray's pun, by which I most emphatically do not mean a "homosexual" economy). The postfeminist play with gender in which differences are elided can easily lead us back into our "pregendered" past where there was only the universal subject—man.

CHAPTER ONE

1. Elizabeth Kolbert, "Literary Feminism Comes of Age," *The New York Times Magazine* (December 6, 1987), p. 110.

2. And a very telling sentence it is. Speaking of the male plot of ambition, he writes, "The female plot is not unrelated, but it takes a more complex stance toward ambition, the formation of an inner drive toward the assertion of selfhood in resistance to the overt and violating plots of ambition, a counter-dynamic which, from the prototypes *Clarissa* on to *Jane Eyre* and *To the Lighthouse*, is only superficially passive, and in fact a reinterpretation of the vectors of plot." A footnote refers us to Nancy K. Miller's work. Given that Brooks in this book is trying to devise a model for reading based on Freudian theory, and given how extensively feminism has discussed the differences between the male's oedipal trajectory and the female's psychic development, it is unconscionable that Brooks disregards all of this feminist work, while noting in passing the greater complexity of the female plot, as well as its difference from and opposition to the male plot that nevertheless entirely preoccupies him. See Brooks's *Reading for the Plot: Design and Intention in Narrative* (New York: Vintage, 1985), p. 39.

3. Elaine Showalter, "Toward a Feminist Poetics," in *The New Feminist Criticism: Essays on Women, Literature, and Theory*, ed. Elaine Showalter (New York: Pantheon Books, 1985), p. 131.

4. Elaine Showalter, "The Rise of Gender," in *Speaking of Gender*, ed. Elaine Showalter (New York: Routledge, 1989), p. 5.

5. See also the two volumes edited by Linda Kauffman, *Gender and Theory: Dialogues on Feminist Criticism* (Oxford: Basil Blackwell, 1989) and *Feminism and Institutions: Dialogues on Feminist Theory* (Oxford: Basil Blackwell, 1989).

6. See Lee Edelman, "At Risk in the Sublime: The Politics of Gender and Theory," in Kauffman, ed., *Gender and Theory*, pp. 213–24.

7. Kauffman, *Feminism and Institutions*, p. 3.

8. Christopher Newfield, "The Politics of Male Suffering: Masochism and Hegemony in the American Renaissance," *differences* 1, no. 3 (Fall 1989): 66.

9. David Leverenz, "The Politics of Emerson's Man-Making Words," *PMLA* 101, no. 1 (January 1986): 39.

10. For a comprehensive anthology of feminist writings on melodrama, see Christine Gledhill, ed., *Home Is Where the Heart Is: Studies in Melodrama and the Woman's Film* (London: BFI, 1987). The notion of melodrama as a text of muteness is Peter Brooks's. See *The Melodramatic Imagination: Balzac, Henry James, Melodrama and the Mode of Excess* (New Haven: Yale University Press, 1976).

11. I am quoting, with permission, from a draft of Cavell's article, "Stella's Taste," forthcoming in his book on melodrama.

12. Juliana Schiesari, *The Gendering of Melancholia: Feminism, Psychoanalysis, and the Symbolics of Loss in Renaissance Literature*, unpublished manuscript.

13. Frank Lentricchia, "Patriarchy Against Itself—The Young Manhood of Wallace Stevens," *Critical Inquiry* 13, no. 4 (Summer 1987): 774.

14. R. Howard Bloch, "Medieval Misogyny," *Representations* 20 (Autumn 1987): 19.

15. Elaine Hansen, "Commentary," *Medieval Feminist Newsletter* 6 (December 1988): 6. Bloch's discussion is filled with typical "deconstructionist" faulty syllogisms—which go to prove that the illogic Bloch sees as characteristic of writing itself becomes especially pronounced in male texts when woman is the subject. I can hardly believe that respectable journals would allow such illogic to pass were the topic any other subject *but* women. And what if our nineteenth-century misandrists were misologist enough to write, "If sperm can be defined as a virulent poison, then any virulent poison can be defined as sperm"?

16. Donald Pease, "Patriarchy, Lentricchia, and Male Feminization," *Critical Inquiry* 14, no. 2 (Winter 1988): 379.

17. Joseph A. Boone and Michael Cadden, eds., *Engendering Men* (New York: Routledge, 1990). On its first page the authors thank Showalter for her inspiration and encouragement.

18. In this final essay entitled, "(In)visible Alliances," the author, Robert Vorlicky, begins by recounting a conversation he had with a female feminist friend about the beating and rape of a female jogger in New York's Central Park. His friend asks, "What is in men to make them do this? . . . Men, and boys, believe they have the right to violate anyone, anytime . . . Men have nothing to offer me, as a woman" (p. 275). Vorlicky is upset that his friend engages in such "essentializing" generalizations about men, and he protests his own exemption from such generalizations and insists on being recognized as a supportive male feminist. As I was reading Vorlicky's essay and considering his decision to center his discussion around the issue of sexual violence against women, I kept being reminded of another article I had read in the first male feminism book edited by Jardine and Smith—Andrew Ross's essay, "Demonstrating Sexual Difference" (*Men in Feminism*, ed. Alice Jardine and Paul Smith [New York: Methuen, 1987], pp. 47–53). There, Ross recounts the case history of the Yorkshire Ripper in order to warn feminists against

essentializing the categories of men and women (e.g., against claiming that all men are rapists), and he argues, "the lesson of Sutcliffe, and others like him, calls for a thorough cultural critique of the codes of necessity that depend upon those very concepts of universality supporting statements about 'all women' and 'all men,' for such statements reproduce the very conceptual apparatus that makes Sutcliffes into killers" (p. 52). But one might well ask who is in greater complicity with the violence supporting patriarchal rule: the female "essentialist" or the male critic who uses such an example to make such a point? For while I have no doubt that Ross did not intend the terrorist effects of teaching some feminists a "lesson" about how their thinking is the kind of thinking that gets them raped and murdered, I nevertheless believe such admonitions serve a policing function which male feminists, conscious only of their good will toward their feminist sisters, need to examine.

That some men are making the same points put forth by men years ago when Susan Brownmiller's study of rape first appeared suggests that feminism has not, in fact, come of age within the academy. There is the same refusal on the part of well intentioned men to see that the issue is not so much *whether* all men are rapists or not, but how all men benefit from a system in which some men rape women (and these benefits must now be understood to include the intellectual capital accruing to men who score points against feminists for their supposed theoretical naiveté).

19. Eve Kosofsky Sedgwick, *Between Men: English Literature and Male Homosocial Desire* (New York: Columbia University Press, 1985). David Van Leer criticizes Sedgwick for "pushing straight and gay men further apart" in "The Beast of the Closet: Homsociality and the Pathology of Manhood," *Critical Inquiry* 15, no. 3 (Spring 1989): 604. See Sedgwick's response, "Tide and Trust," *Critical Inquiry* 15, no. 4 (Summer 1989): 745–57 and Van Leer's reply to that response, "Trust and Trade," in the same issue, pp. 758–63.

20. Lee Edelman, "Redeeming the Phallus: Wallace Stevens, Frank Lentricchia, and the Politics of (Hetero)Sexuality," in Boone and Cadden, eds., *Engendering Men*, p. 50.

21. Eve Kosofsky Sedgwick, "Across Gender, Across Sexuality: Willa Cather and Others," special issue, "Displacing Homophobia," ed. Ronald R. Butters, John M. Clum, and Michael Moon, *The South Atlantic Quarterly* 88, no. 1 (Winter 1989): 53–72.

22. Although an interesting exception is Susan Bordo, "Feminism, Postmodernism, and Gender Skepticism," in *Feminism/Postmodernism*, ed. Linda J. Nicholson (New York: Routledge, 1990), pp. 133–56.

23. Helen Vendler, "Feminism and Literature," *The New York Review of Books* (May 31, 1990), p. 22.

24. See Jonathan Culler, *On Deconstruction: Theory and Criticism after Structuralism* (Ithaca, N. Y.: Cornell University Press, 1982), pp. 43–64. For a critique

of Culler's position, see my "Feminism and the Power of Interpretation: Some Critical Readings, in *Feminist Studies/Critical Studies*, ed. Teresa de Lauretis (Bloomington: Indiana University Press, 1986).

25. Denise Riley, *Am I That Name? Feminism and the Category of "Women" in History* (Minneapolis: University of Minnesota Press, 1988), p. 112.

26. Judith Butler, *Gender Trouble: Feminism and the Subversion of Identity* (New York: Routledge, 1990), p. 3.

27. Quoted in Riley, *Am I That Name?*, p. 100. See Donna Haraway, "A Manifesto for Cyborgs: Science, Technology, and Socialist Feminism in the 1980s," in Nicholson, ed., *Feminism/Postmodernism*, pp. 190–233.

28. Gloria Anzaldúa, "Preface," *Borderlands/La Frontera* (San Francisco: Spinsters/Aunt Lute, 1987), n.p.

29. For a forceful articulation of this point, see Evelyn Brooks-Higginbotham, "The Problem of Race in Women's History," in *Coming to Terms: Feminism, Theory, Politics*, ed. Elizabeth Weed (New York: Routledge, 1989), pp. 122–33.

30. Biddy Martin and Chandra Talpade Mohanty, "Feminist Politics: What's Home Got to Do with It?" *Feminist Studies/Critical Studies*, ed. Teresa de Lauretis (Bloomington: Indiana University Press, 1986), p. 208. For Pratt's narrative, see Minnie Bruce Pratt, "Identity: Skin Blood Heart," in Elly Bulkin, Minnie Bruce Pratt, and Barbara Smith, *Yours in Struggle: Three Feminist Perspectives on Anti-Semitism and Racism* (New York: Long Haul Press, 1984), pp. 11–63.

31. Rita Felski, *Beyond Feminist Aesthetics: Feminist Literature and Social Change* (Cambridge, Mass.: Harvard University Press, 1989, pp. 168–69).

32. Teresa de Lauretis, "The Essence of the Triangle or, Taking the Risk of Essentialism Seriously: Feminist Theory in Italy, the U.S., and Britain," *differences* 1, no. 2 (Summer 1989): 3–37. This entire issue of *differences* is on the topic of essentialism. For other discussions of the topic, see Chris Weedon, *Feminist Practice and Poststructuralist Theory* (Oxford: Basil Blackwell, 1987); and Diana J. Fuss, *Essentially Speaking* (New York: Routledge, 1989). The British journal *m/f*, which is no longer publishing, devoted itself to a rigorous anti-essentialist line. In *m/f* 5 and 6 (1981): 1–4, the editors, Parveen Adams, Beverley Brown, and Elizabeth Cowie, spell out their position. For a telling critique of this position, see Michele Barrett's and Rosalind Coward's reply to this editorial, *m/f* 7 (1982): 87–89.

33. One of the most trenchant critiques of this kind of colonization is Audre Lorde's "An Open Letter to Mary Daly" about the latter's *Gyn/Ecology*, in *This Bridge Called My Back: Writings By Radical Women of Color*, ed. Cherríe Moraga and Gloria Anzaldúa (Watertown, Mass.: Persephone Press, 1981), pp. 94–97.

34. Nancy K. Miller, "The Text's Heroine: A Feminist Critic and Her Fictions," *diacritics* 12, no. 2 (Summer 1982): 53.

CHAPTER TWO

1. Fredric Jameson, "Reification and Utopia in Mass Culture," *Social Text* 1 (1979): 148.

2. Since I published this article, Andreas Huyssen published "Mass Culture as Woman: Modernism's Other," in my *Studies in Entertainment: Critical Approaches to Mass Culture* (Bloomington: Indiana University Press, 1986), pp. 188–207. For an article which shows how gendered metaphors are employed in discussing distinctions between film and television viewing, see Patrice Petro, "Mass Culture and the Feminine: The 'Place' of Television in Film Studies," *Cinema Journal* 25, no. 3 (Spring 1986): 5–21.

3. Ann Douglas, *The Feminization of American Culture* (New York: Avon, 1977), p. 13.

4. Jane P. Tompkins, "Sentimental Power: *Uncle Tom's Cabin* and the Politics of Literary History," *Glyph* 2 (1978): 98. Tompkins is responding directly to Douglas, but all references to Douglas have been deleted in the reprinted version in Showalter's *The New Feminist Criticism*.

5. Manuel Puig, *Kiss of the Spider Woman*, trans. Thomas Colchie (New York: Vintage, 1980), p. 78. Obviously, since this was written the novel has been made into a film; yet I don't feel the film adds anything to the novel (on the contrary).

6. Jean Baudrillard, *In the Shadow of the Silent Majorities or the End of the Social and Other Essays*, trans. Paul Foss, Paul Patton, and John Johnston (New York: Semiotext(e), 1983), p. 33.

7. Roland Barthes, *Image, Music, Text*, trans. Stephen Heath (New York: Hill and Wang, 1977), p. 167.

8. For a discussion of this aspect of Baudrillard's thought in relation to the horror film, see my essay "The Terror of Pleasure: The Contemporary Horror Film and Postmodern Theory," in Modleski, ed., *Studies in Entertainment*.

9. On this point, see especially Michele Montrelay, "Inquiry into Femininity," trans. Parveen Adams, *m/f* 1 (1978): 65–101.

10. Jean Baudrillard, "The Ecstasy of Communication," trans. John Johnston in *The Anti-Aesthetic*, ed. Hal Foster (Port Townsend. Wash.: Bay Press, 1983), p. 132.

11. Nancy K. Miller, "The Text's Heroine: A Feminist Critic and Her Fictions," *diacritics* 12, no. 2 (Summer 1982): 53.

12. Baudrillard, *In the Shadow*, p. 19.

CHAPTER THREE

1. Paul Willemen argues this point in general in "Notes on Subjectivity—On Reading 'Subjectivity Under Siege,' " *Screen* 19, no. 3 (Autumn 1978): 41–70; as

does Annette Kuhn with specific reference to "women's genres." See Annette Kuhn, "Women's Genres: Melodrama, Soap Opera, and Theory," in *Home Is Where the Heart Is: Studies in Melodrama and the Woman's Film*, ed. Christine Gledhill (London: BFI, 1987), pp. 339–49.

2. John Fiske, "British Cultural Studies and Television," in *Channels of Discourse: Television and Contemporary Criticism*, ed. Robert C. Allen (Chapel Hill: University of North Carolina Press, 1987), p. 271.

3. Graham Murdock, quoted in David Morley, *The Nationwide Audience* (London: BFI, 1980), p. 14.

4. Fiske, "British Cultural Studies and Television," p. 272. For a brief critique of this essay, see Meaghan Morris, "Banality in Cultural Studies," *Discourse* 10 (Spring-Summer 1988): 3–29.

5. Barbara Pym, *Less Than Angels* (New York: Harper & Row, 1987), p. 186.

6. Compare Renato Rosaldo's remarks on Le Roy Ladurie's *Montaillou*, in which Le Roy Ladurie ruefully notes that the peasant women of Montaillou never spoke to the inquisitor of their feelings about marriage and explains, "The woman was regarded as an object. . . . The historian finds himself faced with an area of cultural silence on this subject." Rosaldo comments, "What the inquisition record reveals is that peasant women in Montaillou did not tell their interrogators much about their passions in courtship. Whether the issue was skirted because of the women's reluctance to talk about possibly heretical love magic, out of mutual reticence between women and their male inquisitors, or owing to the historian's imputed 'cultural silence,' simply cannot be decided on the basis of available evidence. Nonetheless, Le Roy Ladurie simply declares that the things women fail to tell their inquisitor represent areas of cultural silence." "From the Door of His Tent: The Fieldworker and the Inquisitor," in *Writing Culture: The Poetics and Politics of Ethnography*, ed. James Clifford and George E. Marcus (Berkeley: University of California Press, 1986), p. 82.

7. For one discussion of literary competence, see Jonathan Culler, *Structuralist Poetics: Structuralism, Linguistics, and the Study of Literature* (Ithaca, N. Y.: Cornell University Press, 1975); and for a very different one stressing interpretive communities, see Stanley Fish, *Is There a Text in This Class?: The Authority of Interpretive Communities* (Cambridge, Mass.: Harvard University Press, 1980). The term "cultural capital" is Bourdieu's. See Pierre Bordieu, *Distinction: A Social Critique of the Judgment of Taste*, trans. Richard Nice (Cambridge Mass.: Harvard University Press, 1984). Tony Bennett and Janet Woolacott prefer to speak of "reading formations." See their *Bond and Beyond: The Political Career of a Popular Hero* (London: Methuen, 1987).

8. Janice Radway, *Reading the Romance: Women, Patriarchy, and Popular Literature* (Chapel Hill: University of North Carolina Press, 1984), p. 243n.

9. Annette Kolodny, "Dancing Through the Minefield: Some Observations on the Theory, Practice, and Politics of a Feminist Literary Criticism," in Showalter, ed., *The New Feminist Criticism: Women, Literature, Theory* (New York: Pantheon, 1985), pp. 55–56.

10. The huge body of literature contesting the most basic tenets of classical ethnography is seldom brought to bear self-critically in ethnographic studies of media and mass culture.

11. But for a discussion that challenges Eagleton's pessimism about the "academicization" of literary criticism, see Tony Bennett, "The Prison-House of Criticism," *New Formations* 2 (Summer 1987): 129–44.

12. Recent work on cultural ethnography in general has stressed the point that "culture" is always relational, an inscription of communication processes that exist, historically, *between* subjects in relations of power. See James Clifford, "Introduction: Partial Truths" in Clifford and Marcus, eds., *Writing Culture*, p. 15.

13. So, for example, Ien Ang gathered reader responses to *Dallas* by placing the following notice in the newspaper: "I like watching the TV serial *Dallas*, but often get odd reactions to it. Would anyone like to write and tell me why you like watching it too, or dislike it: I should like to assimilate these reactions in my university thesis." It's interesting to think about what kind of responses she would have elicited had she said she *doesn't* like watching *Dallas*. See Ien Ang, *Watching Dallas: Soap Opera and the Melodramatic Imagination*, trans. Della Cooling (London: Methuen, 1985), p. 10.

14. Robert C. Allen, "Reader-Oriented Criticism and Television," in Allen, ed., *Channels of Discourse*, p. 74. He is here referring to Wolfgang Iser's critique of textual critics.

15. The phrase is Bonnie Zimmerman's. See her "What Has Never Been: An Overview of Lesbian Feminist Criticism," in Showalter, ed., *The New Feminist Criticism*, pp. 200–24.

16. See the Derrida-Searle exchange in *Glyph* 1 and 2 (1977). The article by Jacques Derrida is entitled "Signature, Event, Context," *Glyph* 1: 172–97; John R. Searle's response is entitled "Reiterating the Difference: A Reply to Derrida," *Glyph* 1: 198–208. Derrida's reply to Searle is "Limited Inc abc . . . ," *Glyph* 2: 162–254.

17. J. L. Austin, *How to Do Things with Words* (Cambridge Mass.: Harvard University Press, 1962), p. 26.

18. Ibid., p. 28. Derrida ignores this point in order to make his case against Austin stronger; he speaks of "the conventionality without which there is no performative" in his "Signature, Event, Context," p. 188.

19. Steven Mailloux, however, speaks of "constitutive hermeneutics," which seems to me to be getting close to a notion of the "performative" activity of the

critic. See Steven Mailloux, *Interpretive Conventions: The Reader in the Study of American Fiction* (Ithaca, N. Y.: Cornell University Press), 1982.

20. Jean-Paul Sartre, *What Is Literature?*, trans. Bernard Frechtman (New York: Washington Square Press, 1966), p. 29.

21. Shoshana Felman, *The Literary Speech Act: Don Juan with J. L. Austin, or Seduction in Two Languages*, trans. Catherine Porter (Ithaca, N. Y.: Cornell University Press, 1983), p. 31.

22. Christopher Butler, *Interpretation, Deconstruction, and Ideology: An Introduction to Some Current Issues in Literary Theory* (Oxford: Clarendon, 1984).

23. Derrida, "Signature, Event, Context," p. 186.

24. Ibid., p. 188.

25. Monique Wittig, "The Straight Mind," *Feminist Issues* 1, no. 1 (Summer 1980): 106.

26. Quoted in Felman, *The Literary Speech Act*, p. 117.

27. Felman does observe that Don Juan breaks his promises to men too. But this is to ignore the obvious point that Don Juan's reputation rests exclusively on his ability to "conquer" women; that this behavior also involves the manipulation of men and may even ultimately aim at mastery over other men in no way mitigates the fact that women are the chief victims in this scheme; rather it suggests that a fully politicized analysis must consider the complex interrelationship between Don Juan's heterosexual exploits and "homosocial desire."

28. In addition to Donna Landry, "Congreve Recovered; or, the Limits of Woolf's Feminism," *The Michigan Academician* 17 (1985): 58–69; see the chapter, "Pandora's Box: Subjectivity, Class and Sexuality in Socialist Feminist Criticism," in Cora Kaplan, *Sea Changes* (London: Verso, 1986).

29. Felman, p. 77.

30. Terry Eagleton, *The Function of Criticism: From the Spectator to Post-Structuralism* (London: Verso, 1984), p. 103.

31. Landry, "Congreve Recovered," p. 134.

32. See in this connection Patricia Yaeger's argument that women should refuse to follow Barthes's lead and instead affirm the older term "work" over Barthes's preferred term "text." Patricia Yaeger, *Honey-Mad Women: Emancipatory Strategies in Women's Writing* (New York: Columbia University Press, 1988), p. 48.

33. Virginia Woolf, *A Room of One's Own* (New York: Harbinger, 1957). p. 48.

34. Joan Rivière, "Womanliness as a Masquerade," in *Formations of Fantasy*, ed. Victor Burgin, James Donald, and Cora Kaplan (London: Methuen, 1986), pp. 35–44.

35. See the essay by Homi K. Bhabha which is significantly (for our purposes) entitled, "The Commitment to Theory," *New Formations* 2 (Summer 1988): 19.

36. Ibid., p. 19.

37. Colin Mercer, "A Poverty of Desire: Pleasure and Popular Politics," in *Formations of Pleasure* (London: Routledge and Kegan Paul, 1983), p. 85.

38. Alice Walker, *In Search of Our Mother's Gardens: Womanist Prose by Alice Walker* (San Diego, Calif.: Harcourt Brace Jovanovich, 1984), p. 232.

CHAPTER FOUR

1. J. Glenn Gray, *The Warriors: Reflections on Men in Battle* (New York: Harper & Row, 1959), p. 79.

2. Since I wrote this, Brian de Palma's *Casualties of War* appeared; more than any other film, this one corroborates Theweleit's basic insight. Toward the end of the film, the camera over and over again cuts to shots of the woman who has been raped, mutilated, and repeatedly shot.

3. Klaus Theweleit, *Male Fantasies*, vol. 1: *Floods, Bodies, History*, trans. Stephen Conway, in collaboration with Erica Carter and Chris Turner (Minneapolis: University of Minnesota Press, 1987), pp. 50 and 45. "Homosocial" is Eve Kosofsky Sedgwick's term. See her *Between Men: English Literature and Male Homosocial Desire* (New York: Columbia University Press, 1985).

4. Judith Mayne, "Walking the *Tightrope* of Feminism and Male Desire," in *Men in Feminism*, ed. Alice Jardine and Paul Smith (New York: Methuen, 1987), pp. 62–70.

5. Anthony Wilden, *Man and Woman, War and Peace* (New York: Methuen, 1987), pp. 124–28.

6. I would like to note in passing that this same problem applies to Wilden's film, "A Chorus Line," which seeks to show how women have been objectified in Hollywood, but relies so heavily on quotation, and so little on critical commentary, that it is hard to see how someone who doesn't already deplore this objectification could be led to change his or her perspective.

7. Gustav Hasford, *The Short-Timers* (Toronto and New York: Bantam, 1980).

8. Julia Kristeva, *Powers of Horror: An Essay on Abjection*, trans. Leon S. Roudiez (New York: Columbia University Press, 1982), p. 64.

9. See especially her "Stabat Mater," trans Arthur Goldhammer, in *The Female Body in Western Culture: Contemporary Perspectives*, ed. Susan Rubin Suleiman (Cambridge, Mass.: Harvard University Press, 1985), pp. 99–136. Despite the fact that Kristeva's thought has been embraced by many feminists for rescuing the category of the maternal from the oblivion to which patriarchal theories have tended

to consign it, Kristeva remains very ambivalent about the maternal—an ambivalence that results in her declaring in her recent work her desire for the law (see "Stabat Mater," p. 109). For excellent critiques of this aspect of Julia Kristeva's work, see Kaja Silverman's *The Acoustic Mirror* (Bloomington: Indiana University Press, 1988) and Teresa de Lauretis, "The Female Body and Heterosexual Presumption," *Semiotica* 67, nos. 3/4 (1987): esp. 268–75.

10. Dorothy Dinnerstein, *The Mermaid and the Minotaur: Sexual Arrangements and Human Malaise* (New York: Harper & Row, 1976).

11. Gilles Deleuze, *Masochism: An Interpretation of Coldness and Cruelty*, trans. Jean McNeil (New York: George Braziller, 1971), p. 79.

12. Paul Smith, "Men in Feminism: Men in Feminist Theory," in Jardine and Smith, eds., *Men in Feminism*, p. 35.

13. Alice Jardine and Paul Smith, "A Conversation," in Jardine and Smith, eds., *Men in Feminism*, p. 254.

14. "Women in the Beehive: A Seminar with Jacques Derrida," in Jardine and Smith, eds., *Men in Feminism*, p. 193. To be sure, since the participants remain anonymous, this may very well be a woman speaking. My point remains the same, however, since the person is attempting to think a Derridean strategy and hence to impersonate the man.

15. The word "admiration" is used by Stephen Heath to describe a relationship between feminists and their male sympathizers. See Heath, "Male Feminism," in Jardine and Smith, eds., *Men in Feminism*, pp. 1–32.

16. Cary Nelson, "Men, Feminism: The Materiality of Discourse," in Jardine and Smith, eds., *Men in Feminism*, p. 170.

17. This tendency is more evident in film theory than in literary theory. See, for examples, Gaylyn Studlar, "Masochism and the Perverse Pleasures of the Cinema," in *Movies and Methods*, vol. 2, ed. Bill Nichols (Berkeley and Los Angeles: The University of California Press, 1985), pp. 602–21; D. N. Rodowick, "The Difficulty of Difference," *Wide Angle* 5, no. 1 (1982): 4–15; and Kaja Silverman, "Masochism and Subjectivity," *Framework* 12 (1980): 2–9. An excellent critique of the work of Studlar and Silverman and an analysis of the limitations of Deleuze's work for feminism may be found in Sonia Rein, "Brutality," unpublished paper. In an interesting article on "slasher films," Carol Clover also broaches the subject of male masochism, but does so more tentatively and cautiously than the others named here. See her "Her Body, Himself: Gender in the Slasher Films," *Representations* 20 (Fall 1987): 131–72. In literary and art theory, see Leo Bersani, *The Freudian Body: Psychoanalysis and Art* (New York: Columbia University Press, 1986). Like Deleuze, many of these writers discuss in detail Freud's essay, "A Child is Being Beaten: A Contribution to the Study of the Origin of Sexual Perversions," *The*

Standard Edition of the Complete Psychological works of Sigmund Freud, trans. James Strachey (London: Hogarth, 1974), vol. 17.

18. See, for example, Margaret Randolph Higonnet, Jane Jenson, Sonya Michel, and Margaret Collins Weitz, *Behind the Lines: Gender in the Two World Wars* (New Haven: Yale University Press, 1987). Also see Nancy Huston, "The Matrix of War: Mothers and Heroes," in Suleiman, ed., *The Female Body in Western Culture*, pp. 119–38 and Susan Jeffords, *The Remasculinization of America: Gender and the Vietnam War* (Bloomington: Indiana University Press, 1989). An exception would be Elaine Scarry's book, *The Body in Pain: The Making and Unmaking of the World* (New York: Oxford University Press, 1985). Although Scarry's book is a study of torture and war, the extensive index contains not a single reference to rape, and the work is almost completely unconcerned with issues of gender.

CHAPTER FIVE

1. Katha Pollitt, "The Strange Case of Baby M," *The Nation*, May 23, 1987, p. 683.

2. "Thighs and Whiskers—The Fascination of 'Magnum, p.i.' " is the title of an article by Sandy Flitterman, in *Screen* 26, no. 2 (March–April 1985): 42–59.

3. Sigmund Freud, *Three Essays on the Theory of Sexuality*, trans. James Strachey (New York: Basic Books, 1962), p. 53n.

4. Ibid., *Three Essays*, p. 52.

5. Ibid., p. 53n.

6. Sigmund Freud, "History of an Infantile Neurosis" (New York: Collier Books, 1963), p. 275.

7. Ibid., p. 268.

8. Ibid.," p. 268.

9. Ariel Dorfman, "The Infantilizing of Culture," in *American Media and Mass Culture: Left Perspectives*, ed. Donald Lazere (Berkeley: The University of California Press, 1987), p. 149. See Dorfman's *The Empire's Old Clothes: What the Lone Ranger, Babar, and Other Innocent Heroes Do to Our Minds* (New York: Pantheon Books, 1983).

10. Theodor W. Adorno (with the assistance of George Simpson), "On Popular Music," *Studies in Philosophy and Social Science* 9, no. 1 (1941): 17–48.

11. Editors of *Cahiers du Cinema*, "John Ford's *Young Mr. Lincoln*," in *Movies and Methods*, ed. Bill Nichols (Berkeley: The University of California Press, 1976), p. 526.

12. Laura Mulvey, "Changes," *Discourse* 7 (Spring 1985): 11–30. Juliet Mitch-

ell, *Women the Longest Revolution: Essays in Feminism, Literature and Psychoanalysis* (London: Virago, 1984), p. 291.

13. Marie Balmary, *Psychoanalyzing Psychoanalysis: Freud and the Hidden Fault of the Father*, trans. Ned Lukacher (Baltimore, Md.: The Johns Hopkins University Press, 1982), pp. 7–24.

14. Julia Kristeva, *Tales of Love*, trans. Leon S. Roudiez (New York: Columbia University Press, 1987), p. 46.

15. Mary Gordon, " 'Baby M'—New Questions About Biology and Destiny," *Ms.*, June 1987, pp. 25–28. Janice Doane and Devon Hodges, "Risky Business: Familial Ideology and the Case of Baby M," *differences* 1, no. 1 (Winter 1989): 67–82.

16. Sigmund Freud, "Female Sexuality," in *The Standard Edition of the Complete Psychological Works of Sigmund Freud*, trans. James Strachey (London: Hogarth Press, 1974), vol. 21.

17. Julia Kristeva, *Black Sun: Depression and Melancholia*, trans. Leon S. Roudiez (New York: Columbia University Press, 1989), p. 27.

CHAPTER SIX

1. Quoted in Michael Bronski, *Culture Clash: The Making of a Gay Sensibility* (Boston: South End Press, 1984), p. 185.

2. Kaja Silverman, *The Subject of Semiotics* (New York: Oxford University Press, 1983), p. 183.

3. Jane Gallop performs this kind of reading upon the writings of Lacan himself. See her *Reading Lacan* (Ithaca, N. Y.: Cornell University Press, 1985).

4. Peter Lehman, "*In the Realm of the Senses*: Desire, Power and the Representation of the Male Body," *Genders* 2 (Summer 1988): 95.

5. See Barbara Ehrenreich, *The Hearts of Men: American Dreams and the Flight from Commitment* (New York: Doubleday, 1983). The term "domestic mystique" is Peter Filene's. See *Him/her/self: Sex Roles in Modern America* (New York: Harcourt Brace Jovanovich, 1975).

6. See Dana Polan's discussion of "tinkering" as an American mythology and its relation to narrative. *Power and Paranoia: History, Narrative, and the American Cinema, 1940–1950* (New York: Columbia University Press, 1986), pp. 86–87.

7. Franz Kafka, *The Metamorphosis*, trans. Stanley Corngold (Toronto: Bantam, 1972), p. 58.

8. See Kaja Silverman, *The Acoustic Mirror: The Female Voice in Psychoanalysis and Cinema* (Bloomington: Indiana University Press, 1988).

9. Jacques Lacan, *Feminine Sexuality*, ed. Juliet Mitchell and Jacqueline Rose, trans. Jacqueline Rose (New York: Norton, 1982), p. 85.

10. For a discussion of masculinity as mask, see also Paul Hock, *White Hero, Black Beast: Racism, Sexism and the Mask of Masculinity* (Bristol: Pluto, 1979), esp. pp. 94–105.

11. See Teresa de Lauretis's feminist analysis of Lotman's work in *Alice Doesn't: Feminism, Semiotics, Cinema* (Bloomington: Indiana University Press, 1984), pp. 116–21.

12. See the three articles in the special issue on "Male Trouble" in *Camera Obscura* 17 (1988)—Constance Penley, "The Cabinet of Dr. Pee-wee: Consumerism and Sexual Terror," pp. 133–54; Ian Balfour, "The Playhouse of the Signifier," pp. 155–68; and Henry Jenkins III, "Going Bonkers!: Children, Play and Pee-wee," pp. 169–94. For another analysis of Pee-wee as a gay male cult figure, see Bryan Bruce, "Pee-wee Herman: The Homosexual Subtext," *CinéAction* 9 (Summer 1987), pp. 3–6. For a discussion of Pee-wee from a perspective closer to my own (as well as for a discussion of *Gorillas in the Mist*, which I will be discussing in the next chapter), see Marsha Kinder, "Back to the Future in the 80s with Fathers & Sons, Supermen & PeeWees, Gorillas & Toons," *Film Quarterly* (Summer 1989): 2–11.

13. Balfour, "The Playhouse of the Signifier," p. 158.

14. Jack Babuscio, "Camp and the Gay Sensibility," *Gays and Film*, ed. Richard Dyer (New York: Zoetrope, 1984), p. 46. For other discussions of camp, see Mark Booth, *Camp* (London: Quartet Books, 1983), and Andrew Ross, "Uses of Camp," *No Respect: American Intellectuals and Popular Culture* (New York: Routledge, 1989).

15. Of course, this is more or less Susan Sontag's point when she says that camp's stress on style is aimed at "neutralizing moral indignation," "Notes on Camp," *Against Interpretation* (New York: Dell, 1969), pp. 291–92.

16. Babuscio, "Camp and the Gay Sensibility," p. 44.

17. For an interesting discussion of the ways the "homosexual lifestyle" shaped the larger culture see Dennis Altman, *The Homosexualization of America, the Americanization of the Homosexual* (New York: Saint Martin's Press, 1982).

18. Gilles Deleuze and Felix Guattari develop this point in *Anti-Oedipus: Capitalism and Schizophrenia*, trans. Robert Hurley, Mark Seem, and Helen R. Lare (New York: Viking, 1977), and *A Thousand Plateaus: Capitalism and Schizophrenia*, trans. Brian Massumi (Minneapolis: University of Minnesota Press, 1987); and Alice Jardine comments upon it in *Gynesis: Configurations of Women and Modernity* (Ithaca, N. Y.: Cornell University Press, 1985), pp. 208–26.

19. See especially her essay "The Mark of Gender," *Feminist Issues* 5, no. 2 (Fall 1985): 3–12.

20. Valie Export, "The Real and Its Double: The Body," *Discourse* 11, no. 1 (Fall–Winter 1988–89): 25.

21. On this point, see the debate between Hélène Cixous and Catherine Clément in *The Newly Born Woman*, trans. Betsy Wing (Minneapolis: The University of Minnesota Press, 1986), pp. 147–60.

22. Noelle Caskey, "Interpreting Anorexia Nervosa," in *The Female Body in Western Culture: Contemporary Perspectives*, ed. Susan Rubin Suleiman (Cambridge, Mass.: Harvard University Press, 1985), p. 185.

23. Ira Paneth, "Wim and His Wings," *Film Quarterly* 42, no. 1 (Fall 1988): 2.

24. bell hooks, "Representing Whiteness: Seeing *Wings of Desire*," *Zeta Magazine* 2, no. 3 (March 1989): 38.

25. Jean-François Lyotard, "Can Thought Go On Without a Body?," *Discourse* 11, no. 1 (Fall–Winter 1988–89): 84.

26. Caskey, "Interpreting Anorexia Nervosa," p. 184. For another interesting discussion of anorexia, see Susan Bordo, "Anorexia Nervosa: Psychopathology as the Crystallization of Culture," in *Feminism and Foucault: Reflections on Resistance*, ed. Irene Diamond and Lee Quinby (Boston: Northeastern University Press, 1988), pp. 87–118.

27. Fredric Jameson, "Postmodernism and Consumer Society," in *The Anti-Aesthetic: Essays On Postmodern Culture*, ed. Hal Foster (Port Townsend, Wash.: Bay Press, 1983), pp. 111–25.

28. But for a feminist analysis see Janice Doane and Devon Hodges, *Nostalgia and Sexual Difference: The Resistance to Contemporary Feminism* (New York: Methuen, 1987).

29. In addition to many of the essays in Suleiman, for example, there is the work in progress on the grotesque body by Mary Russo. See her "Female Grotesques: Carnival and Theory," *Feminist Studies/Critical Studies*, ed. Teresa de Lauretis (Bloomington: Indiana University Press, 1986), pp. 213–29.

CHAPTER SEVEN

1. See the discussion of the film in Patricia Erens, *The Jew in American Cinema* (Bloomington: Indiana University Press, 1984), pp. 101–06.

2. Homi K. Bhabha, "Of Mimicry and Man: The Ambivalence of Colonial Discourse," *October* 28 (Spring 1984): 131. Other texts by Bhabha that I draw on here include: "The Other Question: Difference, Discrimination and the Discourse of Colonialism," in *Literature, Politics and Theory: Papers from the Essex Conference 1976–84*, ed. Francis Barker, Peter Hulme, Margaret Iversen, and Diana Loxley (London: Methuen, 1986), pp. 148–72; "The Commitment to Theory," *New Forma-*

tions 5 (Summer 1988): 5–24; "Sings Taken for Wonders: Questions of Ambivalence and Authority under a Tree Outside Delhi, May 1817," in *"Race," Writing, and Difference*, ed., Henry Louis Gates, Jr. (Chicago: University of Chicago Press, 1985), pp. 163–84.

3. Thomas Cripps, *Slow Fade to Black: The Negro in American Film, 1900–1942* (New York: Oxford University Press, 1977), p. 37.

4. Bhabha, "Of Mimicry and Man," p. 126.

5. One might note that for Bhabha mimicry is like camouflage, like being "mottled," "*not* harmonising." Ibid., p. 125.

6. For a discussion of this scene from the point of view of a black spectator, see Manthia Diawara, "Black Spectatorship—Problems of Identification and Resistance," *Screen* 29, no. 4 (Autumn 1988): 66–79.

7. Bhabha, "Of Mimicry and Man," p. 132. For other articles discussing the ambivalent nature of minstrelsy, see Sylvia Wynter, "Sambos and Minstrels," *Social Text* 1 (1979): 149–56; and Susan Willis "I Shop Therfore I Am: Is There a Place for Afro-American Culture in American Commodity Culture," in *Changing Our Own Words: Essays on Criticism, Theory, and Writing by Black Women*, ed. Cheryl Wall (New Brunswick, N.J.: Rutgers University Press, 1989), pp. 173–95.

8. Ibid., p. 128.

9. See Luce Irigaray, *Speculum of the Other Woman*, trans. Gillian C. Gill (Ithaca, N. Y.: Cornell University Press, 1985).

10. Bhabha, "The Other Question," p. 179.

11. Ibid., p. 170.

12. Cripps, *Slow Fade to Black*, p. 155.

13. X. J. Kennedy, "Who Killed King Kong?," in *Focus on the Horror Film*, ed. Roy Huss and T. J. Ross (Englewood Cliffs, N. J.: Prentice Hall, 1972), p. 109.

14. See René Girard, *Deceit, Desire, and the Novel: Self and Other in Literary Structure*, trans. Yvonne Freccero (Baltimore, Md.: Johns Hopkins University Press, 1972), and Eve Kosofsky Sedgwick's discussion of Girard's work in terms of "homosocial desire," in her *Between Men: English Literature and Male Homosocial Desire* (New York: Columbia University Press, 1985), pp. 21–25.

15. Henry Louis Gates, *The Signifying Monkey: A Theory of Afro-American Literary Criticism* (New York: Oxford University Press, 1988), pp. 108–09.

16. Laura Mulvey, "Visual Pleasure and Narrative Cinema," *Screen* 16, no. 3 (Autumn 1975): 6–18.

17. For examples, see Patricia Mellencamp, "Made in the Fade," *Ciné-Tracts* 3, no. 3 (Fall 1980): 13; Bill Nichols, *Ideology and the Image* (Bloomington:

Indiana University Press, 1981), pp. 104–32; and E. Ann Kaplan, *Women and Film: Both Sides of the Camera* (New York and London: Methuen, 1983, pp. 49–59.

18. Lea Jacobs, "The Censorship of *Blonde Venus*: Textual Analysis and Historical Methods," *Cinema Journal* 27, no. 3 (Spring 1988): 21–31.

19. For a controversial discussion of race, gender and spectacle, see Sander L. Gilman, "The Hottentot and the Prostitute: Toward an Iconography of Female Sexuality," in *Difference and Pathology: Stereotypes of Sexuality, Race, and Madness* (Ithaca, N. Y.: Cornell University Press, 1985), pp. 76–108.

20. Isaac Julien and Kobena Mercer, "De Margin and De centre," *Screen* 29, no. 4 (Autumn 1988): 5.

21. Claire Johnston, "Women's Cinema as Counter-Cinema," in *Sexual Strategems: The World of Women in Film*, ed. Patricia Erens (New York: Horizon Press, 1979), p. 136.

22. For a discussion of the complex relations between racism and anti-Semitism, see Elly Bulkin, Minnie Bruce Pratt, and Barbara Smith, *Yours in Struggle: Three Feminist Perspectives on Anti-Semitism and Racism* (New York: Long Haul Press, 1984).

23. For an interesting discussion of this, see Peter Stallybrass and Allon White, "Below Stairs: the Maid and the Family Romance," in their *The Politics and Poetics of Transgression* (Ithaca, N. Y.: Cornell University Press, 1986), pp. 149–70.

24. Jane Gaines, "White Privilege and Looking Relations—Race and Gender in Feminist Film Theory," *Screen* 29, no. 4 (Autumn 1988): 12–27. In this article, which has a strong ideological axe to grind, since Gaines is attacking psychoanalytic film theory, Gaines tries to prove that psychoanalysis cannot be of use in discussing the issue of race. I hope I have shown that this is not necessarily the case, even though people who have *used* psychoanalysis may be racially biased: such bias is hardly sufficient to discredit the entire discipline.

25. Valerie Smith, "Black Feminist Theory and the Representation of the 'Other'," in *Changing Our Own Words: Essays on Criticism, Theory, and Writing by Black Women*, ed. Cheryl A. Wall (New Brunswick, N. J.: Rutgers University Press, 1989), p. 45.

26. Hazel Carby, *Reconstructing Womanhood: The Emergence of the Afro-American Woman Novelist* (New York: Oxford University Press, 1987), p. 17.

Chapter Eight

1. Andrew Ross begins his chapter on pornography in *No Respect: Intellectuals and Popular Culture* (New York: Routledge, 1989) with the question, "Pornography from a woman's point of view?" (p. 171). He subsequently refers to pornography as a realm of "empowerment" on several occasions. See the recent article on

pornography by Gertrud Koch, "The Body's Shadow Realm" *October* 50, no. 1 (Fall 1989): 3–29. Although Koch is a noted German feminist film critic, she does not mention a single woman who has written about pornography: thus do feminist critics contribute to the eradication of women within scholarship, even scholarship on such a quintessentially feminist topic.

2. Ross, *No Respect*, p. 194. But see the essay by Scott MacDonald, "Confessions of a Feminist Porn Watcher," *Film Quarterly* 36, no. 3 (Spring 1983): 10–17, which in fact does offer some cogent explanations for men's attraction to pornography. For another, although less personal discussion of men's attraction to pornography, see Alan Soble, *Pornography: Marxism, Feminism, and the Future of Sexuality* (New Haven: Yale University Press, 1986).

3. Geoffrey Nowell-Smith, "Minnelli and Melodrama," in *Home Is Where the Heart Is: Studies in Melodrama and the Woman's Film*, ed. Christine Gledhill (London: BFI, 1987), pp. 70–74.

4. Bronski, *Culture Clash: The Making of a Gay Sensibility* (Boston: South End Press, 1984), p. 53.

5. Michael Moon, "Disseminating Whitman," special issue, "Displacing Homophobia," ed. Ronald R. Butters, John M. Clum, and Michael Moon, *The South Atlantic Quarterly* 88, no. 1 (Winter 1989): 255.

6. "Disclaimer" is a term used by Robin Wood to denote aspects of plot or the existence of characters whose sole purpose is to assure us of the protagonists' heterosexuality. See his *Hollywood from Vietnam to Reagan* (New York: Columbia University Press, 1985), p. 229.

7. D. A. Miller, *The Novel and the Police* (Berkeley: University of California Press, 1988), pp. 192–220.

8. In addition to Bersani, see Jeffrey Weeks, *Sexuality and Its Discontents* (London: Routledge, 1985), pp. 231–35; and Simon Watney, *Policing Desire: Pornography, AIDS, and the Media* (Minneapolis: University of Minnesota Press, 1987), pp. 58–76.

9. Leo Bersani, "Is the Rectum a Grave?" in *AIDS: Cultural Analysis/Cultural Activism*, ed. Douglas Crimp (Cambridge Mass.: The MIT Press, 1988), p. 219.

10. Ibid., p. 215. See also Catharine A. MacKinnon, *Feminism Unmodified: Discourses on Life and Law* (Cambridge, Mass.: Harvard University Press, 1987); and Andrea Dworkin, *Intercourse* (New York: The Free Press, 1987).

11. Gayle Rubin, "The Leather Menace: Comments on Politics and S/M," in SAMOIS, ed., *Coming to Power: Writings and Graphics on Lesbian S/M* (Boston: Alyson, 1981), p. 221.

12. Kaja Silverman, "Masochism and Male Subjectivity," *Camera Obscura* 17 (1988): 36.

13. Adrienne Rich, "Compulsory Heterosexuality and Lesbian Existence," *Signs* 5, no. 4 (Summer 1980): 80–81.

14. See, for example, Gayle Rubin, "Thinking Sex: Notes for a Radical Theory of the Politics of Sexuality," in *Pleasure and Danger: Exploring Female Sexuality*, ed. Carole S. Vance (Boston: Routledge and Kegan Paul, 1984), pp. 307–8.

15. See Robin Linden, ed., *Against Sadomasochism: A Radical Feminist Analysis*, (East Palo Alto, Calif.: Frog in the Well, 1982).

16. Parveen Adams, "Of Female Bondage," *Between Feminism and Psychoanalysis*, ed. Teresa Brennan (New York: Routledge, 1989), p. 262.

17. Rubin, "Thinking Sex," p. 279.

18. Rosalind Coward, *Female Desires* (New York: Grove Press, 1985), pp. 92–106.

19. See my discussion of the food motif in Alfred Hitchcock's *Frenzy* in *The Women Who Knew Too Much: Hitchcock and Feminist Theory* (New York: Routledge, 1988), pp. 101–14. In addition to Claude Lévi-Strauss, *The Raw and the Cooked: Introduction to a Science of Mythology*, vol. 1., trans. John and Doreen Weightman (Chicago: University of Chicago Press, 1969), we could also invoke in this discussion Julia Kristeva's work on Biblical abominations in *Powers of Horror: An Essay on Abjection*, trans. Leon Roudiez (New York: Columbia University Press, 1982).

20. Teresa de Lauretis, "The Essence of the Triangle or, Taking the Risk of Essentialism Seriously: Feminist Theory in Italy, the U.S., and Britain," *differences* 1, no. 2 (Summer 1989): 22–27.

21. Judith Butler, *Gender Trouble: Feminism and the Subversion of Identity* (New York: Routledge, 1989), p. 137. Butler does not allude to the fact that "parody," and related concepts like "mimicry," "mimesis," "masquerade," and "carnival," are hotly contested categories in feminist writings as well as (we have seen) in writings about colonialism. For another affirmative assessment of parody in the context of lesbian existence, see Sue-Ellen Case, "Towards a Butch-Femme Aesthetic," *Discourse* 11, no. 1 (Fall–Winter 1988–89): 55–73.

22. Teresa de Lauretis, "Film and the Visible," forthcoming in *How Do I Look?*, ed. Douglas Crimp, Bay Press.

23. Pat Califia, "Among Us, Against Us: The New Puritans," *Caught Looking*, ed. Kate Ellis et. al. (Seattle, Wash.: The Real Comet Press, 1988), p. 22.

24. Linda Williams in her book *Hard Core: Power, Pleasure, and the Frenzy of the Visible* (Berkeley: University of California Press, 1989) discusses the ways pornography may be seen as attempting to deny the woman's difference even when it seems most to flaunt it.

25. Susan Griffin, *Pornography and Silence: Culture's Revenge Against Nature* (New York: Harper & Row, 1981), pp. 111–12.

INDEX OF FILMS

Alien Nation, 118

Batman, 98, 109
Big, 96–99, 101, 105, 108
Big Top Pee-wee, 91–92, 95, 103–104
Birth of a Nation, 118, 124
Blonde Venus, 120, 127–28

Casualties of War, 173n2
Chorus Line, A 173n6
Clara's Heart, 131, 133
Color Purple, The, 131
Coming to America, 116, 118
Crossing Delancey, 129–30, 133, 134

Dead Poets Society, 136, 137–40, 145, 150
Devil and Miss Jones, Part 3, The, 160–163
Devil's Playground, The, 138

Fatal Beauty, 132
Frenzy, 182n19
Full Metal Jacket, 61–62, 64, 66, 73–74
48 Hours, 145

Gallipoli, 138
Ghost, 132–34
Gone with the Wind, 43
Gorillas in the Mist, 121–26, 127–28

Heartbreak Ridge, viii, 62, 64–65, 66, 71, 72

In the Realm of the Senses, 92
Incredible Shrinking Man, The, 93–96, 105, 110

Jazz Singer, The, 115, 129
Jumping Jack Flash, 132

King Kong, 121–22, 124, 126

Last Temptation of Christ, The, 109
Lethal Weapon, 136, 141–45, 150, 162, 163
Lethal Weapon 2, 136, 141–45, 162
Love Story, 39

Married to the Mob, 96
Moon Over Parador, 119
My Man Godfrey, 117

Pee-wee's Big Adventure, 95, 100, 104
Picnic at Hanging Rock, 138
Platoon, 72–73

Riddles of the Sphinx, 104

She Must Be Seeing Things, 158
Stella Dallas, 8–9
Sur un Air de Charleston, 126

Tequila Sunrise, 145
3 Godfathers, 84–85
Three Men and a Baby, 7, 33, 76–84, 86–89
Three Men and a Cradle, 76, 88
Tightrope, 64
Top Gun, viii, 62, 62, 67, 70–72, 73, 145
Twins, 95–96

Wings of Desire, 104–09, 162
Witches of Eastwick, The, 70

Young Mr. Lincoln, 85

INDEX

Adams, Parveen, 152–154, 157, 168n32
Adorno, Theodor W., 83
Alexander, Martha, 154
Allen, Robert C., 46, 171n14
Althusser, Louis, 15, 17, 42
Ang, Ien, 171n13
anorexia, 101–102, 110–11, 130, 141, 153, 178n26
Anzaldúa, Gloria, 18–19
Aristotle, 14
Austen, Jane, *Northanger Abbey*, 40, 56
Austin, J.L., 46–47, 49–50, 52–53, 56–58, 171n18

Baby M., 76–77, 87
Bakhtin, Mikhail, 6, 86
Balmary, Marie, 86
Barthes, Roland, 25, 31, 52, 172n32
Basinger, Kim, 78
Baudrillard, Jean, 24, 30–34, 36, 169n8
Baym, Nina, 10
Bennett, Tony, 170n7, 171n11
Bersani, Leo, 136, 146–154, 156, 159
Bhabha, Homi K., 54–56, 116, 119–120, 123, 127, 132, 173n35
bisexuality, 78
Bloch, R. Howard, 11, 166n10
body: and gender, 92, 101, 102–111, 130, 137, 141–42, 144, 146; maternal, 130; black woman associated with, 133
Bonaparte, Napoleon, 56

Boone, Joseph A., 11–12, 166n17
Booth, Mark, 177n14
Bordo, Susan, 167n22, 178n26
Bourdieu, Pierre, 170n7
Boy George, 90
Bright, Susie, 160–62
Brooks, Peter, 3, 8, 165n2, 166n10
Brown, Beverley, 168n32
Brownmiller, Susan, 65, 67, 167n18
Bruce, Bryan, 177n12
Bulkin, Elly, 180n22
Butler, Christopher, 49–51, 55
Butler, Judith, 17–18, 132, 157–58, 161, 182n21

Cadden, Michael, 11–12, 166n17
Califia, Pat, 159–60
camp, 99, 103, 155, 157, 161, 177n14
Carby, Hazel, 134
carnival, 85–86
Case, Sue-Ellen, 182n21
castration anxiety, 16, 22, 67–68, 78–79, 82–83, 93, 97
Cather, Willa, 13
Cavell, Stanley, 8–11
Chodorow, Nancy, 41, 88
Cixous, Hélène, 16
Clifford, James, 171n12
Clover, Carol, 194n17
Collins, Joan, vii
colonialism and colonialist discourse, 17, 116, 120, 182n21
Columbo, 106, 108
Coward, Rosalind, 153
Cowie, Elizabeth, 168n32

Cripps, Thomas, 116, 124
Crossroads, 40
Culler, Jonathan, 15, 167–68n24, 170n7

Dallas, 45, 171n13
Daly, Mary, 168n33
Danson, Ted, 77
Dante, Alighieri, 80
De Beauvoir, Simone, 15, 17
De Lauretis, Teresa, 20, 156, 157, 173–74n9, 177n11
De Palma, Brian, 173n2
De Saussure, Ferdinand, 15
deconstruction, 4, 10–11, 50, 166n10
Deleuze, Gilles, 68–70, 73–74, 101, 155–56, 174n17, 177n13
Derrida, Jacques, 15, 42, 46–47, 49–50, 54, 70, 171n18, 174n14
Devito, Danny, 95
Dick Talk, 92
Dickens, Charles, *David Copperfield*, 51
Dickinson, Emily, 140
Dietrich, Marlene, 127–128
Dinnerstein, Dorothy, 88
disavowal, 22, 54, 81–83, 85, 90, 96, 119, 122–24, 128, 156, 161
Diawara, Manthia, 179n6
Disney, Walt, 78, 83
Doane, Janice, 87, 178n28
Dorfman, Ariel, 83
Douglas, Ann, 24–26, 28, 31, 169n4
Dreyfus, Richard, 119
Du Bois, W.E.B., 127
Dworkin, Andrea, 135–36, 146–48, 151, 159, 161
Dynasty, vii

Eagleton, Terry, 43, 53, 171n11
Eastwood, Clint, 62, 64, 71
Edelman, Lee, 6, 12
Ehrenreich, Barbara, 90, 93, 96
Emerson, Ralph Waldo, 7–9, 12
enunciation, 54–55, 57
essentialism: in theories of femininity, 54–55, 57, 101, 157–58; in relation to race, 115; in relation to masculinity, 166n18

ethnographic criticism, 34–44, 46, 48, 53, 58, 171n10
Export, Valie, 101–02, 110

Falcon Crest, 36
Falk, Peter, 105–06
Fanon, Frantz, 120
Farr, Susan, 153
father, 52, 58, 90, 157; in war films, 70–74; in masochistic fantasies, 69–70, 155; in *Three Men and a Baby*, 76–89; in *3 Godfathers*, 76–89; pre-oedipal, 86–88; in *The Jazz Singer*, 115; in *Coming to America*, 117; in *Dead Poets Society*, 139
Felman, Shoshana, 47–49, 52–53, 57, 172n27
Felski, Rita, 20
fetishism, 22, 54, 81, 90, 116, 120, 122, 125, 127–28, 156, 158, 162–3
Fish, Stanley, 42, 50, 170n7
Fiske, John, 39, 44, 170n4
Ford, John, 77, 84–85
Fossey, Dian, 121–26
Foucault, Michel, 15, 18, 33, 157
Frankfurt School of Social Research, 37, 48, 67
Freud, Sigmund, 18, 22, 44, 78, 130, 165n2; "A Child is Being Beaten," 69, 174–75n2; "The Wolf Man," 80–82; on masculinity, 100; on art, 111
Full House, 88

Gaines, Jane, 180n24
Ganz, Bruno, 105, 109
Gates, Henry Louis, 126
gay studies, 5–6, 12; *see also* homosexuality; lesbianism
gender studies, 5, 12–15, 92
Gibson, Mel, 145
Gilbert, Sandra, 10
Gilman, Sander L., 180n19
Girard, Rene, 125, 179n14
Goldberg, Whoopi, 131–33
Goldmann, Lucien, 50
Gordon, Mary, 87
Grant, Cary, 128
Gray, J. Glenn, 61, 72
Gray, Ursula, 61

Griffin, Susan, 163
Griffith, D. W., 124
Guattari, Felix, 68, 101, 177n13
Gubar, Susan, 10
Guttenberg, Steve, 79
gynocritics, 4–5

Hall, Stuart, 37
Hansen, Elaine, 11
Happy Days, 98
Haraway, Donna, 18
Hasford, Gustav, 66
Hawks, Howard, 85
Hawthorne, Nathaniel, *The Scarlet Letter*, 7
Heath, Stephen, 174n15
Hegel, G.W.F., 30, 32
Herman, Pee-wee, 7, 85, 91, 95, 99–100, 111, 141–42, 177n12
Hitchcock, Alfred, 5, 106, 182n19
Hoberman, J., 63
Hock, Paul, 177n10
Hodges, Devon, 87, 178n28
Holtby, Winifred, 16
homoeroticism: *see* homosocial relations
homosexuality, 156, 159, 162; in *Kiss of the Spider Woman*, 27–30; and *Top Gun*, 63; and *Three Men and a Baby*, 82; and *3 Godfathers*, 85; and Pee-wee Herman, 99–100, 103, 177n12; and *Lethal Weapon*, 143–44and pornography, 143–51; *see also* lesbianism
homosocial relations: 63, 173n3 179n14; in *Top Gun*, 71; in *Three Men and a Baby*; 82, 85; in *Big*, 97; in *Gorillas in the Mist*, 125; in *Dead Poets Society*, 138–39; in *Lethal Weapon*, 141, 144; in *The Devil and Miss Jones, Part 3*,161; in *Don Juan*, 172n27,
hooks, bell, 20, 106
Huyssen, Andreas, 169n2
hysteria, 137, 139–40, 161; male, 77, 79, 82, 85, 100, 143; female, 101, 103

Irigaray, Luce, 119, 163
Irving, Amy, 129
Iser, Wolfgang, 171n14

Jameson, Fredric, 23, 111
Jardine, Alice, 69, 177n18
Jews in film, 115, 129
Jung, Carl, 102

Kafka, Franz, "The Metamorphosis," 94–95
Keats, John, 56
Kennedy, X.J, 121–22
Kuhn, Annette, 170n1
Kierkegaard, Sören, 52
Kinder, Marsha, 177n12
Koch, Gertrud, 181–2n1
Kolodny, Annette, 42
Krieger, Murray, 42
Kristeva, Julia, 18, 62, 67–68, 86–88, 157, 173–74n9, 182n19
Kubrick, Stanley, 61–62, 72–74

Lacan, Jacques, 9, 15, 18, 33, 49, 52, 54, 58, 81, 90, 95–96
Ladurie Le Roy, 170n6
Landry, Donna, 53–54
Laverne and Shirley, 98
Lehman, Peter, 92
Lentricchia, Frank, 10–12
lesbianism, 6, 12–13, 19, 146, 151, 159, 163, 182n21; and sado-masochistic practices, 135–36, 147, 150, 152–60, 162
Leverenz, David, 7–9, 11
Lévi-Strauss, Claude, 153, 182n19
Lewis, Jerry, 85, 100
Lorde, Audre, 168n33
Lotman, Jurij, 98, 177n11
Lovelace, Linda, 161
Lyotard, Jean-François, 10, 110

MacDonald, Scott, 181n2
MacKinnon, Catharine, 135–36, 146–48, 151–52, 159, 161
Madonna, 39
Mailloux, Steven, 171–2n19
male feminism, 6–7, 64, 68–69, 73–74, 166–67n18, 174n15
Mapplethorpe, Robert, 145
Marcuse, Herbert, 148
Marshall, Penny, 98
Martin, Biddy, 19–20
Marx, Karl, 52

Marxism, 10, 12, 23, 27–31, 36–37, 41–42
masochism, 29–30, 142, 144, 155; female, 9–10, 149; male, 7, 68–69, 73–74, 149–50, 152, 155, 174n17
masquerade, 54, 96, 103, 115, 182n21
mass culture: theories of, 7, 23, 35–36
Mazursky, Paul, 119
McLaughlin, Sheila, 158
melancholia, 9
melodrama, 8–10, 137
Melville, Herman, 24
Mercer, Colin, 57
Miller, D.A., 145
Miller, Nancy K., 22, 33, 165n2
Milton, John, 56
mimesis, 126
mimetic desire, 125
mimicry, 116–17, 119, 125–26, 132, 146, 179n5, 182n21
minstrelsy, 119, 179n7
Mitchell, Juliet, 86
Mitchell, Margaret, *Gone with the Wind*, 43
Mohanty, Chandra, 19–20
Molière, *Don Juan*, 15, 49, 52, 172n27
Morley, David, 38–41, 43–44
Morris, Meaghan, 170n4
mother, 90, 151; in melodrama, 9; pre-oedipal, 67–69, 70, 86–87; in masochistic fantasies, 68–69, 70, 155–57; surrogate, 76–77; in *Three Men and a Baby*, 82; in *3 Godfathers*, 84; in *Big*, 98; in narrative, 98, 108; in *The Jazz Singer*, 115; black woman as, 120, 128, 130; in *Clara's Heart*, 131; symbolic, 156–57
Mulvey, Laura, 86, 127
Murphy, Eddie, 116, 118
My Two Dads, 88

narrative theory, 3, 98, 143
Nationwide, 38–41, 57
Nelson, Cary, 74
Newfield, Christopher, 7
Nicholson, Jack, 70
Nicholson, Linda J., 14
Nietzsche, Friedrich W., 52
Nowell-Smith, Geoffrey, 137

oedipus complex, 72, 91–92, 115, 117, 131, 165n2
Oedipus Rex, 60, 64, 86, 131
Oshima, Nagisa, 92

Pease, Donald, 11
pedophilia, 78, 85, 152
Pee-wee's Playhouse, 102, 111
Penley, Constance, 99–100, 103
performance, 101, 103, 128, 132, 158
performative aspect of criticism, 22, 45–58, 171–2n19
Pesci, Joe, 143
Petro, Patrice, 169n2
Pfeiffer, Michelle, 145
Plato, 119
Polan, Dana, 176n6
Pollitt, Katha, 76
popular culture: see mass culture, theories of
pornography, 5, 135–36, 145–46, 152, 159–63, 180–81n1, 181n2, 182n24
postfeminism, 3, 6, 8, 10–13, 90, 92, 105, 130, 135–36, 163
postmodernism, 14, 18, 27, 83, 90, 99, 101, 103, 110–11
poststructuralism, 15, 22, 103
Pratt, Minnie Bruce, 19, 180n22
Propp, Vladimir, 144
public sphere, 20, 43
Puig, Manuel, *Kiss of the Spider Woman*, 24, 27–32, 34, 94, 169n4
Pym, Barbara, *Less Than Angels*, 35, 40, 45–56

Racine, Jean Baptiste, 50
race: theories of, 17, 116–21, 126–27, 180n19, 180n22; and feminist theory, 17–22, 127–34, 180n24; in *The Jazz Singer*, 115–16, 129; in *Coming to America*, 116–18; in *Alien Nation*, 118; in *Birth of a Nation*, 118–19, 124; in *Gorillas in the Mist*, 121–27; in *King Kong*, 121, 124, 126; in *Blonde Venus*, 127–28; in *Crossing Delancey*, 129–130, 133–34; in *Clara's Heart*, 131, 133; in *The Color Purple*, 131; in *Ghost*, 131–35; in *Jumping Jack Flash*, 132; in *Fatal Beauty*, 132; in

Lethal Weapon, 140–41, 143, 162–63; in *The Devil and Miss Jones, Part 3*, 162–63
Radway, Janice, 41–45
rape, 32–33, 51, 61, 65, 67, 69, 131, 166–67n18, 173n2
reception theory: *see* ethnographic criticism
Rein, Sonia, 174n17
Renoir, Jean, 126
Reubens, Paul: *see* Pee-wee Herman
Rich, Adrienne, 151–52, 159
Richardson, Samuel, 39
Riley, Denise, 16, 20–22
Riviere, Joan, 54
Rodowick, D.N., 174n17
romances, 35, 40, 41–45, 47
Rosaldo, Renato, 170n6
Ross, Andrew, 135, 166–67n18, 177n14, 180–81n1
Rubin, Gayle, 135, 149, 152–53
Russell, Kurt, 145
Russo, Mary, 178n29
Ruth, Dr., 79

sadism, 69
sado-masochism: *see* lesbianism and sadomasochism
Salome, Lou Andreas, 80–81
SAMOIS collective, 152–54
Sartre, Jean-Paul, 42, 47–49
Schwarzenegger, Arnold, 95
Screen criticism, 36–38
Sedgwick, Eve Kosofsky, 12–13, 167n19, 173n3, 179n14
Selleck, Tom, 79
Scarry, Elaine, 175n18
Schiesari, Juliana, 9
Shakespeare, William, 16, 54–56, 140; *Othello*, 16
Showalter, Elaine, 3–6, 11, 166n17, 169n2
Silver, Joan Micklin, 129
Silverman, Kaja, 90, 95, 149, 173–74n9, 174n17
simulation, 30–31, 38
Smith Barbara, 180n22
Smith, Paul, 6, 69–70
Smith, Valerie, 133
Soble, Alan, 181n2
Sontag, Susan 177n14
speech acts, 47, 49–50, 54, 57

Stallone, Sylvester, 90
Stern, William, 87
Stevens, Wallace, 10–11
Stowe, Harriet Beecher, *Uncle Tom's Cabin*, 24–26
Studlar, Gaylyn, 174n19
subculture, 37–38, 41–43
Swayze, Patrick, 132

Theweleit, Klaus, 61–63, 67–69, 173n2
Tompkins, Jane, 26, 169n4
Truth, Sojourner, 21–22
Twain, Mark, *Adventures of Huckleberry Finn, The*, 97

utopian aspect of feminist thought, 20, 22, 48, 53

Van Leer, David, 167n19
Vendler, Helen, 13–14
Von Sternberg, Josef, 127
Vorlicky, Robert, 166n18

Walker, Alice, 57
war, 61, 62, 74; with Iraq, viii; in films, 61–66; with Vietnam, 70, 71–73, 142–43
Wayne, John, 84, 90
Weeks, Jeffrey, 147
Weir, Peter, 138
Wenders, Wim, 104–105, 109, 111
Whitehead, Mary Beth, 87
Whitman, Walt, 137–38, 140
Wilde, Oscar, 13, 137
Wilden, Anthony, 61, 65–67, 73, 173n6
Willemen, Paul, 169n1
Williams, Linda, 161, 182n24
Williams, Robin, 138
Wittig, Monique, 81–82, 101, 110
"Wolfman," The, 81–82
Wollstonecraft, Mary, 17
woman's film, the, 8
Wood, Robin, 181n6
Woolacott, Janet, 170n7, 171n11
Woolf, Virginia, 52–58
Wynter, Sylvia, 179n7

Yaeger, Patricia, 172n32

Zimmerman, Bonnie, 171n15